MOTHERLAND

A Philosophical History of Russia

Lesley Chamberlain

OVERLOOK/ROOKERY
NEW YORK, NEW YORK

MOTHERLAND

This edition first published in The United States of America in 2007 by
The Rookery Press, Tracy Carns Ltd
in association with The Overlook Press
141 Wooster Street
New York, NY 10012
www.therookerypress.com

Cataloging-in-Publication Data is on file at the Library of Congress

Printed in the United States of America
FIRST EDITION

ISBN 978-1-58567-952-2
ISBN-10   1-58567-952-6

1 3 5 7 9 10 8 6 4 2

ACKNOWLEDGMENTS
I am indebted to Jane Robertson for her care with the manuscript, to Alexander Pyatigorsky who commented on an early draft, and to my husband, as always.

A NOTE ON TRANSLITERATION
Names in the text are transliterations of the Russian originals e.g. Lev Tolstoy, not Leo, following a composite of UK library styles. Exceptions are well-known anglicizations like Alexander (not Aleksandr) and the surname Herzen (not Gertsen), and where writers have themselves Europeanized their names e.g. Alexandre Koyré, Alexandre Kojève. Aleksei remains in its Russian form. Ilyich (not Il'ich), another exception, is a concession to easy reading. I have preferred the ending 'y' to 'i' or 'ii' — thus Dmitry, not Dmitri, Dostoevsky, not Dostoevskii. Solovyov, Gorbachov and similar names stressed on the final syllable are offered as a better guide to pronunciation than the familiar endings in -iev/-ev. References in the notes and the bibliography follow the style of individual publications.

The power of the spirit is only as great as its expression, and its depth only as deep as it dares to extend itself in its exposition and lose itself.

Hegel, *The Phenomenology of Spirit*

Russian coming to terms with European civilization during the nineteenth century was significant not only for Russia. However confused and amateurish a process it often was, however much it was impaired by inadequate information, false perspectives, by prejudice and passion, there was at work in it an extremely sure instinct for the things that were unsound and critical in Europe.

Erich Auerbach, *Mimesis*

Contents

CONTENTS

Preface

In 1996 I had a conversation with Isaiah Berlin who was then in his eighties and doyen of the history of Russian thought in Britain and America. Tea for me, tomato juice for him, in a stifling summer London, in a café on Piccadilly. Russia had recently shed its Soviet shackles, and Berlin had returned there to meet students at the St Petersburg conservatoire. 'It's just the same, nothing has changed.' His happiness was palpable. The world of his 'remarkable' decade essays of 1955–6, a moving evocation of nineteenth-century Russian intellectual life, had come true before his eyes. In ten passionate years from 1838 to 1848 a generation of idealists had dreamed of Russia's moral rebirth. Yet this emotional high point was hardly the whole story of Russia's philosophical beginnings. As a student of Russian intellectual history I had always hoped he would say more. I asked him now: 'Why, if you know this and I know it, why doesn't everyone know that Russia is a culture without reason?' The conversation became awkward. Did I know how the rich lived, he asked. Silence on my part. We passed on to the disappearance of the working class from the modern world, and the fate of Marx.

It was a strange encounter, which help revived an old project. To write a philosophical history of Russia had long seemed to me as attractive as it was difficult. Philosophy in Russia? Isaiah bypassed the question by highlighting the good moments. Academic historians meanwhile wrote histories of the political and social ideas preceding Communism. Since Soviet Russia officially banned all views out of true with Marxist-Leninist orthodoxy, the Revolution of October 1917 was a neat cut-off point. Although a few stalwart souls worked on admirably, looking for where 'Soviet philosophy' revealed its freer Russian origins, the general view was that for most of the twentieth century philosophy was pushed aside to make way for a compulsory monolithic ideology.

But Russia's philosophical history needs to be described in a new way, especially now it is a free country. Russia has engaged with Western philosophy with tragic intensity and has made an eccentric, poetic, original contribution that has scarcely been written down. Thirty years ago, when I was not quite Isaiah's student in Oxford, I began considering the ideas set down here. The task might have been finished sooner.

Years passed which took me to Communist Russia as a news reporter in 1978–9 and as a writer in 1992, 1993 and 1996. I worked a little on classical Western philosophy in quieter moments. Russian philosophy had almost nothing in common with that analytical discipline. Yet philosophy remained the key to the mystery of that country and culture.

The story told over the following pages – and it is mainly a story of hope and belief, not a series of arguments – is intended to provide a missing piece in Western understanding of a country which is a 'mother-land' to its own people but a strange 'otherland' to outsiders. An outline of more familiar nineteenth-century intellectual history is followed by essays on the continuous substance of Russian belief over two centuries. Professional philosophers may want to skip many of my pages, though as postmodernists they will surely appreciate the difficulty of criticizing a body of ideas which is interrupted and unfinished, but which tells a story.

There are good reasons for assuming Russia does not have philosophy. On the other hand it is not the *Russian* view, and, as for the Western view, it seems clear to me that the Cold War had much to do with making the simple negative view the desirable one. Retrospectively I am always surprised how thirty years ago Russian thought – the positive substitute for philosophy – was presented as a remarkably coherent and consistent subject. It seemed to Western scholars inevitable that nineteenth-century 'social and political' thought, standing in for an absence of academic philosophy, paved the way for the Bolshevik Revolution. It would surely be fair to say that the discipline of Russian thought had its political reason to exist because the West urgently needed to understand how the Revolution was made and how a short century of totalitarian Soviet rule ensued. Here was a discipline which could make sense of something alien and threatening and to a certain extent tame it.

The Cold War approach gave a retrospective coherence to the Western view of the Russian intelligentsia which was not nearly so evident in Russian practice. A single focus on what made Marxism take root and what caused the Revolution had, for instance, mostly to bypass religious thought and it had to dismiss all the ideas that captivated Russian minds for a century but which didn't fit the Communist mould. After the long nineteenth century it was assumed that diverse interests and values no longer shaped twentieth-century Russian life under a totalitarian regime.

In contrast to this view, one of my key premises is that Russian intellectual experience over the last two hundred years has been of a piece, and that what we have to understand is the 'long tradition', from 1815 to 1991, of a country which sits uncertainly on the Western fringe in an alternative cultural space. Through its seventy-four-year duration Soviet Russia was also still Russia, though many factors were exaggerated for the worse.

It was the habit of a past Western era not to dwell on the absence of Western-style academic philosophy in Russia for reasons of politeness. It was almost as if it was ungentlemanly to draw attention to weaknesses the enemy couldn't help. As one of the leading historians of the period put it, to seek out Russian philosophy would risk presenting 'an impoverished picture of Russian thought'.[1] The convention was in one way well-intentioned. It expressed a desire to admire Russia for its positive otherness. Fifty years ago, defining the territory, Isaiah Berlin himself wrote: 'The case of Russia . . . is not hopeless. Russian thinkers there have been – thinkers, but not eminent philosophers.'[2] In Isaiah's case the distinction followed from a genuine concern not to exclude from the 'philosophical' picture all that was remarkable about Russian thought, above all the lives and characters of men like Herzen and Belinsky, Tolstoy and Dostoevsky, and all those humanitarian qualities which kept the tradition of thought close to literature.

But by what it omitted this approach also defined that Cold War anxiety to present Russia as a definite and knowable cultural phenomenon: to master the negative side of Churchill's 'puzzle wrapped in an enigma'. Part of the task of students in the West studying Russian intellectual history was to show that the mystery was susceptible to Western understanding; and in that respect to show that Russia could be brought into line with an enlightened postwar world. It seems to me clear that Russia was never necessarily any of these things. It remained an 'otherland', intelligible to itself perhaps, but poorly grasped from outside. Perhaps the most estranging factor for viewers from the outside is the way Russia and the West seem to occupy the same cultural territory, and yet to have colonized it quite differently, so that their versions of the world compete and overlap. Russia and the West are neither compatible nor incompatible, just enduringly 'other' and faintly uncomfortable in each other's company. For as long as this was not admitted it was a kind of inverted geo-cultural snobbery for historians to say, in effect, ah this wild, sad country, we can find a place for it yet, in our wisdom. The Russians, even in moods of deep self-criticism, do not see themselves like this. Their world is simply their own.

I include in my history a range of considerations. One is that Russia's experience of philosophy has curiously anticipated a breakdown of Western trust in reason. That is why it is possible to take a new look at the Russian phenomenon through postmodern eyes. Another of my claims is that Russia's moral tradition remains its strongest legacy. My final speculation is that, if there was no real break in Russian self-perception in 1917, the change may come now, in the twenty-first century, in the wake of the Soviet failure. Tentatively I have dated the 'long tradition' 1815 to 1991. I hope that latter date has meant the end of intellectual self-defeat for Russia, given the painful experience of two short centuries.

I have tried to recreate in this book the pain of Russia's experience of itself. It is ironic but not historically unusual for this to be attempted by an outsider. Many of the best books about Russian thought have been written by non-Russians, and, as this history will show, Western writers and philosophers have often been borrowed and even adopted as honorary Russians in the cause of Russian self-definition. In my case I have surrendered myself quite willingly, in the hope of being useful.

It may be asked who are these 'Russians'? What is this 'Russia' that is a 'motherland' to itself and an 'otherland' to outsiders? Not every Russian is the same. Not everyone stands for the same idea of the country. Especially not now. To which I would reply two things. First, Russian thought has spent much of its time and energy defining a specific Russian way of seeing and doing things. To the extent that there is Russian philosophy it has asked and continues to ask not 'What is truth?' but 'What is Russian truth?'. Secondly, it was the great insight of one nineteenth-century thinker, Pyotr Lavrov, that Russia wanted to define itself as an ethical category. In trying to trace the development of Russia's self-understanding I have assumed this sense of the people and the nation trying to see themselves, especially with the help of Western philosophy, in terms of a new, probably unattainable definition of the good man in Russia and the good life.

Of all the aspects of Russia which still need elucidation and under-standing I have concentrated on the experience of philosophy because it lies at the heart of Russia's encounter with the West and its quest for self-definition. How can it be neglected? Central to Russia's experience of itself as a different place has been its startlingly consistent rejection of

Descartes, and the value of 'I think, I am'. It is startling because to reject Descartes is tantamount to rejecting modern philosophy and the modern (but not the postmodern) West.

In many ways this rejection of Western rationalism has spelled disaster for Russia. Reason is the backbone of the Enlightenment values by which Europe, as set out so recently by its Draft Constitution, still tries to live. The philosophy of Descartes holds dear values for individual freedom and integrity, and for the impartiality of science, which are among the great achievements of the modern world. To be a culture without reason is like being a mammal without a backbone. But what Russia set in reason's place – even from the early nineteenth century – was a moral quest, and this ethical gain has to be offset against the rational loss. Russian thinkers wanted to find a moral way of being, what philosophers would call a moral ontology, and this is what above all marks out Russia's 'long tradition'. The Soviet experiment was only part of that quest. The Communist idea was also, lest we forget, a moral idea.

This is not a book which flatters Russia, but also not one which tries to make it sort-of-Western and therefore sort-of-amenable. It considers a world prey at one extreme to appalling intellectual tampering with the real lives of diverse human beings and, at the other, to anarchic rebellion to save real lives from just that tampering.

Why, once again, is the subject so difficult? I would like to bring the reader's attention back to my observation that the body of philosophical thought in question is so unfinished that it almost has to be invented before it can be dissected. In the West, as is well known, modern philosophy developed at the beginning of the seventeenth century out of medieval theological disputes. Scholastic arguments abound in Descartes, not least in his pious attempt to prove the existence of a God who would bless the creation of secular science. After Descartes, the great rationalists of the later seventeenth and early eighteenth century, Spinoza and Leibniz, prolonged the engagement with religious dogma which anchored their works, and Descartes, firmly in the history of Judaeo-Christianity.

But this was not the case in Russia, where Russian Orthodoxy was a church of the common people with very little dogma. Orthodoxy's authority lay with the Hellenistic Church Fathers, but its real power was the sung liturgy. Not by coincidence did Orthodoxy stress as its most important component the moment of full, active worship in which it was felt God was present in the community. It was almost as if this moment could not be written down, for that would entail grasping the present and perfect moment which, by definition, no mere mortal could do. 'Neither "heaven descending upon earth", nor earth longing for heaven . . . In the Ancient Russian Church the divine is felt to dwell . . . right there present in the shrine in all the holy objects that fill it . . . The complete incarnation of the spiritual in the material is one of the essential tendencies of the Russian religious mind.'[3] The twentieth-century émigré scholar who vividly described the Russian religious mind, Georgy Fedotov, and who made the point about the relative absence of theology, found in a medieval source a neat confirmation of a non-dogmatic church. Its own priests described it as 'a tongue-tied maiden'.[4]

The tongue-tied maiden, the silent medieval Russian Church, is as much the precursor of Russian philosophy as the Western Church of Western philosophy, but with an evidently different outcome. As late as the early nineteenth century it was the influence of German philosophy which persuaded Russian religious thinkers to write down what the Orthodox world-view entailed and thus through a German style of thought, and reaction to it, to approach philosophy for the first time. The religious thinkers became philosophers because the Russian religious spirit had to be committed to the page for the sake of national pride and to hold Russia's own against the rationalist West. But they made the transition so late!

I have no doubt that Russia has something to add to philosophy. A passion for truth, a desire to resolve impossible questions, has been part of the intellectual culture for two hundred years. Isaiah Berlin celebrated the circles of the 1830s, whose discussions, I imagine, a Russian Plato would have written down as the founding dialogues, had he only existed. What *The Republic* was to classical Athens, a Russian Plato's *Motherland* might have been to Russia. Absurdly at times I try to compensate for the missing Russian Plato, for which I can only ask the reader's indulgence. As for the scholar-writer in whose footsteps I have been following since our Piccadilly tea, I have come to see him as a Russian thinker in his own right, a stealthy philosophical renegade a little uncomfortable in analytical Oxford, who often took up Russian themes and expressed a Russian point of view when he was apparently writing about other things.

Preface to the U.S. Edition

Motherland takes the risk of generalizing about what Russian philosophy is and, against the grain of Western sophistication, accepts that it has a strong national core. What has to be the primary topic, even if one is looking in from outside, is a long-sustained internal debate about 'Russian truth'. In the thirty-five years I've been writing in various forms about Russia and its unique ways, the only satisfactory approach has seemed to me to become a temporary insider and this applies to philosophy as much as to art and politics and travel. For the philosophy project 'The Motherland Thinks about The Motherland', albeit replete with the problems of exclusive self-reference, might have been a more comprehensive title. That said, one of my critics a few years ago deemed the result of my approach at once terribly clever and curiously inconsequential, taking upon itself, unnecessarily, the faults of a notoriously indefineable tradition. It would be slippery of me to suggest cleverness and inconsequentiality, plus a great deal of moral intensity, were part of what I set out to show. Readers will judge for themselves.

Russian truth is a controversial entity and my view is that it is part art, part social and political campaign, part religious devotion and part argument. Like art in Tolstoy's definition, Russian philosophy goes to work in a sphere of emotional infectiousness, punctuating its efforts with political *cris de coeur*, and sometimes supplementing the whole with borrowings from and criticisms of Western philosophers. At its heart is a system of values it would like to see realised as the right way for the moral man to live and which dream carries a particular urgency given the nearly always critical state of Russian politics and society. In Part II of this book, its heart, I refer to the drive for a moral philosophy of being or an ethical ontology as fundamental to Russian philosophy in its broadest sense. A moral philosophy of being is the aim of 'Russian truth', and one is left in no doubt that its scope is sweeping and its power gripping. It is akin to a novel by Dostoevsky and Dostoevsky himself is a Russian philosopher. Yet philosophy has also to work with definitions and arguments. It can't, even stretching the definition, be a matter only of emotional energy and extraordinary metaphorical and sensational pictures. It is this powerful mixture of elements in the Russian tradition which led me to announce just now that I would be 'showing something' as much as arguing it. In fact I would be telling and showing and arguing a number of things simultaneously. They add up to my sense of what 'Russian truth' is.

Pressure to make the subject intelligible to curious newcomers led to the suggestion that I write a basic history of what used to be called 'Russian nineteenth-century political and social thought' to get the narrative underway. So be it. Essentially this was the Cold War approach to Russian philosophy. It selected those themes in the history of ideas that apparently led to the Bolshevik Revolution of 1917. If the West could understand this tradition, it could understand what made Russia, until the ideological collapse of 1991, Communist. Writing a new version of it more than a decade after that collapse, I particularly enjoyed picking out ideas that were socialist but not Marxist, theories of history that went directly back to Hegel, rather than via Marx, and, amid the many communally-driven ideals, bursts of praise for individual freedom and dignity. There was no inevitability about the Communist outcome of the nineteenth-century tradition, although in a separate later chapter on Lenin, comprising Section III of the book, I show how he capped it with a monstrous simplification.

Section II, coupled with Section IV, looks at Russian philosophy as it never was considered during the Cold War. Had it been, 'the evil empire' might have been less easy to dismiss as the infernal enemy. Writing about the Russian spiritual-national impetus which affects everything in Russian cultural life, but specifically, in the philosophical context, notions of goodness and truth, I find myself with one foot in the insider camp and one in the outsider camp, primed both to appreciate and to criticize. Actually this isn't such an unusual position. It was roughly that held by the liberal religious philosophers whom Lenin expelled from the country in 1922 and who, in the meantime, have become the subject of my next book, *Lenin's Private War*.

At the heart of *Motherland*, it has to be said, comparing Russian philosophy with its Western counterparts, I discern a failing which I think has never been sufficiently emphasized in the West, namely that here is a tradition which emphatically rejects Descartes, the West's father of reason and modern science. Descartes is rejected because the typical seeker after Russian truth refuses to omit the emotional and faith components from the picture of knowledge. The immediate consequence seems to me a tradition which suffers from a lack of concern for objectivity and, indeed, as the expelled philosophers of 1922 put it, no respect for the difference between true and false.

Ironically the post-Enlightenment, post-modern West has discovered for itself the chaotic consequences of abandoning the truth goal over the past forty years. At the same time it has brought into mainstream philosophy, from the margins of literature and faith, imagination and the life of the body, all kinds of experiences that can hardly be called untrue and somehow ought to belong to a modern sense of what is and what is good. In this respect Russia in its rejection of Descartes was way ahead of the West at the same time as way behind it a century ago. It was in its philosophical partiality at once superior and inferior. So one reason for the interested outsider to read about Russian truth-seeking today would be to realize the affinity between the post-modern and the Russian religious-philosophical. Surely it's the case that knowledge is more than the product of 'I think, therefore I am' and truth more than what I alone can arrive at. But one has to keep in mind the dubious moral practicality of leaving frontiers open and definitions unfinished and undermining personal warranty. I have in passing traced an ironic line whereby the Austrian poet Rilke translated his awareness of Russian spirituality into a body of German poetry which inspired Heidegger and half the world. Thus the Russian tradition helped to lay the foundation for the upheaval in Western metaphysics, the overthrow of the tradition from Plato to Descartes, by Heidegger, although some would say the right place for both Rilke and Heidegger is still not philosophy, but poetry. Taking these various factors into consideration I suggest that the Russian predilection for the non-rational has to be seen in both its negative and positive consequences. To see the religious philosopher Blaise Pascal as a kind of counter-figurehead, acceptable to Russia where Descartes was not, I find, following the suggestion of Lev Shestov, extremely helpful. I am only saddened that many Russians seem unwilling to accept anything at all negative about their national quest for truth.

To enlarge on the positive outcome for the project, I dwell admiringly on what I call the quest for 'the good man in Russia'. It is salutary to witness this constant moral concern, which has the same simple insistence as that of Plato and which from the early nineteenth century is fundamentally opposed to Anglo-American Utilitarianism. But it is salutary too to see where the quest for the good man leads to a tampering with knowledge, and even with scientific results, in the interests of the good society, comprising the collaboration and community of good men. How easily it could all go wrong!

As I make these comments on that specifically philosophical Russian tradition which I have isolated in order to bring out its peculiar characteristics, readers will begin to see how it joins up again with the tradition in social and political thought with which *Motherland* opened. Of course they are not separate. But at different times in Russia themes and values common to both traditions have taken on quite different political shadings, and one needs to see the origins, alongside the contexts in which they have been put to work, to grasp the whole still elusive picture. The complex and tangled world of Russian 'values' is surely why Western understanding of the country and its culture and politics, so caught up with Western political notions of 'left' and 'right', has so often been wide of the mark. It would be a great joy to me if this book could make better foreign understanding of Russia more likely in future. Understanding, as I have found in the course of my research, doesn't necessarily lead to approval, but it is a vast improvement on ignorance.

I don't want to underplay the link between Russian philosophy and art, by which I mean literature and poetry. Many of those figures who in the West are called Russian writers, like Dostoevsky and Pasternak and Solzhenitsyn, are also philosophers in the Russian sense. Perhaps the best introduction to Russian philosophy qua Russian truth I have ever read was written by Nadezhda Mandelstam, wife of the poet, in her memoir *Hope Abandoned* (chapter 29). One critic of the U.K. edition of *Motherland* told me he preferred not to have his Russian literature spelled out as philosophy but rather to leave things as they were. Well, what can I say? Another was indignant about the relative absence of Tolstoy, who has long been regarded as a kind of key in England to what is good about old Mother Russia. But I think Tolstoy is the wrong track to go down too far, if what one wants to understand is Russia, and not England.

Finally I would like to comment on the relative absence of proper names in this prefatory essay and in the crucial second part of this book. In the course of my work I found it was the ideas that reached across the board, and not who was expounding them in some partial and specific context, that mattered. That suprapersonal and communal element in its makeup is also part of the definition of Russian truth and helps to account for how it survived the Soviet period and still uncertainly continues.

L.C. London March 2007

PART I

The Making of the Intelligentsia

The Russian Revolution and Russian philosophy share a common origin. They begin not with an idea but with a political class and its discontents. That class was the nineteenth-century Russian intelligentsia, which defined itself by agitating for social reform. Its members, *intelligenty*, were critical thinkers who regretted the primitive political state of their country under tsarism. The first and second generation were mostly sons of the *dvoryanstvo* – the nobility or gentry – though by the mid-century a good proportion came from less elevated classes. Typically they were the sons of priests and teachers. Their educational level was patchy for the first half-century, except for a privileged few who studied abroad. But always the passion for ideas was great, as readers of Russian literature know. When a member of the pre-revolutionary intelligentsia encountered a new, progressive idea from the West it immediately suggested either a better Russian future along Western lines, or a new way to distinguish a peculiarly Russian future. The intelligentsia divided accordingly – albeit very roughly – into Westernizers and Slavophiles.

The life of the modern intelligentsia, and with it philosophy in Russia, can be seen as beginning with the French Revolution, delayed in its impact in Russia by about thirty years. In this light it is possible to identify five nineteenth-century generations who laid intellectual foundations still in place today. The first-generation Russian *intelligenty* were a handful of men, active in the 1820s, deeply affected by the French Revolution, either directly as a political inspiration or indirectly through the German philosophy they studied. The second age of the intelligentsia was marked by the 'beautiful souls' of 1838–48. After 1848 the 'new men' emerged, followed by the Populists of 1866–81, although in all these periods there were writers, and also religious thinkers, who fitted under no single heading. The dates can only be approximate. Finally came the men intellectually active in the 1890s, Lenin's generation, all of whom began with the lesson of Marx. The generation split to produce Russia's finest philosophical and cultural achievement to date, the Silver Age. Through these five ages – and six casts of mind – nineteenth-century Russian intellectual life ranged much more widely than the twentieth-century Communist legacy suggested. The Russian Revolution acted as a funnel, directing a small portion of the available ideas towards one ideological end. To recapture the history one has to freeze the funnel process and reverse it. Since many of the ideas current in nineteenth-century Russia are still with us, this must also indicate that there is a European treasury to rediscover.

1

The Men of the 1820s

Nearly all the men of the 1820s who helped create modern intellectual life in Russia were born within ten years of the French Revolution: the political reformer Nikolai Turgenev in 1789, the philosopher Professor Mikhail Pavlov in 1793, and the writer Pyotr Chaadaev in 1794. A slightly younger generation was represented by Prince Vladimir Odoevsky, born in 1804. (The pronunciation of this writer's surname is worth noting, because unusually the stress falls on the second 'o'.) In the period which began around 1815 and could be stretched to 1836 or 1838, a mixed picture of these men and their world comes to the fore: of well-educated army officers like Nikolai Turgenev agitating for reform; of university professors like Pavlov and literary journalists like Odoevsky teaching new ideas; and of Chaadaev, a writer whose *Philosophical Letters* made a unique contribution to Russia's future by proposing to draw a line under an unfruitful past. Political optimism and a new openness to Western ideas drove Russia forward after the victory over Napoleon. That hope came crashing down after the failure of the first public protest against the autocracy, in December 1825. The rebels were either executed or exiled to Siberia.

The Decembrists named by historians after that 1825 political disaster were members of the nobility who had variously studied abroad and seen action with their regiments. Theirs was a touching story of idealism wildly miscalculating the effects of reasonable action in an unreasonable country. On 14 December 1825 they withdrew their obedience on the parade grounds of St Petersburg and in the Ukraine and fired a few shots, somehow to convey the spirit of their demands for the abolition of serfdom and the creation of a written constitution. The gesture suddenly gave Enlightenment reason a meaning in Russia. To the horror of its Romanov rulers this vast inchoate country of a few intellectuals and millions of peasants began to think publicly about liberty.

In the words of the foremost non-Russian historian of intellectual Russia, when the Napoleonic Wars ended with Tsar Alexander I's march into Paris at the head of the Holy Alliance, young Russian campaigners allowed themselves to become inspired by 'the "juridical world view" of the Enlightenment, according to which legal and political forms determined the revolution of society'.[1] For some eight to ten years it seemed possible that Russia might become a liberal country. Alexander, who had been tutored by a liberal Swiss, promised a constitution and made positive changes in education. The foundation of St Petersburg University in 1819 was a milestone. Nikolai Turgenev (no relation of the later novelist Ivan), took as his reformist goal the abolition of serfdom and formed a Union of Welfare to discuss Russia's liberal prospects. He tried not to spark panic in ruling circles, unlike the openly republican Pavel Pestel who wanted the autocracy destroyed.[2]

But despite La Harpe, the Swiss teacher who had 'turned [his] thoughts towards freedom', Alexander became frightened by unrest when his household regiment mutinied in 1820.[3] A series of military rebellions and revolutions broke out across Europe, and Nikolai Turgenev and his friends retreated to the conspiratorial shadows.[4] After the Greek uprising in 1821, John Capodistrias, who had been the tsar's adviser, left Russia to fight for his country. The Pole Adam Czartoryski, another St Petersburg court adviser, also returned home, albeit to a Poland that had vanished except in spirit. Between 1772 and 1795 Poland as an independent territory had disappeared into the Russian, Prussian and Austrian empires, just as European peoples were becoming aware of their intrinsic value. National awareness would be as much of a thorn in imperial Russia's side for the next century as progressive sentiment at home. As the liberal flame died, Alexander succumbed to pressure from Metternich in Austria to keep a tight hold on his empire. Dismayed, the tsar lost himself in religious mysticism. When he died suddenly in 1825 the Decembrists seized their chance to profit from the brief interregnum and failed. Alexander's brother Nicholas I took the throne by handing out sentences of execution and exile to the conspirators. Nikolai Turgenev saved his life by escaping abroad.

The new tsar, Nicholas I, the Metternich-style 'gendarme of Europe', a man who loved playing with soldiers, would now become the scourge of the nascent Russian intelligentsia. Suspicious of the liberal political implications of reason, he made it his first act, early in 1826, to purge the universities of their philosophy departments.

Activity in those departments was hardly extensive and hardly revolutionary. The subject was in its infancy and the German metaphysics the students studied was remote from daily life. Its capacity to thrill lay in its cosmic harmonies and world historical predictions. But the imperial authorities were worried by the threat of atheism, much as seventeenth-century Catholic England had worried about the devilish Hobbes. For the same reason Descartes had refrained from publishing his scientific views, fearing to be condemned by the Inquisition like Galileo. Late, as always so fatefully late, Russia woke up to a political fear of philosophy. The tsarist authorities took atheism to be synonymous with reason and since reason was linked to the upheaval of 1789 what more justification did they need to silence its practitioners? The Russian autocrat was the little father, *tsar batyushka*, God's representative on earth, whose authority should not be brought into question by a few new-fangled thinkers asking questions about nature and knowledge and the meaning of life.

Professors Mikhail Pavlov, Ivan Davydov and Dmitry Vellansky, who taught courses in the metaphysics of Friedrich Schelling at Moscow and St Petersburg universities, were the men at risk. Pavlov (1793–1840) brought back some volumes of Schelling from Germany, and his notes based on Schelling's lectures.[5] Alexander Herzen, one of the intellectual giants of the century, later commented that it was Pavlov who made German philosophy 'at home' in Moscow and that he had a gift for doing this 'with unusual clarity of exposition'.[6] Pavlov also published articles in the characteristically named 'fat' journals which played a vital role in the development of Russian literature. By this route the beginnings of Russian philosophy seeped out of the academy and into society.

Pavlov founded and edited the journal *Athenei*. In a three-way colloquy, which he wrote in the style of a classical dialogue and published in the first number in 1828, a character called Xenophon began sceptically: 'Yes, man is a trope of the soul, and nature is infinite finitude. What could be clearer?' But the conversation soon eschewed irony to introduce the 'Absolute' as the key to universal understanding. The Schellingian Absolute was an energy inherent in all things, creating a fundamental affinity, or, as Schelling called it, *identity*, between the world of nature and the world of the human mind. Schelling's philosophy, characteristic of the Romantic period, argued that because man and the world around him are of the same substance, everything about that world can be known, hence the claim to absolute knowledge which in pre-Romantic thought was only possible in the mind of God.[7]

The sense of 'Philosophy' or 'Science' or 'Reason', written large and conceived as a short-cut to universal understanding, gilded the attraction in a backward country of a potential discipline of cogent thinking. But even the earliest Russian teachers had to admit the threat of vulgarization and misuse. In Pavlov's dialogue a second character, Pomyast, represented unchecked enthusiasm for the one Idea that would solve everything, a position which drew criticism from a third participant, Menon, that Russia might thus embark on a superficial and self-destructive path. Pomyast accepted the opaque formula that 'truth is the character of the mind, and therefore comprises our need' but such empty speculation distressed Menon who wanted to see greater value placed on empirical knowledge. Quoting Schelling in German, from the 1805 *Ideas Towards a Philosophy of Nature*, he reminded Russian readers that philosophy explained how experience was possible, but did not make up for not knowing the facts in other fields. When philosophy's job was done, moreover, and introspection could go no further, men would naturally come back to their religious faith. This sentiment may have been put in to please the censor. At heart Pavlov's article was a positive exposition of a new German Idealist philosophy, suggesting not only that absolute knowledge was possible but that men were driven from within to seek it. German Idealism did threaten a backward, autocratic state. It proposed introspection, for which every man had an innate capacity, as the way to a new individualism and independence of mind. Individuals were becoming introspective, and critical, as part of a universal process by which the world would become more perfect. No one man or state could resist that process because it was natural: an inner need or demand, some kind of inherent force, was driving every particular thing towards its true fulfilment. The Russian professors and their students felt the power of that *inner* truth which had been declared a universal human need.

Suspended between the new wisdom and the old Christian faith, the Russian philosophy of Pavlov's day challenged autocratic power which justified itself by divine sanction, though by such convoluted and indirect means that its opponents surely did not detect the real thrust of the argument. Atheism was the obvious enemy but the real threat was greater than they could imagine. Schellingism was liberating two great forces, nature and the individual. Schelling's definition of metaphysics contained a project to change subject peoples into confident self-empowered nations and transform oppressed subjects into individuals bursting with the means to self-expression. From a work published in 1811 Schelling defined metaphysics as:

1) What creates states organically and makes a mass of people of one heart and being, that is, a people [*ein Volk*].

2) That by means of which the artist and the poet, through intense feeling, reproduce in the language of the senses eternal and primal images.

3) This inner metaphysic, which equally inspires the statesman, the hero of the battlefield, the heroes of religion and science, is something which is equally repelled by the so-called theories which the *bien pensant* allow to deceive them, and by the flatness of empiricism, which comprises the opposite of the former.

4) All metaphysics, whether it expresses itself speculatively or practically, rests on the talent to conceive of the many as directly in the one, and by the same token the one in the many; in a word it rests on a sense of totality.

5) Metaphysics is the opposite of all mechanism; it is an organic manner of feeling, thinking and behaving.[8]

In 1832 another dialogue of Pavlov's appeared in the well-known journal *Telescope*, in which a philosophical materialist – a man who believed that matter not mentality was the prime mover of reality – was converted to a Schellingian idealist view of nature. The Russian idealist now accepted that 'every phenomenon in nature is the externalization of an inner essence'. Four years later, Pavlov published a book, *The Basis of Physics*, in which he stressed how the individual was alive in the midst of, and inwardly bonded with, a living nature. The emphasis in the new philosophy was on what was natural or organic, as opposed to what was constrained by arbitrary, man-made rules.

Dmitry Vellansky (1774–1847), who taught in St Petersburg, had begun the Romantic revolution in Russian ideas some years before Pavlov. After studying at a Kiev religious academy, he qualified for the task by taking courses in medicine and natural science at German universities, where he also heard Schelling and Schellingians lecture. When he died *The Medical Journal of Russia* hailed him as 'the Russian Schelling' and regretted that his early work was little recognized. The reader may well ask why *The Medical Journal of Russia* should be so interested in philosophy. The still slightly odd answer was that technically Vellansky occupied the chair of botany at the Medical Academy of St Petersburg. The title of his post was a way of disguising the refractory subject he really taught. Similarly Pavlov was nominally a professor of agronomy.

Vellansky thought of himself as the founder of Schellingism in Russia. He introduced new concepts of the natural world drawn from what he termed 'theosophy'. He was ridiculed even in his own time for his vagueness, although when he offered a reward of 5,000 roubles to anyone who could disprove scientifically any of his claims no challenger came forward.[9] He was more a bearer of the new than an interesting mind in himself. Yet the moment he marked in Russia was clearly recognized by the *Great Soviet Encyclopedia* of 1971, which recorded: 'Vellansky expressed the dialectical thesis concerning the general connectedness of phenomena, their binary nature and the struggle of polar opposites as the source of development.' Here, in Russian Schellingism at its most general, in dialectical materialism at its most opaque, was the link that would carry Russian thinkers on from Schelling to Hegel, and thence to Marx and to Lenin.

Dialectical materialism, the house philosophy of Marxist-Leninism, the sine qua non of a short century of Soviet self-justification, belonged in truth to an era of Romantic speculation. Back in the early nineteenth century, students of Vellansky were struck by the proposition that truth arose out of the interaction of matter and ideas. Vellansky taught them that the resulting cultural product moved with an inherent dynamic towards a progressive goal. A century later, not nature but the economics of the class struggle produced the dialectical energy to move the world forward. Raisa Gorbachov, the wife of the last Soviet leader, was a university teacher of the 'science' of dialectical materialism right up to the end of the Soviet phenomenon.

Ivan Davydov (1794–1863) delivered a lecture in Moscow in 1826 entitled 'On the Possibility of Philosophy as Science' in which he expounded Schelling's philosophy of identity. Our minds are made in such a way that through introspection we can know everything in the world. The lecture was said to be based on Schelling's *On the Possibility of Any Form of Philosophy* (1795). Once again, albeit in a roundabout and technical way, a small Russian audience heard the message that truth empowered individuals, and that the very search for truth was part of an organic thrust forwards, likewise of nature and culture. Davydov, who studied philosophy, knew Latin and wrote a thesis on the early English empiricist Francis Bacon, tried to deflect political attention from his subject by telling his students – or was it the police agent among them? – that he saw no conflict between the new philosophy and traditional Christian belief. But Russia was still reeling from the Decembrist insurrection and Davydov delivered his inaugural lecture to a department in Moscow just about to close. The authorities simultaneously closed the philosophy departments in St Petersburg and at Kazan'. That thriving university 500 miles due east of Moscow on the Volga, where Lenin would later study, needed watching as much as the 'asiatic' and 'European' Russian capitals.[10]

The most lamented victim of the 1826 purge was yet another university Schellingist, Alexander Galich (1783–1848). He never really recovered from weeks of interrogation and persecution which took his profession away from him. Galich studied in Göttingen and Helmstedt and on his return submitted a thesis based on Schelling's philosophy of nature. A man with original ideas living in reactionary times, he couched his dissertation in the form of a letter to an imaginary interlocutor, and added a survey of the history of philosophy from Ancient India. Vellansky examined it and found Galich's approach vague, personal and poetic. But Galich, who had a positive reputation for wit as well as brains, got his doctorate and permission to teach at the St Petersburg Pedagogical Institute, providing that his thesis – 'full of such new ideas and appealing to only a few specialists' – was not published. Also he was obliged to stick to state-approved textbooks for his lectures.[11]

The critic and mid-century man of letters Alexander Nikitenko found Galich to have a rare and critical mind, of whom the likes of Vellansky could hardly be the judge. According to Nikitenko, who later worked at the Ministry of Public Instruction and wrote about the strain of taking responsibility for censorship, Galich did not need to see all questions answered or even embraced by a single system of thought. He taught what Schelling wrote but he was not a Schellingist. Galich instructed his students: 'The human mind has a surprising talent for bending under the burden of its own weighty inventions and this unnatural position threatens it with collapse at any minute. You should learn to find the centre of gravity and weigh it against your own strength, in order to stay on your feet and walk straight.'[12] One of the many quiet, backroom tragedies of Russian philosophy was Galich's demotion to book-keeping in a grocery store, where, isolated among ledgers of mundane calculation, he took to drink.

Like the work of Henri Bergson a hundred years later, Schelling's thought appealed to enthusiasm and poetic and religious sentiment, and Galich and Pavlov warned against its indiscriminate adoption. Intelligent authorities might have accepted that above all in respect of its warnings their teaching was genuinely educational.

On the other hand it was too late for those authorities, and, though they might persecute individual thinkers, the fire of modernity had already been lit, however anti-modern the empire. Not only were the universities teaching Schelling, but private enthusiasts like Prince Odoevsky and his aristocratic circle were meeting in discussion groups. On these occasions Odoevsky used to don a black velvet cloak and call himself Faust. Goethe's learned doctor could not stem his appetite for knowledge despite nearly destroying himself and wrecking the life of young Margarete, but the Romantic rebel and the mystical seer in Faust were appealing traits for a young foreigner to adopt. Odoevsky's friends included Vil'gelm Kyukhel'beker and Dmitry Rozhalin, both close to the poet Pushkin. The friends banded themselves together as 'wisdom lovers' or *lyubomudry*, to pool their ideas. As well-endowed members of the nobility, several of them had the means to pay Schelling a personal visit.[13] The Russian influence of Schelling, a Romantic thinker well known in Germany, acknowledged in Europe, obscure in England, has generally been strikingly underestimated by Western scholars. He laid the foundations for an unlimited Russian appetite for German Idealism over the next two centuries.

Odoevsky (1804–69) in this respect, and also thanks to his unusual writing, was a leading figure. A multi-talented dilettante, after studying literature and philosophy at the Moscow Pension for the Nobility, he became deeply impressed by Schelling in the mid-1820s, and from 1824 to 1825 edited a Schellingian periodical called *Mnemozina*. Kyukhel'beker and the young poet Dmitry Venevitinov contributed articles. The name *lyubomudry* is usually translated as 'lovers of wisdom' but literally means 'philosophers'. It was a Slav calque on the Greek which allowed the generation of Russian Schellingists to distinguish themselves from the *philosophes* of the French Enlightenment. Whether this strategy was sincere – Odoevsky denigrated the encyclopaedists as 'chatterboxes' – or whether this was yet another choice of nomenclature to appease the censor we will never know, only that Odoevsky trod carefully with the political authorities, knowing how suspicious they were, and later became a censor himself. After December 1825, though he had no part in the conspiracy, he was almost arrested because of the role his friend Kyukhel'beker played, which earned him a sentence of exile. Odoevsky closed his conversation circle, occupied himself with his civil service job, and only reopened it some years later.

Odoevsky was mystically inclined and conservative in politics and temperament, characteristics which urged him both to enthuse for

German Idealism and to want to educate his country. His conservatism was not of the hidebound 'Official Nationality' type, widespread in the 1830s, which wished to keep all liberal Western influence out of Russia.[14] Though snuffed out by the Decembrist panic soon after its birth, *Mnemozina* published such pieces as Kyukhel'beker's account of his visit to Schelling, a translation of Germaine de Staël on Kant, aphorisms from Schelling and others, and Pavlov 'On the Ways of Understanding Nature'. The state of philosophy in Russia was parlous, Odoevsky underscored in its pages. Not a single academic course in philosophy existed in Russia nor a dedicated journal. The courses did exist of course, but not under their own name, since they lacked government blessing. Odoevsky wanted, as Galich before him, to compile a philosophical dictionary outlining 'all the major philosophical systems'. He lived up so zealously to his sense of *noblesse oblige* that he proposed examinations in moral and social competence for his companions in the nobility, who were bound by their class origin to be guardians to the people. It was thus at least in part via Schelling that Plato's political spirit took root in modern Russia. It lived on in the conservative romanticism of a man like Odoevsky and it remained in place in Russian education through much of the nineteenth century, just as it did in a much more advanced country like England, with the difference that England had learned its classical lessons through direct study of the Greek.[15]

Later Odoevsky reworked the experience of his *lyubomudry* years into a book, *Russian Nights* (1844), which mixed the genres of fiction, memoir, speculation and criticism, in a way that had no parallel in Russian literature of the day and still seems very modern. The 'Nights' offered not only a unique portrait of the philosophical atmosphere of the years when German Idealism first held Russia under its spell but also delivered engaging thoughts on ethics, language, music and literature. Odoevsky was 'just what we mean by Russian thinker, an active and comprehensive mind, stubbornly striving to unite all the fragmented aspects of [his] knowledge', a Soviet critic observed in 1981.[16]

The man who nevertheless towered over the first generation of the intelligentsia was Pyotr Chaadaev (1794–1856). In 1836 Chaadaev, who like a few men of his Russian generation still wrote in French, was arrested, interrogated and kept under house arrest for eighteen months until he confessed to having been 'mad'. His crime was to have alleged in his *Philosophical Letters* that because of its traditional bad ways, rooted in tsarism and the Orthodox Church, Russia had no cultural past and no good civilization of its own and could only go forward by joining with Catholic Europe. The 'Letters' had been written in 1831 but were only published in Russian, in *Telescope*, five years later because of their evidently explosive content. *Telescope*'s editor Nikolai Nadezhdin had his journal closed down as a result and was left in financial difficulties. Chaadaev's proposition was absurd and evidently insulting in imperial circles. But for the new critical generation it lit a torch. It was not necessary to agree with the proposed remedy to see that it spoke the truth about Russia's backwardness.

Chaadaev's ideas and fate were not interesting to Marxists and later Marxist-Leninists because he was a conservative and a believer. He did not count as a major player in the history of revolutionary thought, and for these reasons only ever received specialist attention in the West, and that forty years ago. His interests developed too early for him to become a Hegelian. He stressed the importance of individual dignity and how assimilating classical European civilization would benefit Russia. His inspiration for change in Russia came from the post-revolutionary Ultramontane Catholicism of Felicité Lammenais in France. Ultramontanism was, paradoxically, a call to return to a more traditional, reverential society shaped by transcendent moral values and with a sense of the limitations of human knowledge.

But the very idea of education was revolutionary in Russia, given the obscurantism of those in power. Thus when Chaadaev steeped himself in conservative sources it was to produce a magnificent denunciation of a country which was refusing to reach for the light.

There is a certain detail in life which is not connected with physical being, but which concerns the intelligent man; it shouldn't be neglected: there is a regime for the spirit just as there is a regime for the body; one has to know how to submit to it. This is old wisdom, I know; but I think that in our country it very often still has all the merit of a new discovery. It is one of the most deplorable things of our strange civilization that we still have to discover truths which are the most trivial elsewhere, even among peoples a lot less advanced than we are in some respects. The point is that we have never walked alongside other peoples; we don't belong to any of the great families of the human race; we are neither of the West nor the East, and we have the traditions of neither the one nor the other. As if we were situated outside time, the universal education of the human race has not reached us yet.

The true development of the human race in society has not yet begun for a people as long as life has not grown more regulated, easier, gentler than it was amid the uncertainties of its first age. In the case of societies which orient themselves without convictions and without rules, even in daily matters, and life lacks a constitution, how can one expect the seeds of the good to take root? What appertains is the chaotic fermentation of things in the moral sphere, comparable to the upheavals of the earth which preceded the present state of the planet. We are still there.[17]

Would Chaadaev's love of European high culture have been acceptable had it not led him directly to attack the institution of serfdom in Russia? Not really. Serfdom was the conspicuous badge of Russian barbarity which any Western-inspired educational advance threatened. With his European education, Chaadaev's immediate predecessor Alexander Radishchev (1749–1802) had seen the writing on the wall thirty years earlier and been imprisoned and sentenced to hard labour in Siberia for his frankness.

Serfdom degraded the whole of society and kept it from modern cultural progress. Reason was Chaadaev's chief concern, but how could reason flourish in a country which lacked respect for the dignity of individual human beings? Reason was the product of centuries of intellectual and cultural refinement, not just a measuring instrument. What was the value of a country that had failed to inherit the universal ideas of good and evil, truth and falsehood, and duty, justice and law? These were Chaadaev's questions, which he followed up by blaming Russian Orthodoxy for the country's deprivations. Because Russia was divorced from the Roman Catholic Church the classical tradition had not been transmitted, nor the fruits of medieval scholasticism and the Renaissance.

When Chaadaev was put under pressure by his interrogators he tried to stick to his views, but he was overwhelmed by self-blame. The public apology forced upon him mirrored the split in his heart:

> Love of one's country is a beautiful thing, but far more beautiful is the love of truth ... It's true that we Russians were always rather careless about what was true and what false. That's why it doesn't do to get very angry with a society for being sorely touched by a somewhat caustic tract addressed to its weaknesses. That's why I assure you I'm not at all cross with this good public which indulged me for so long. I am trying to come to terms with my strange position – coldbloodedly, without any irritation.[18]

Chaadaev's personal fate was emblematic of the potential personal fates of all the men over the next 150 years who would carry Russia's intertwined philosophical and revolutionary traditions forward. He stood for a defining moment in the early life of the intelligentsia. As the first Russian thinkers became aware of the wealth of European philosophy – and with it the attractions of a liberal education – they realized that their first priority in spreading enlightenment in Russia must be to oust the autocracy. Whatever interests they might have held dear in pure scholarship, however much some might have been tempted to value art and personality and speculative philosophy higher than politics – and there were always a small apolitical number – Russian circumstances forced political change to the top of the agenda. Chaadaev's personal fate took up much of a famous study of *Nicholas's Gendarmes and Literature 1826–1855* written (in Russian) by the historian Mikhail Lemke on the eve of the demise of tsarism and published in 1908. Lemke's work highlighted the basic civic freedoms liberal *intelligenty* were still agitating for in 1905, eighty years after the Decembrist Insurrection.[19]

2

The Beautiful Souls

The chief differences between the men of the 1820s and those of the 'remarkable' decade of 1838–48 were the quickening of the moral pulse that fired Chaadaev's protest and the search for models and leaders to spread the new idea of the good life. Alexander Herzen (1812–70) and Vissarion Belinsky (1811–48), the two foremost men of the age, threw themselves body and soul into the struggle to educate and free a country crippled by obscurantism and inhumanity. Through them the intelligentsia put a new value on what the novelist Ivan Turgenev would call 'leading' or 'central' personalities, who could embody the force for change.[1] Herzen and Belinsky were not only ardent anti-tsarists and socialist pioneers but highly distinctive individuals whose life and work had great general significance. German and French thought shaped their education. Indeed, Herzen is one of the few men in nineteenth-century Russia – and anywhere ever – to have understood Hegel. But the chief impulse of these 'remarkable' men was to use philosophical ideas to fuel protest and reform. In this respect they were 'publicists' more than philosophers, which was an important factor in the making of the intelligentsia. Nevertheless, on the side of philosophy, exposed to Hegel's view of reason as the power of history, they were (to co-opt Vellansky here, since he didn't die until 1847) the first generation to theorize in recognizably pre-Marxist terms about Russia's future. They took from German metaphysics reasons why Russia should move away from tsarism towards a better life.

They felt their calling. Like characters in Schiller's plays, the kind of texts their Romantic education was steeped in, they consciously acted out their rebellious parts on the stage of history. During the thirty-year reign of Nicholas I, when writers were exiled to remote parts of Russia, journals were suppressed, and censorship meddled in everything, Belinsky and Herzen represented heroic defiance in the name of irresistible rational progress. The Third Department, the tsar's intellectual police and censorship organ, put all Russia's literary journalists under pressure to conform to the policy of Official Nationality, which amounted to supporting the tsar and the Orthodox Church, and a fair number did out of conviction. But Belinsky and Herzen refused. They formed a determined, colourful and characterful intelligentsia as it had never existed before. Despite not being philosophers, their lives represented Russian philosophy in the making. Their fates would come to matter to Russia in the same way as Socrates' life and death mattered to Plato and the whole of Western civilization.

Isaiah Berlin pictured them in the finest essay he ever wrote as a historian of ideas:

Imagine then a group of young men, living under the petrified regime of Nicholas I – men with a degree of passion for ideas perhaps never equalled in a European society, seizing upon ideas as they come from the West and with unconscionable enthusiasm, and making plans to translate them swiftly into practice . . . They were conscious of being alone in a bleak world, with a hostile and arbitrary government on the one hand, and a completely uncomprehending mass of oppressed and inarticulate peasants on the other, conceiving of themselves as a kind of self-conscious army, carrying a banner for all to see – of reason and science, of liberty, of a better life.

Like persons in a dark wood, they tended to feel a certain solidarity simply because they were so few and far between; because they were weak, because they were truthful, because they were sincere, because they were unlike the others. Moreover they had accepted the romantic doctrine that every man is called upon to perform a mission beyond mere selfish purposes of material existence; that because they had had an education superior to that of their oppressed brothers they had a direct duty to help them towards the light . . .[2]

Belinsky, the son of a provincial doctor, had to support himself and was often in financial difficulties. Not allowed to complete his education at Moscow University because of a play he wrote attacking serfdom, he threw himself into literary criticism and journalism. He became known for his passionate involvement with one favourite idea after the next, often expressed in 'private' letters to friends. (They would be published in a less censorious age and comprise almost his best work.) He was a tragicomic figure who wrestled with the truth not least because he felt his own limitations. An autodidact, he ran the gamut of changes in terminology and philosophical allegiance. Yet he never lost sight of the core values of honesty, dignity and justice he was seeking for society. His moral urgency characterized the epoch. As he once rebuked the more worldly Turgenev: 'We have not yet solved the problem of the existence of God, and you want to eat.'[3]

Belinsky's knowledge of Goethe and Schiller, Schelling, Fichte and Hegel – those great German figures who stood like volumes of a living encyclopaedia on the shelves of the early Russian thinkers – was fragmented and inevitably superficial. Belinsky couldn't read German and relied on Herzen and Turgenev and their mutual friend Mikhail Bakunin for a version of the latest theories. But he got the gist and responded very much as the men of the 1820s had done, taking the view that Absolute Reason was a panacea. Where he differed was in the passion with which he applied that panacea to social evils. Belinsky insisted that philosophy should provide solutions to man's unhappiness by delivering a single, total, all-reconciling theory of progressive humanity. On how it could be done he wrote mnemonic notes to himself, as here in his early 'Fichtian' phase: 'Man was the last and the greatest effort of nature in its striving to attain self-consciousness. The human organism was an individual [*lichnost'*], was the tool of rational consciousness . . .'[4] One idea, reason, held the world together, if only men could see it. 'Thought or the idea, in its undifferentiated, universal meaning, that is what should be the object of man's learning. Outside the idea everything is a phantom and a dream; only the idea is essential and real.'[5] But only a year later he would write to Bakunin: 'That I *am* [my italics] will always be for me higher than that I *know* and the wise words . . . that it's this way logically but in practice different will always be wise for me.'[6] In his subsequent Hegelian phase Belinsky thought not Fichte the 'subjective' Idealist but Hegel the 'objective' Idealist could now instruct him in the way to be, because the object was 'reality'. '*Reality* is the watchword and the slogan of our age, reality in all things – in beliefs, in science, in art and in life. This powerful, courageous century won't tolerate anything false, counterfeit, weak, diffuse, but loves everything powerful, strong and essential.'[7]

A crisis ensued when Belinsky realized that the *concept* of reality put just as much strain on real lives as any other abstraction. Life as it was lived was more complex than any concept could grasp. Through 1841 the powerful letters Belinsky wrote to his friend Botkin expressed his disillusion with philosophy as a guide to life, at the same time as his immense frustration with a Russia unwilling or unable to realize its cultural potential as a modern country.

Social being, social being – or death! That's my slogan. What is it to me that the general lives when the individual [*lichnost'*] suffers? What is it to me that a genius on earth should live in the sky when the crowd flounders in the mud? What is it to me that I understand the idea, that the world of the Idea has been revealed to me in art, in religion, in history, when I cannot share it with all the people who should be my brothers in humanity, my neighbours in Christ, but who are alien to me and enemies by virtue of their ignorance? What is it to me that for the chosen there is happiness, when the majority does not even suspect it is possible?[8]

The way European Romantic literature extolled the special genius of every people or nation excited Belinsky's generation to imagine what Russia could become. It would become a genuine and valuable culture, only when? Just as Marx was describing Russia as 'semi-Asiatic', Belinsky was prompted to think of it as a never-never land. He called it unreal because it had no civil institutions. Its philosophers were bound to be outsiders, if not unreal themselves.

Our fond (and rational) dream was always to raise up all our life to reality, and consequently our mutual relations; but look what happened! The dream was just a dream and will remain so. We were phantoms and will die phantoms but it's not our fault and we have nothing to reproach ourselves with. Reality arises out of the soil, and the soil of every reality is society. The general without the particular and the individual is real only in pure thought, but in real evident reality it is an onanistic, dead dream. Man, that is a great word and a great business, when he is a Frenchman or a German or an Englishman. But are we Russians great? No! Society looks upon us like diseased growths on its body, and we look upon society as on a heap of rotten dung. Society is right, we are even more right. Society lives by means of a certain quantity of well-known convictions, in which all its members coalesce like the rays of the sun meeting in a glass used for burning. They understand each other without saying a word. This is why in

France, in England, in Germany people who have never seen each other before and are strangers can recognize their kinship, embrace and weep – some on the public square in a moment of rebellion against despotism and for the rights of humanity, others perhaps over the question of bread, a third group over the unveiling of a monument to Schiller. There can be no activity without a goal and without activity no life. The source of interests, goals and activity is the substance of societal life. Is that not clear, logical and true? We are people without a native country, no, worse than not having a country, we are people for whom their native country is a phantom, and it is no surprise that we too are phantoms, that our friendship, our love, our strivings, our activity, is all phantom.

And yet:

I have never met people with such an insatiable hunger for life, with such huge requirements of life, with such a capacity for self-abnegation in the service of the Idea, as us.[9]

Belinsky continued to work for seven years after the *annus mirabilis* of 1841, struggling with ill-health and laying the foundations for a school of literary criticism which, if hardly of benefit to art for its own sake, yoked the cause of literature to social improvement in a bond that lasted two centuries. No one who reads Belinsky even 150 years after his death can deny they have met the first good man in its philosophical history, a wayward Eastern Socrates.

Dear Vasily . . . as you told me on our last meeting, I am a *fact of Russian life*. But just look what a monstrous and misshapen fact! I understand Goethe and Schiller better than those who know them off by heart, and I don't know German, I write (and

25

sometimes quite well) about humanity, and I don't even know what Kaidanov knows. So should I feel guilty? Oh no, a thousand times no! I think, just give me the freedom to act on society for ten years, and then if you like I'll string myself up. In three years perhaps I would have regained my lost youth, would have learned not just German but Greek and Latin, would have acquired some basic knowledge, and would come to love work and find strength of will. Yes, sometimes I feel deeply that this is the radiant awareness of my calling, not the voice of petty self-love, which is trying to justify my laziness, apathy, weakness of will, my lack of strength and the rubbish of my nature . . . So only one thing is left: we'll have to hope to die soon. That is the best thing. Meanwhile goodbye for now. My eyes are closing. I'm sleepy.[10]

Alexander Herzen was such a different man: suave, confident, an aristocrat by birth and nature, half-German on his mother's side, and superbly educated. He read Goethe and Schiller, Schelling, Hegel, Feuerbach and the German mystics in the original German, and Saint-Simon and Fourier in French, so he was more able than any of his contemporaries to shape his ideas in a European context. But he shared Belinsky's antipathy towards the autocracy and the blight of serfdom. Here was the supreme moral issue for every Russian thinker. In his three volumes of memoirs, *My Past and Thoughts*, he remembered with distaste his father's mistreatment of serfs on the family estate. He began to make revolutionary waves while still a student in Moscow and quickly found himself rusticated. A rich man determined to help the Russian cause, he would spend much of his life in involuntary foreign exile. He made homes-from-home in Paris and London, and wrote and campaigned in journals of his own creation against the autocracy. Seen from within the revolutionary tradition Herzen has long been admired for devoting his life's work to the cause of social improvement and political liberalization in Russia. Yet he was always an individualist in his thinking and his style of life. He matured as a reformer rather than a revolutionary and his real protest was against comfortable complacency anywhere.

His hopes began with European socialism. As the future looked from around 1838, the beginning of the 'remarkable' decade, if France could become the founding socialist society, then what was to stop socialism spreading, even eventually to Russia? But Herzen's socialism was always his own. He admired a pre-Marxist socialism in which a morally and aesthetically superior way of life could be freely chosen by rational men and women. His ideal society was more meritocratic than egalitarian and he advocated neither a 'bourgeois' nor a 'proletarian' path to social justice. He never became a mouthpiece for any fixed ideology. He was a political liberal, an idealist and an individualist who, after his socialist hopes for Europe collapsed, thought peasant socialism the best course for peasant Russia combined with a continuing stratum of high intellectual culture for the educated classes.

The crisis in his moral thinking came in 1848 when the French reformist government under Louis-Philippe, in which the socialist hope for better lives for industrial workers lay, failed to carry forward a programme of social and political welfare. Let down by Philippe Egalité, Herzen had a choice: either to brand the disappointing European political Left as selfish individuals unable to practise what they preached, and to go on hoping that good men would choose the socialist path one day; or to change his view of human nature. He changed his assessment of men. Interested in good behaviour in the way paved by classical thinkers from Cicero to Castiglione, Lord Chesterfield to Schiller, Herzen accepted that 'a man only does something seriously when he's doing it for himself'. He came to see that human nature – and therefore the clue to what motivated action – was a mixture of selfish egoism and genuine benevolence; any attempt at the good society had to respect that. Personal morality, which might lead to good results for society, did not follow from a calculation, or from obedience to a rule. Mostly it was the result of impulse. These things he set down in '*Omnia mea mecum porto*' ('I carry all that is mine with me'), the last chapter of his classic account of his 1848 crisis, *From the Other Shore* (1850).[11]

Already before 1848 Herzen was a writer on moral topics. Moral education, or the betterment of Russia, he wrote, needed individuals of character and spirit. Individuals had to improve in this all-round way, not so much to be good as to be truly individual, before the country could improve generally. In his long essay *Dilettantism in Science* (1843) he campaigned for a rigorous scientific and a rich artistic culture inspired by European models. One great example was the 'spiritual aristocracy' exemplified by Goethe.

Herzen was unique among the intelligentsia in combining liberal individualism with a dislike of the utilitarian-individualistic way of life he felt was taking hold of the West and was also causing Western culture to deteriorate from the Goethean gold standard. Herzen wanted an educated Russia of a style which no one else dreamed of in his day. His advocacy of Russian peasant socialism was always admired by historians of the revolutionary movement, but, now that that context is no longer the only one possible for understanding Russian intellectual history, he seems all the harder to place. Russian writers and thinkers have never found him the same inspiration as European and American scholars did forty to fifty years ago. His ideas show he was half-European not only by blood.

A problem for the political Left has been Herzen's very unsocialist contempt for societies levelled by their democratic and egalitarian impulses. In *From the Other Shore* he had a doctor put the case for the aristocratic ideal he linked with Goethe and Schiller in the classical Weimar period. An eighteenth-century European culture like this, with a direct reach back to the Renaissance and Antiquity, should be Russia's model, Herzen said. Liberal individualism needed to buy itself a share of this cultural geneaology if it was to flourish in Russia. But with the same despair as Chaadaev and Belinsky Herzen saw the defence of individualism as a lost cause. The result for the defender could only be personal unhappiness, if he could not escape abroad.

> I see in the present and the past knowledge, truth, moral strength, the striving for independence, love of beauty in a small handful of people who are treated as enemies, lost in an environment which does not sympathize with them. On the other hand I see the tight-fisted development of the remaining strata of society, with their narrow ideas, based upon tradition, their limited needs, a few strivings towards the good, a few feeble impulses towards evil... The mass is only a good when it is faceless. The development of the unique individual, that charming phenomenon, is what everything free, talented and strong works towards.[12]

Herzen was anti-bourgeois, which didn't make him a premature Marxist class warrior, but in this respect a Russian Nietzsche, proclaiming the need for aesthetic sensitivity and moral individualism. Anti-conventional and angry, he despised the dullness of carefully ordered, secure lives for the way they seemed to breed servility, timidity and blindness to beauty.

> The form of life is becoming less and less beautiful and gracious. People shrink back, are afraid, all of them live like shopkeepers, and the morals of the petty bourgeoisie have become the common outlook; no one rejects the settled way of life.[13]

He wasn't alone in his aesthetic-moral vision. All his 'remarkable' generation were anti-philistine. As they reached for the first time to define the good man in Russia and the good society, the 'remarkable' intelligentsia were adamant their country should not be home to a European-style petty bourgeoisie. But what should the good man be then, and how can Russia give him life? And what is the ethical opposite of bourgeois? That Russian virtue is not yet clear. But the definition presumed in *Dilettantism in Science* and *From the Other Shore* is that, with a certain dislike of common egoism taken for granted, the good man in Russia is stylish and not provincial. 'Bourgeois' is simultaneously an aesthetic and a moral description and tries to illustrate the way the two spheres are linked. Herzen suggested that it was provincial to be self-centred, to be morally petty, to be aesthetically clumsy. It was stylish to be an individual. One way of expressing the point might be to say that the good man in Russia is at home in the whole world, not just his own village. The metaphor, with links to the great vision of intellectual and cultural development Hegel outlined in *The Phenomenology of Spirit* (1807), is implicit in much of what Herzen writes about the good man and the good life.

It underlies what he dislikes about the rise of academic and scientific specialization in the nineteenth century. In *Dilettantism in Science* he attacks the narrowness of cultural life in Germany, France, England and Russia. The contemporary worlds of Russian and European learning are full of one-sided specialists more likely to maximize clumsiness and confusion in the world than contribute to real humanist progress. Narrowness of outlook, and the inability to live fully, cannot characterize the good man in Russia. For Herzen the good man will never be a technocrat.[14]

Not to extend his concerns beyond his own immediate needs and worries is the characteristic of a small man. The good man in Russia doesn't have to be a social activist, doesn't have to be a person of expressly good deeds, but he must have a certain roundness as a person. He must know the world of other men from inside, not just as an onlooker or a theorist. In a vision which inspired Hegel, and now Herzen, Goethe famously said that talent grew in solitude but character nurtured itself in the stream of the world. Like his mentor Hegel, Herzen's ethics were about talent and character coming together in an idea of the good man as a man-*in*-the-world.

People are egoists because they are personalities ... Not to acknowledge this is to undo a person, to make him a sterile, insipid, characterless being. We are egoists, and that's why we can work for independence, prosperity and the recognition of our rights, why we hunger for love, and seek activity.[15]

Herzen hated any sign of non-freedom and insisted we should be slaves to nothing: not to language and set ways of thinking, not to nature, not to governments, and not even to a vision of the future. The good society derives its greatest benefit from individual, integrated personalities.

We shall not seek a harbour anywhere else but in ourselves, in the awareness of our unlimited freedom, our autocratic independence. Saving ourselves by this means we shall set ourselves up on that brave and wide terrain, which is the only one on which a free life in society can develop – if it is at all possible for human beings. If people would sooner or later get the idea of saving themselves rather than saving the world, of liberating themselves rather than liberating humanity, how much they would do towards saving the world and liberating mankind.[16]

Herzen was a great reader of Hegel, though not in a way that fitted the revolutionary tradition. *Dilettantism in Science* and *Letters on the Philosophy of Nature* (1845–6) were devoted to praise for what Herzen saw as the true scientific or rational mentality, which strove for disinterested knowledge of objective reality. We have to abandon self-reference to take in new, unknown material. We must give away the truth we know, practise mental courage, *otvaga znaniya*, in order to regain truth at a higher level. In one way this was only a very general lesson. It was Hegel stripped of his over-emphasis on the progressive metaphysics of history to reveal a solid model for individual scholarly and psychological education in the interests of society. What Herzen grasped about Hegel, however, his unique virtue, was the alternative his system of thought offered to British and American Utilitarianism. The Utilitarian theory of society envisaged the pursuit of self-interest to maximize the amount of utility or pleasure in society generally. It was interested in the social product, not the actual moral quality of individuals. But Hegel was interested in maximizing the amount of reason in society, through individual self-development. Hegel gave Herzen too much, more than he could use in responding with unprecedented philosophical depth to the problem of Russian backwardness.

In particular *Dilettantism in Science* responded to the fear Chaadaev had expressed, that Russians cared little to distinguish truth from falsehood. A real grasp of science in the German sense of *Wissenschaft*, in Russian *nauka*, was the answer. That meaning of 'science' embraced scholarship, the human sciences and the hard sciences. It set the accent on accuracy, neutrality and integrity. Hegel, a German Descartes, not related to the cautious French rationalist in kind but playing a parallel role, had written the most up-to-date 'discourse on method'. Herzen hoped this method would build the good society and good men in Russia.

The good man in Russia was a moral-aesthetic concept never named but born in the 'remarkable' decade. It was the way Herzen and Belinsky and their contemporaries thought about each other. As Berlin put it in his essay 'A Remarkable Decade':

> The . . . members [of the intelligentsia] thought of themselves as united by something more than mere interest in ideas; they conceived themselves as being a dedicated order, almost a secular priesthood, devoted to the spreading of a specific attitude to life, something like a gospel.[17]

The term 'remarkable' decade belonged to the critic Pavel Annenkov, whom Berlin went on to quote:

What was demanded was a certain intellectual level and certain qualities of character... They protected themselves against contacts with anything that seemed corrupt... and they were worried by its intrusion, however casual and unimportant. They did not cut themselves off from the world, but stood aloof from it, and attracted attention for that reason; and because of this they developed a special sensitiveness to everything artificial and spurious. Any sign of a morally doubtful sentiment, evasive talk, dishonest ambiguity, empty rhetoric, insincerity, was detected at once, and ... provoked immediate storms of ironical mockery and merciless attack ... The circle resembled an order of knighthood, a brotherhood of warriors; it had no written constitution. Yet it knew all its members scattered over our vast country; it was not organized but a tacit understanding prevailed. It stretched as it were across the stream of the life of its time, and protected it from aimlessly flooding its banks. Some adored it; others detested it.[18]

The philosophical encouragement for this attitude came from the German metaphysics and literature the 'remarkable' men read. There the budding good man in Russia met the German 'beautiful soul', whom Schiller defined as one who had so absorbed the lesson of the good that it was second nature to him. His thoughts were his deeds.

A beautiful soul is so called, when the ethical feeling of all a person's sentiments has become so secure that he can allow his emotions to lead his will without fear, and is never in danger of getting into conflict with the resolutions of his will.[19]

Because Schiller was a disciple of Kant, the beautiful soul left an imprint of Kantian moral idealism on the Russian intelligentsia which it never lost.

While setting the standard for the moral life the beautiful soul also suggested the right attitude to knowledge. The Russian idealists accepted with alacrity that Romantic marriage of ethics and knowledge – of being and knowing, of values and facts – which would prove so enormously fruitful and enormously dangerous in the history of European ideas. For Schelling, the good man was one who could understand the totality of nature and man's place within it. The right way of life was right because it cleared a right way of seeing. For the right way of life introspection and imagination were required in equal part. Art was needed, to give roundness and breadth. Odoevsky's reading of Schelling in the 1820s persuaded him that the task for the good man in Russia was to understand his instinct and feel his reason.[20] Kant had said that art existed at the crossing-point of reason and feeling and so the Romantics were set on course. The good man in Russia was now a rich personality abundantly able to connect the material with the spiritual, the desirable with the real.

Suddenly the concept of the beautiful soul was present in Russian life, and the 'remarkable' men used it to praise each other, as in this memoir of the poet Venevitinov by the future Slavophile thinker, Ivan Kireevsky.

Anyone who thinks his way with love into the works of Venevitinov (for love alone gives us full understanding) will recognize there a philosopher permeated by the revelation of his age; he will recognize a deep, original [samobytny] poet whose every feeling is illuminated by thought, whose every thought is warmed by the heart; whose dream is unadorned by art but born of itself beautiful; whose best song is his own life, the free development of his full and harmonious soul. For nature generously endowed him with her gifts and maintained their diversity in equilibrium. For that reason everything beautiful was native to him; that is why in knowing himself he found resolved all the secrets of art, and in his own soul he could read the outline

34

of the highest laws, and contemplate the beauty of creation. For that reason nature was accessible to both his mind and his heart ... The harmony of mind and heart was the outstanding characteristic of his soul, and even his imagination was more the music of ideas and feelings than the play of inventions. This testifies to the fact that he was born all the more for philosophy than for poetry.[21]

Ivan Turgenev took the beautiful soul as a guide to the personality of Nikolai Stankevich (1813–40), a little-known Russian thinker but one who was a dear companion to Belinsky and Herzen until his premature death in 1840.

[Stankevich's] spirit never drooped, and everything he talked about, whether it was the ancient world, art, sculpture and so on was full of higher truth and some kind of fresh beauty and youth ... Stankevich had that effect on others because he didn't think of himself, he was genuinely interested in others and, as if he didn't notice it himself, carried others with him into the realm of the Ideal. No one argued in such a lovely and human fashion. There was no trace in him of phrase-mongering. Even Tolstoy wouldn't have found it in him ... Stankevich was bigger than average build, and very good looking ... he had lovely black hair, a high forehead, small grey eyes; his gaze was loving and cheerful ... when he smiled his lips crinkled up slightly, but very kindly – in general his smile was extraordinarily welcoming and generous ... in his whole being, in his movements there was a kind of grace and unconscious *distinction* [original in English] – as if he were a son of the Tsar, unaware of his heritage ... he had an almost childlike naivety which was all the more moving and surprising given his mind ... he was very religious – but rarely spoke of religion.[22]

The cult of what the American psychologist William James would later call tender-mindedness became deeply rooted in this Russia of the 1830s, when the newly married Herzens and their friends the Ogaryovs acted out the philosopher's right attitude to the world on their joint wedding night. The two couples threw themselves on their knees before a crucifix, prayed together and kissed each other in the spirit of Christ. The historian Martin Malia observed of this scene that it was 'the very apotheosis of Schiller's aesthetic education: four beautiful souls united in love and God and the cosmos.'[23] Perhaps not the cosmos in Schiller's case, for this was more Schelling's province, and Schiller himself was an atheist. But clearly these were the romantic years in Russia, when the pursuit of truth and the pursuit of friendship and love had a freshness comparable with Plato.

Odoevsky and his friends sat up all night discussing virtue.[24] Searching for a similar definition, Galich wrote that the young philosopher must be able to think and feel as a *typical* human being and be able to maintain within himself a wholeness which kept his various impulses in harmony. He must be able to pair imagination with reason and be lucid in both heart and mind. He should have the practical goal of humanity before him at all times. With these qualities he would be on the right path to divine knowledge [*bozehstvennaya nauka*] and might emerge as one of philosophy's chosen few:

You are distinguished from the mass of ordinary souls and heavenly powers educate and guide you invisibly. For without a certain mood of the soul [*nastroenie dushi*] our science is in vain and our searching unfruitful.[25]

Annenkov summed up the 'remarkable' atmosphere the new good Russians conjured up.

All took the moral factor as the starting point for any activity, whether in life or in literature, all acknowledged the importance of aesthetic demands on themselves and on works of the intelligence and the imagination, and not a single member of the circle ever entertained the idea that one could do without, for instance, art, poetry and creative work generally in the political education of people any more than in life ... moral good consisted in the aesthetic cultivation of one's own self, i.e. in acquiring a sensibility for the True, the Good and the Beautiful, and developing an invincible organic revulsion for ugliness of any shape or kind ... It was his belief that the study of the basic ideas in the creative works of true artists could serve as a good device for elevating oneself to the level of Rational man and Purified Personality.[26]

The sentimental good man made a deep impact in Russia, and in the novel *The Brothers Karamazov* (1879–80) Dostoevsky would later rediscover his qualities as a quasi-religious figure in his portrait of Alyosha Karamazov as a beautiful soul. As an achievement in philosophy the Russian beautiful soul expressed values which no one yet knew how to set down systematically, but which could only be conserved in a non-technocratic, anti-utilitarian culture where literature and philosophy would have honoured places.

The idea of the beautiful soul in Russia produced charming creatures, whose world revolved around philosophy and poetry. They were weak men in a country about to discover its urgent need for revolutionary leaders and teachers. Many of them were personally weak, like the novelist Turgenev, who reproduced that weakness in his stories of 'superfluous men' who had no place in a world of social and political activism. With the exception of Herzen, all the early Russian beautiful souls were politically weak, as was every other genuine individual in Russia. But they were deeply attractive as people a little disabled by their unworldliness.

A last addition to the beautiful soul generation must be the Slavophile Aleksei Khomiakov (1804–60), although technically, like Odoevsky, he was suspended between the generations. Khomiakov was another nobleman and dilettante. He was at some time a cavalry officer, poet, publicist, historian, agronomist and inventor. In this last respect he took a 'silent motor' to the Great Exhibition in London that was so loud the neighbours where he was staying complained. A sympathetic memoir depicts him as an impressively bold and masculine type, who led a life at once glamorous, poetic and simple. He seems to have chosen a very attractive path, never finding his way to the front of a classroom, but applying himself to problems of philosophy and theology while being able to wander around his country estate admiring the stars in the sky. He was a typical scion of an old, aristocratic Russian family, bound by a service ethic to his country. Commissioned in the army, he distinguished himself in battle against the Turks in Bulgaria in 1828–9, but as soon as he was free of his obligations he preferred that rustical-philosophical life which gave him time to read and think.[27]

He travelled as a young man, spending the years 1825–6 in Paris learning to write plays which were not to be his distinction in life. His early friends were the future Decembrists, army officers whose patriotism he shared, but whose rebellion he condemned. He travelled abroad and loved England, the way other nineteenth-century Russian conservatives would. On their honeymoon trip, he and his wife took an extended detour home through northern Italy and central Europe, where he was able to use his excellent foreign languages. His German was as fluent as his French and English, which in turn allowed him to correspond and keep in personal contact with Western writers.

As a thinker he was close to Venevitinov and Odoevsky, and counts as an honorary member of the Schellingist *lyubomudry*. His work contains all the hallmark references to Kant and Fichte, Schelling and Hegel, of the Romantic generation. At the same time he inherited his mother's religious faith and remained a devout believer. He became an expert in theology and his essays on the ways of Orthodoxy compared with those of Western Churches were translated into French and German. A long correspondence followed with the conservative English churchman, expert on the Anglican liturgy and sometime Bishop of Worcester, Samuel Palmer. Herzen, a very different type of man, found Khomiakov endlessly argumentative, but surely here was a man of parts of whom Herzen should have approved, at least for Russia's sake. Khomiakov's friends found him lively and lovable and valuable and when he died unexpectedly of cholera in 1860, there was great sadness at the loss of a theological master.[28]

Khomiakov's under-appreciated philosophy synthesized the two streams of influence upon him, German Idealism and Orthodoxy. Critical of Hegel's rationalist metaphysics, Khomiakov nevertheless grasped why the most dynamic and detailed system of secular reason the world had ever known was not to be dismissed lightly. The word philosophy is appropriate in Khomiakov's case, although it should not be taken to mean that he worked for long years to perfect his systematic account of the meaning of life. Like many Russians after him he preferred, and was at his best, amending the work of others. The comments on Hegel in the 'Letter on Philosophy to Yu. F. Samarin' were written shortly before his death.

He wrote there that Hegel's abstractions were the rock on which Russian affection for German Idealism foundered. The 'Letter', which belonged to his last decade, has no exact date and possibly he was slow to write down suspicions which Belinsky had voiced fifteen years earlier. The question Belinsky had raised, and Khomiakov now explored, was whether these German abstractions really described reality. What was it they were true of? Surely not of lived life. How could something called reason make sense of all human experience? Khomiakov took particular exception to the generative aspect of Hegel's system: the notion that ideas bring reason-as-life into being. Khomiakov thought Hegel was obsessed with life as an intellectual process to the point where he assumed the growth of ideas meant everything. Hegel was wrong because reality has an existence independent of what men think about it.

> Hegel's whole system represents only the possibility for the *concept* [my italics] to develop itself into the full diversity of actuality and to culminate in the actuality of spirit.[29]

To emphasize the word 'concept' while reading this sentence makes Khomiakov's meaning plain. When concepts are applied, some residue of the real and the present moment is left behind ungrasped. The proposition is important. Khomiakov's preferred approach to truth laid one of the twin foundations of Russian philosophy. (The other foundation was laid by Odoevsky, with whom Khomiakov shared a critical view of the West, despite those happy travels.)

Seen from pre-industrial Russia, the social and cultural aspects of industrialization were unattractive to Russian noblemen like Odoevsky and Khomiakov. Would it be too much to think Khomiakov displayed his silent motor at the Great Exhibition in criticism of all the new noise in the world? Khomiakov accused Hegel of being too much concerned with the *manufacture* of reality. He was philosophy's answer to a slightly vulgar nineteenth-century industrial entrepreneur, as the Russian nobleman saw him. Accompanied by a great deal of terminological brouhaha, his very mind resembled a 'factory process.'[30]

The dawning sense of Russia's different situation, the cultural lag which meant Russia still had time to choose a different path, could be expressed in so many different ways. The philosophical has usually been ignored. But it was the acute awareness of how Russia was different, and might save itself for a better future, that prompted a model of knowledge distinct from the latest Western theories. As technical expertise – the result of the application of instrumental reason – threatened to exhaust the definition of what reality meant, Khomiakov wanted Russia to retain a grasp of simple truth. From Khomiakov's point of view, all human beings had an essential knowledge of reality prior to any logical analysis, or technical use, they might make of it. Instrumental knowledge was not the beginning of their relationship with the world, only a subordinate part of it. Really to know the world we have to simplify ourselves intellectually and revert to a mode of immediate apprehension.

Hegel's model of knowledge, which rested on a sharp division between the individual and the world he perceived, and all the painful and stimulating complexity resulting from that split, absorbed the new socio-economic fact that, in the vanguard of history, millions of rural workers were leaving their homes to work in the alien milieu of towns and factories. Economic progress exemplified the ways of the Hegelian mind, as Hegel would have claimed, or, the explanation materialists would prefer, Hegelian mind took its shape from rapid contemporary social and economic change.[31] Whichever came first, mind or matter (and Hegel in 1807 was ahead of German industrial history), Khomiakov accepted the connection between economics and mentality but applied it to Russia with a different result. Russia was not so far advanced as the West, therefore its mode of knowledge was different. By choice it might remain different.

Hegelian man's struggle with the alien world cost him pain. Could this account of truth be right? Why should the pursuit of truth cost individuals their happiness and feeling of being at home in the world? Why should the nineteenth century cost Russians dear, when they still had a choice? Many Russians, and not just conservative thinkers, wanted to hold on to native forms of community in Russia. Khomiakov's philosophical achievement was to justify that wish with a vision of knowledge linked to happiness.

Like many philosophers Khomiakov had a negative and a positive project. His negative project was to attack Hegel. His positive work was to try to capture the presentness and community so valued by traditional Russian culture with a concept of his own, *sobornost'*.[32] *Sobornost'*, from the noun *sobor*, meaning a cathedral and reflecting the general idea of a gathering, was in effect religious community elevated to a principle of being. It was the idea which, with two definitions of knowledge as faith attached to it, made the first Russian philosophy of knowledge possible. The first definition captured our immediate knowledge of the world prior to the logical activity of reason. Khomiakov claimed that by this intuitive knowledge we can distinguish between the real and our mind's fantasy. We know immediately and thus without reflection whether our idea of an object coincides with the object itself. His second definition of knowledge described the complete understanding we can have of the world when all our faculties act in concert. In both these definitions Khomiakov embraced a favourite Russian and Schellingian idea, that knowledge arises not out of confrontation with the world but a coming-together. Schelling called the product of the synthetic faculty '*Mitwissenschaft*', 'knowledge-with'. Khomiakov's knowledge theory was based on a double sense of community: among men and between men and objects. With a rich religious tradition to support him, reflecting a belief in God and man as of one substance, Khomiakov proposed an ideal mode of consubstantial knowledge, or cognitive love, whereby the individual became one with the thing perceived.[33]

Khomiakov's friend and fellow religious thinker Ivan Kireevsky (1806–56), whose notebooks passed to Khomiakov when he died, set up a similar positive goal for Russian philosophy when he wrote in those notes of an ideally 'integral knowledge', distinguished from 'logical knowledge'. Integral knowledge requires us to participate with our whole being in knowledge, and also to realize that we cannot seek knowledge in social isolation. Intellectual judgement is only effective when it emanates from being-in-community. Being-in-community is the right inner condition of the thinking soul.[34] Corresponding to 'integral knowledge' for Kireevsky is 'organic personality', another allusion to Russia's desire not to be industrialized, neither socially nor epistemologically.[35] The Russia of Khomiakov and Kireevsky preferred to remain one step behind, in a more beautiful and harmonious world than any utopia the conflictual West promised.

The decade or so when Russia began to think of itself as a potential good society made up of good men was 'remarkable' precisely because it awakened the idea of Russia as a unique culture in relation to Europe. Belinsky and Herzen worked in a world in which reference was increasingly made to the *Russian* truth which Absolute Reason would reveal. Philosophy is a universal discipline, but this approach need not be rejected as unacceptable if one thinks back to how Plato, for whom Socrates represented the best of Athens, was dazzled by the competing philosophical merits of Syracuse. Geographical and political entities have often defined contrasting approaches to, and evaluations of, the pursuit of truth.

One of the first instances of 'Russian truth' occurred in an early Kireevsky essay, 'The Nineteenth Century' (1832). The idea was duplicated in many pieces of lesser journalism. Reflecting the passions of the era a decade later Odoevsky would devote the last of his 'Russian Nights' to the Russian way. Historicism taught that national cultures find themselves in different stages of development along their unique path to self-fulfilment. To reflect upon this process was what made the nation self-aware. The very business of finding one's nation caught up in meaningful self-reflection was a national landmark. So the Russian intelligentsia, by virtue of its own existence, could congratulate Russia on entering the modern world.[36]

The national element pressurizing philosophy in the Romantic era was strong, but it was not difficult to translate out of nationalese into conceptualese. Philosophy could be called Russian, and about Russia, and still be universally useful. In Europe, historicism generated parallel ideas of French and German 'truth', which set up contrasting models of truth in relation to freedom. The German Romantics, intimidated by the French Revolution, defined German freedom as an inner state, not to be gained by French political violence. Fichte in his *Addresses to the German Nation* and Schelling in that extraordinary 1811 book *On the Nature of German Science* both labelled as German a metaphysics which began with the freedom of the individual to give the world meaning out of his own thoughts. The 'German' position was a rebellion from social constraints on liberty, but a revolt that, for Schelling and Fichte, who were accordingly styled 'subjective' Idealists, only happened in imagination. Hegel found this initial German position inadequate. He refused to stop at the milestone of defensive inwardness which for him was only part of modern liberation. The story would be complete when consciously free individuals found themselves reintegrated in a complex free society. Hegel's German vision, in his capacity as an 'objective' Idealist, was modern society with a plus sign after it; it was the de luxe model thanks to the amount of reason it incorporated. Progress would obtain when individual freedom became outward and social again, confidently worldly but incorporating the deep and formative experience of German inwardness. The message was in-tended to uplift the Germans after Napoleon had dealt such a blow to their antiquated, despotic states. Such rational modern freedom was everything the nineteenth century should hope for. Hegel put forward a grand cultural ideal, which not surprisingly made a great impact: on the alas rather simple thinking of his successor Ludwig Feuerbach, and in 'remarkable' Russia itself.

When Feuerbach wrote in the late 1830s that philosophy must become Franco-German, he meant that a philosophy adequate to the progressive age should combine German Idealism's interest in mind/spirit (*Geist*) with French eighteenth-century materialism. Not an easy task, because they were normally thought of as opposite approaches to nature, the one involving a priori mental syntheses, the other restricting itself to empirical data. But Hegel had made the synthesis of materialism and idealism – the synthesis of syntheses – attractive. As a result, everywhere his name was known, synthesis became a potent general idea and a way of thinking about the future. In early nineteenth-century Russia, many articles and essays expressed the thought that Russian culture might move beyond present European one-sidedness towards something more perfect.

Both Kireevsky and Chaadaev's editor Nikolai Nadezhdin came out in print with speculation that Russia's task was to unite cultural and philosophical opposites. Nadezhdin's name is unknown outside Russia but he was particularly prescient about how Russia would reach this goal by revealing the social-material bonds or ties in which true intellectual wisdom consists.[37] A strong version of the Russian historicist vision was that the West was a graveyard out of which a new Russian-led European culture would be born. The graveyard was quite a metaphor for the negative moment Hegel said was entailed in all progress, in order for Western society to reach its complex future goal. Dostoevsky liked it so much as an incentive he revived it forty years later, for it almost contained an incentive to kill the West off.[38]

If synthesis was the pattern of the fashionable argument, the nation or 'the people' was its substance. The emerging nation was the token of progress. German Romanticism celebrated the freedom of nations to fulfil their natural destiny free from the fetters of empires and autocrats. Nations, as living entities, bore inside themselves the seed of what they could ideally become. The Russian Westernizers admired the Hegelian idea because it showed how Russia was bound to throw off tsarist oppression as it progressed along its natural path.

Having established a model for a great synthetic culture, Romantic nationalism then had one more task in Russia: to set the idea of the people – the *narod* – against the tsarist state. The Slavophile Kireevsky of the 1840s, and Khomiakov as he always was, rejected the Western model of national progress but allowed German Idealism to stimulate a new awareness of their own nation as the product of its people and their folk ways. Kireevsky's wife, it is said, was the first to point out the similarity between some of Schelling's pronouncements and those of the Church Fathers which had long ago become the daily habit of worship of a religious people. Her observation exemplified how men like her Slavophile husband were not immune to Western ideas, but preferred to find Russian parallels.[39]

Where, in one of the first visions of utopian socialism, the French thinker François Fourier imagined *phalanges* of 1,600 persons, occupying a common building or *phalanstère*, engaging in agricultural work, and sharing the yield of the land and the profit, Khomiakov and Kireevsky suggested that Russia would better refer to the ancient peasant socialist community, since such co-operative communities were still in place in the 1840s and didn't need to be invented on abstract principles. The Russian community was called the *obshchina*, from the word *obshchy*, meaning general or communal, and the concept was powerful. The Slavophiles based their entire outlook on a classic distinction they made forty years before the German sociologist Ferdinand Tönnies (1855–1936), between societies and communities.[40]

Herzen agreed with the Slavophiles on the desirability of this unique, embedded Russian form of socialism. In fact there was hardly a Russian thinker before Lenin who did not want Russia to be itself. So what was the difference between the Westernizers and the Slavophiles in the end? It was in their underlying philosophy of ethics in relation to knowledge. The Slavophiles were religious conservatives, the Westernizers atheist progressives, which put them in different philosophical camps with regard to science and reason. The Slavophiles, perfectly represented in this respect by Khomiakov, were sceptical of the civilizing power of reason. Given Hegel's model of progress, which started with naive community, passed through an age of individualism and social fragmentation, and moved on to a more complex kind of society than community, the Russian Westernizers looked forward to that social complexity; the Slavophiles preferred to stay with naive community. These differences of direction did not deter men in either camp from believing Russia's future was unique and lay apart. But it did affect what was to be done to make this difference work for Russia in a concrete way, linked to social reform if not revolution. The next three generations would throw up a storm of conflicting ideas.

3

The New Men

The year 1848 was a terrible setback for progressive Western politics and likewise a nadir for early socialism in Russia. As the French socialist cause was defeated on the Paris barricades 1,000 miles away, Nicholas I put the Russian universities under quasi-military control, stepped up the censorship of books, and sat on the press. Unrest among the Poles in the Russian empire added to a fear that Russia too would soon erupt. In 1848 Sergei Uvarov, the man who had invented the ideology of Official Nationality and held the tsar's realm together for fifteen years, was astonished to lose his job as Minister of Public Instruction, and de facto chief censor, for being insufficiently conservative. When Belinsky died the same year it was clear an age had passed in which no progress had been made politically. The Crimean War (1853–6) subsequently diverted an unhappy country from its domestic issues. Yet there was light ahead, for when Nicholas died in 1855 he made way for his son, Alexander II, who finally liberated the serfs, in 1861.

At this time Russia passed intellectually into the hands of 'the new men', who tried a more practical experiment than hitherto any good or 'remarkable' men had proposed. They aimed to build a society which, if it was not Western, was a recognizable relative of Western middle-class models, based on 'the rationalist ideals of radical bourgeois democracy'.[1] In many ways it was a strange age, combining utopian socialism and, of all the world-views which might have proved unpopular in Russia, Utilitarianism. Both were rationalistic and both were from the West.

Nikolai Chernyshevsky (1828–89), who proposed that goal of radical bourgeois democracy, published an annotated Russian edition of J. S. Mill's *Principles of Political Economy* early in his career. The experience of the English Mill instructed him in the Utilitarian outlook, at the same time as the German Feuerbach persuaded him that Russia's future no longer lay with metaphysics but with the new science of man. Feuerbach, that rather simple thinker, had a 'medical-materialist' reason for discarding metaphysics. He thought that both Hegelian Idealism and Christian faith squandered cultural energy by dividing human nature into real and ideal aspects. 'Mankind' itself was a promise of something that didn't exist.[2] Chernyshevsky wrote his most significant essay, 'On the Anthropological Principle', to honour Feuerbach's move out of pointless, enervating metaphysics and into social welfare. Such should also be the Russian way forward.

A man must be regarded as a single being having only one nature ... a human life must not be cut into two halves, each belonging to a different nature ... every aspect of man's activity must be regarded as the activity of his whole organism, from head to foot inclusively, or if it is the special function of some particular organism we are dealing with, that organ must be regarded in its natural connection with the entire organism ... Anthropology ... always remembers that the process as a whole, and every part of it, takes place in a human organism ... [exemplifying] the operation of the laws of nature.[3]

What mattered to Chernyshevsky was not a beautiful abstraction like mankind but real men and women and their immediate needs. To his

Feuerbachian enthusiasm for seeing those physical needs met he added a moral Utilitarian outlook that might have been expressed by Mill or Bentham:

> A careful examination of the motives that prompt men's actions shows that all deeds, good and bad, noble and base, heroic and craven are prompted by one cause: a man acts in the way that gives him the most pleasure ... the fact that good and bad actions are prompted by the same cause does not, of course, diminish the difference between them.[4]

Chernyshevsky had to accept, against the Russian grain, that even though Utilitarianism didn't distinguish between intrinsically good and bad deeds, what made it valid was its interest in their best possible social result. He made his concession because of the flourishing society, the common good, Utilitarianism promised. Chernyshevsky succumbed to the difficulties many people have with Utilitarianism, but he made an effort to overcome them. Under Mill's influence he thought he had found in self-interest the best explanation of what makes men act. The theory was a most useful tool for any thinker engaged in a programme of social change.

Chernyshevsky's simple convictions can be traced consistently throughout his thought. He was a materialist in so far as he believed that there was no invisible human nature in addition to man's natural being and that therefore questions about man could be answered by the natural sciences. (This Feuerbachian belief made philosophy redundant as a first-order discipline.) As a Utilitarian he believed that the well-tuned society derived its energy from men's natural selfishness.

If Chernyshevsky was a philosopher at all then it was in the sphere of social ethics. His function was to help make man's home in the world more comfortable through critical encouragement of the sciences. The notion of the good society as 'home' had been provided by Hegel, but the new idea was that not a discipline of spirit, but social science and consequent social and political reform were the way to make it happen. Faith in science to provide social solutions made Chernyshevsky a 'pre-positivist', that is, a direct precursor of those slightly younger men of the Populist years who would come under the spell of Auguste Comte and Herbert Spencer in the 1870s and bring a passion for science to Russia.[5] 'The science of social material welfare that is usually called political economy' will stop society making bad use of its members, Cherny-shevsky wrote, very much with the accent on science as the focus of hope. If conflicts still arise in society because individuals have incommensurate goals, that is because social institutions are not yet rational enough to iron them out.[6] The name of his short-lived pupil and friend Nikolai Dobrolyubov (1836–61) is usually bracketed with Chernyshevsky's to populate the story of revolution in Russia, but philosophically Chernyshevsky was the 'new man' to exceed all others.

Chernyshevsky had no doubt that human beings were rational. His novel *What is to be Done?* (1864) focused on a series of fictional characters who embodied the Utilitarian philosophy of rational egoism, coupled with Feuerbachian materialism and adapted for Russian use. One after another those characters took control of their lives, formed realistic aims and showed how human goals could be worked out 'with mathematical precision'. The title of the novel was an exemplary Utilitarian question about how Russia could become the co-operative socialist society favoured by its positive characters. The answer was to take a materialistic view of man, and to get rid of weakness of will, pessimism, guilt, tragic inevitability, by changing the social and economic conditions which might make him irrational.[7] Lenin, always interested in galvanizing sluggish Russia into action, would be an unrivalled admirer of *What is to be Done?*

The trend towards simplification was not, however, a happy one for Russian thought, and when Chernyshevsky also used art criticism to express his social optimism, the result was the most unsubtle aesthetic ever invented, which entirely subordinated art to the smooth running of the human machine.

> Let art be content with its fine and lofty mission of being a substitute for reality in the event of its absence, and of being a manual of life for man. Reality stands higher than dreams, and essential purpose stands higher than fantastic claims.[8]

Efficient lives led by free men was Chernyshevsky's goal. His reign was the dullest moment in Russian intellectual history before the advent of Sovietism.

Yet in the very deadness of his bourgeois – by English standards, lower-middle-class – and technocratic vision for Russia Chernyshevsky was something like Russia's answer, adapted, but recognizable, to Adam Smith. Smith, as the pioneer of libertarian economics, was the mind behind the successful nation of small shopkeepers Victorian England became. Smith, a sophisticated mind, believed – although given his sophistication perhaps the metaphor was not quite serious – that an 'Invisible Hand' naturally evened out private and public interests when individuals engaged in free exchange and competition as the basis of the social order.[9] Chernyshevsky believed in a socialist version of this socio-economic machinery which freed men and women to lead private lives in the common interest, helping to build up social capital. *What is to be Done?* laid down a blueprint for a new mixed class of urban Russians, workers and professionals, seamstresses and doctors, to flourish in a decent, hard-working society in which exchange and competition were tempered by the rational inclination to social justice.

Chernyshevsky established a Russian model for 'the new science of political economy'. But really the emphasis was more on morals than economics. No sooner was the political idea established than it seemed as if some native genie had put a different fuel into the social machine. It was as if Chernyshevsky could do nothing but become a representative of the Russian spirit, even though he was trying to work with British-style Utilitarianism. The Utilitarian society where it was rational to be selfish slipped into a Russian community where it was decent to be unselfish and you could call it rational if you liked. The new man in Russia would take responsibility for, and share responsibility with, his neighbour. He would bring to a Russian version of Western-style radical bourgeois democracy the sense of community from a Russian village.

Two problems gape wide open in Chernyshevsky's thinking. One is whether human happiness and social well-being are actually calculable by reason. The second concerns the ramifications of Utilitarianism merging with the Russian political-communal vision. For, supposing that Russian society considers itself rational because its philosophers have said it is, because these philosophers call progress what can be worked out according to calculations based on sociological facts; supposing that, against its self-perception, this Russian society is really driven by a spiritual-communal dream: who then is to make those judgements about happiness and well-being and on what basis are they still scientific? A channel opens up for authoritarianism to establish itself in the name of Utilitarian reason and Chernyshevsky already exemplifies how it will take its course. He judges that wealth makes bad use of men. It 'does more harm than good to society as a whole ... this is revealed [to him] with mathematical precision.'[10]) To involve science in this pronouncement is to suggest that all rational persons, given the facts, must conclude wealth is bad for humankind. The matter does not involve subjective values at all, only the objective scrutiny of facts. But it is extremely difficult to be objective about wealth; and the subjective difficulty wouldn't necessarily disappear even if we accepted a free-market philosophy for the general good. In Chernyshevsky's day there was already a Russian ethical longing for a 'science' to explain how money is bad for human nature and the tendency to tack on a Western social theory to make the ethical claim plausible.

Chernyshevsky was the son of a priest and all his life was driven by his impatience with the degrading social consequences of autocracy. Imprisoned in the Peter and Paul Fortress in St Petersburg for his continuing opposition to serfdom – existing injustice turned out to be hardly dented by the emancipation of the serfs in 1861 – he led a martyr's life. From prison, having written his famous novel behind bars, he was sentenced to hard labour in Siberia, where he remained for almost twenty years in poor health, a broken man. For a good man it is a sad fact that he was not so much a prophet of revolution as a distant herald of the entropy and unhappiness that would follow it in the Soviet century.

Dmitry Pisarev (1840–68), who suffered a fate comparable to Chernyshevsky's in his short life, was the more interesting personality, probably because of the conflict of coming from a gentry family in a lower-class age. His social background, together with the religious piety his mother taught him, caused him so much anguish at university, where he realized he had things wrong, that he suffered a nervous breakdown and attempted suicide. He wrote that it was only coming to write for a women's liberal journal in 1861 that 'forced me out of my confined cell into the fresh air'.[11] Liberated from within, he put pen to paper on his loathing for the tsarist state, for which he too was soon in prison. He finished most of the writing he would ever do there before his release in 1866. Two years later he was dead, drowned, either by accident or his own intention, in the Baltic Sea.

Unlike Chernyshevsky Pisarev was an individualist and exactly because of that a unique radical reformer in mid-nineteenth-century Russia. He was most interested in improved individual psychology to build a better world. Like Chernyshevsky he was impressed by the materialist and rational credentials of Utilitarianism but easily found himself taking up the most moral position that school offered, which was Mill's 'higher' or ideal' view. Senseless egoism like 'that of a child stuffing cakes' was not the same thing as the prudent egoism of 'building inexhaustible stores of fresh pleasure for his entire future', he wrote.[12]

In one of his essays Pisarev swapped the terms around so radically that selfishness came to express one of the most ascetic-heroic models ever put forward in Russian literature. He was evidently trying to marry the beautiful soul ideal of the previous generation with the new demand for good men to contribute actively to a benevolent political order. What he came up with, the man who takes care of his own needs fully, the man who ensures that his whole personality is realized, could have been proposed by Herzen.

That is the selfishness of the new men, and to that selfishness there are no bounds: for that, indeed, they will sacrifice everyone and everything. They love themselves passionately. They respect themselves to the point of worship. But even in relation to themselves they cannot be blind and condescending; they must be on their guard to maintain their love and their respect for themselves at every given moment. Still more precious in their eyes than their love and respect are the direct and sincere relations of their analysing and controlling ego to the ego that acts and orders the external conditions of life. If the one ego were unable to look the other boldly and resolutely in the eye, if the one ego took it into its head to answer the demands of the other with evasions and sophisms, and the other ego meanwhile dared to shut its eyes and to be content with the vain excuses of the first, the result of this shameful confusion in the soul of the new man would be such despair and such convulsive horror at his own paltry and defiled person that he would surely spit in his own face and then, having thus befouled himself, would plunge headfirst into the deepest slough.

The new man knows perfectly well how implacable and pitiless he is toward himself. The new man fears himself more than anything else; he is a force, but woe betide him if this force ever turns against itself. If he commits any abomination which

produces internal discord within himself he knows that there will
be no cure for that discord but suicide or insanity.[13]

Pisarev makes all his remarks about the good life with a bias towards
the need for self-cultivation. Society needs a constant infusion of fresh
intellectual energy, which means nurturing ourselves on the best literature
and history. To educate and liberate ourselves is the best contribution we
can make to the general utility. Despite the quote for which he is
misleadingly famous, that boots are better than Shakespeare, which makes
him sound like a Russian Bentham, Pisarev's world is full of zest and
passion and a love of individual excellence. He puts forward a notion of
moral self-presence which strives to remove all metaphysical impediments
to being good here and now; and he endorses that fundamental link, so
dear to Russian thought, between morality and knowledge. There is a
truth of existence – and a way for Russia – which only the morally self-
present man can perceive.

The notion of moral self-presence is one I have derived from
metaphysics and adapted to ethics to try to get at that link between
knowledge and goodness so dear to Pisarev. Classical philosophy talks
about things being identical with themselves or self-present. Moral self-
presence would be moral self-possession. It would mean no gap
between what a man is and what he does: a lack of parallax brought
about not by the quality of his reason (as in so much moral theory from
Aristotle to Richard Hare) but by the integrity of his being-in-the-
world. Postwar French existentialism tried to set up an ideal like this by
banishing 'bad faith'. The Marxists had their notion of *praxis*. The
impulse in every case was to pin down some integral connection
between what a man thinks and what he does, and thus to be philosophically at ease with what motivates action. But moral self-presence
in all the models that come to mind also includes a notion of self-
liberation.

Pisarev was almost a contemporary of Nietzsche and when he struck the note of self-liberation he captured that aspect of the Nietzschean revolt against idealism which was a love of tangible life in the here and now, not enslavement to comfortless and ill-adapted abstractions. Feuerbach wrote of the terrible waste when a man directed his energy and zeal and love at an empty space. Nietzsche, who owed far more to Feuerbach than is generally acknowledged, wept when he first understood how easy it was for a man not to live fully. Pisarev had a similar personal experience: that shedding of false piety which launched his brief and tragic philosophical career.

Pisarev incurs many labels – materialist and positivist chief among them – but his inheritance from Feuerbach mingles self-liberation with the liberating effects of science. He is pro-science and pro-reason, and he dislikes inwardness rather as if Hegel has convinced him it was a sick and imperfect state of the soul. Aged twenty-one he wrote boldly about the shortcomings of Plato's Idealism from this fresh, outward-looking, practical point of view.

Plato is unquestionably entitled to our esteem as a powerful mind and a remarkable talent. The colossal mistakes this talent made in the sphere of abstract thought derived not from weakness of mind, shortness of sight, or timidity of thought, but from the predominance of the poetic element, from *deliberate contempt for the testimony of experience* [my emphasis], and from an overweening desire, common in powerful minds, to extract the truth from the depths of one's own creative spirit instead of examining and studying it in particular phenomena.[14]

As Nietzsche said, man – the man of classical humanism – must be overcome. As Hegel and Herzen said, subjectivism is debilitating. The good man needs to be able to make his way in the real world. Pisarev was their brother in spirit.

The good thing about Pisarev is that the liberation he wanted for himself he wanted for all men, and it was what pushed him into wanting a science of psychological self-liberation.

> I think that humanity can be fully revealed only in an integral individuality which has developed naturally and independently, untrammelled by service to various ideas, an individuality that has not wasted its strength in struggling against itself.[15]

He was one of the Russian 'nihilists' because of his crusade against convention but more significantly he followed that line of self-liberation from Nietzsche through Freud which is one of the great achievements of modern European thought. He wrestled with Russian philosophy's chief problem: how to reconcile individuality with selflessness. He represented the 'physician heal thyself' peak of what is generally called the Russian Enlightenment – before Russian circumstances, combined with his own fragile psychology, swallowed him up.

The Russian Enlightenment, so steeped in the Utilitarian outlook, was a vital way-station on the road to revolution and to the kind of society which was established after it. But what revolutionary history never used to stress was that Utilitarianism in Russia by any name always had vociferous opponents. Leontiev, Dostoevsky and Solovyov were three of the most powerful and individualized voices of the nineteenth century who all insisted that society needed individuals moral in themselves, not just cogs in the utility machine.

Konstantin Leontiev (1831–91) defended moral individualism as the only way Russia might compensate for the Renaissance tradition it never had. In this he resembled Herzen. Unlike the Hegelian Herzen, however, he divorced the good man from any socializing process of history and, with a new emphasis on imagination, made the good man's values eternal again. Leontiev was a lone voice exaggerating the importance of the creative free spirit to combat an age flattened by scientistic prescription and the pursuit of the average. A Russian Nietzsche of a different kind from Pisarev, Leontiev was an aesthetic radical. He admired the Renaissance and the social and political benefits of aristocracy it demonstrated. Here were weapons to fight against the 'universal utility' and 'the liberal-egalitarian process' which had taken hold in nineteenth-century Europe. And yet Leontiev experienced a typically Russian conflict between what he owed to himself as an individual and a self-humbling ingredient in his very strong religious faith, which sharply curbed his Nietzschean *joie de vivre*, and finally inclined him to enter a monastery. What remained to him was to defend the spiritual against the Utilitarian.

Leontiev believed in a medieval withdrawal into contemplation. He suggested that the fully rounded individual did not depend for his self-perfection on a free society, but would benefit from a repressive one which would encourage introspection. The good society for Leontiev was usefully repressive, as it was for Plato. It beneficially constrained individuals to focus their spiritual energies only on universal ideas. It burned mediocre books and second-rate works of art to keep standards high. Leontiev's position is as impossible today as Plato's: radically undemocratic and anti-egalitarian in its dictatorial idealism. On the other hand, if Leontiev didn't exist this writer would beg God to invent him, for, like Dostoevsky, Leontiev believed that beauty could change the world. His value in mid-nineteenth-century Russia was as an antidote to averageness and dullness and a reminder of mystery. He deliberately provoked the 'new men' by writing that 'the highest degree of social material prosperity and universal political justice would be the highest degree of a-morality.'[16]

Thus when Fyodor Dostoevsky (1821–81) in *Notes from Underground* (1864) famously satirized the Utilitarian impulse to secure universal happiness he was only amplifying existing spiritual opposition to the 'new men'. In all of his fiction, but most famously in *Notes*, Dostoevsky rejected the Benthamite felicific calculus. The individual man was too unpredictable a creature for others to know the key to his happiness. Happiness wasn't a science. Dostoevsky also grasped that the Utilitarian way, as it might be implemented in the name of socialism in Russia, as a dictatorship ruled over by the materialistic social sciences, threatened something sacred to individuals. He stressed the inviolability of a man's personal space and his freedom to decide what kind of man morally he wanted to be. If these spaces were violated, not only would true happiness disappear from the world but, what amounted to the same thing, spirituality would wither.

Dostoevsky was a defender of individuality, and yet a tormented one, who just as often repudiated it. In particular it was difficult for him to square the Western idea of the good man being a self-cultivating individual with the Russian Orthodox idea that the good man belonged unselfishly to a religious community. Having read Kant and Schiller and encountered Hegel, he was drawn to Faustian men of will at the same time as he was horrified by what seemed to befall Russians who went the Western individualist way. When Dostoevsky's fictional characters acquired – in America or elsewhere abroad, or through their foreign reading – the ideas of reason, they instantly found themselves without moral guidance. They were spirits who set out on the Hegelian journey to maturity, only to find that there was no reason to guide them in place of God. They suffered terribly from the consequences of atheism.

In *The Devils* (1871–2) Shatov, whose name means the vacillator, the insecure one, tried America, tried Russia again, as did his amoral hero and mentor Stavrogin. When Stavrogin was complicit in Shatov's murder, it was as if he had arranged to have an inconvenient aspect of himself removed, namely the problem of belief in God. Not to doubt his own faith would mean a man could accept any condition of Russia as God's will, but having come into contact with Western reason this faith was hard to sustain. Intelligent Russian souls were caught between two extremes. In *Crime and Punishment* (1866–7) Raskolnikov, inspired to self-determination by his Western reading, made a perverse effort at 'rational' self-fulfilment by killing an old woman. The course of the novel then traced the slow retrenchment of this false individuality back into Russian spiritual community.

It seemed to Dostoevsky that individuality as the West understood it, and even if it was linked to social reform in the West, could only be sustained in Russia at the price of hatred, lust and murder. A definition of the good man in Russia could not exclude a quiescent religious element. No Russian good man could have knowledge just through himself, independent of his religious community, and that could be the only good Russian way forward.

Vladimir Solovyov (1853–1900) was less pessimistic about individualism and proposed a strong version of it for Russian philosophy. He was an equally determined opponent of the unspiritual. The son of one of Russia's finest nineteenth-century historians, and grandson of a priest, he was the first Russian thinker to create a system of mystical values to rebut the pressure from the Utilitarianism, materialism and positivism which buttressed the growing revolutionary tradition. After an Orthodox upbringing his first experience of the world brought contact with atheism, materialism and socialism, all of which interested him briefly. But already in his teens he was reading the philosophers who would most influence him: Spinoza, Kant, Fichte, Schelling and Hegel, and Schopenhauer. He studied natural sciences in Moscow, then read for a second degree in history and philology. A postgraduate year at the Theological Seminary at Sergiev Posad (in Soviet times, Zagorsk), 1873–4, lends credence to the idea that he inspired Dostoevsky's fictional character Alyosha Karamazov. The two men were close friends and intellectual sparring partners.[17] After his studies at the Seminary Solovyov published his master's thesis on *The Crisis in Western Philosophy*, began teaching in Moscow, and a few years later moved to St Petersburg, where, continuing to publish and lecture, he became a famous name. His university career was cut short when he appealed in a lecture for clemency towards the terrorists who had killed Alexander II. From that year, 1881, until his death in 1900, he was banned from further public instruction and worked independently.

His gentle personality seems to have been rather feminine in the old-fashioned sense and his temperament mystical. He had supernatural visions as a boy, and in a short autobiographical work, *Three Meetings*, described three encounters with Sophia, the second of which happened in the British Museum, where he spent time reading up on mysticism in 1875. His reading surely helped the second vision along. The third summoned him from London to Egypt, where he nearly died because he wore his dark London suit in the desert and the Bedouins took him for an evil spirit. He didn't marry, but had a great interest in an imagined cosmic eros. For him Sophia, the Russian equivalent of the Eternal Feminine, was an aspect of God. Andrzej Walicki writes that 'his nature was childlike and trusting, and he tended to see everything in spiritual terms, as "a reflection of the invisible world"; but although he preached acceptance of "worldliness" through its "transfusion by godliness" he could not come to terms with his prosaic everyday life'.[18]

Solovyov's starting-point was one familiar from classical Russian literature: that human beings have spiritual needs, that everything flows from the values established by the inner life, which gives our existence a moral meaning.

> In the realm of moral ideas, philosophical thought, for all its formal independence, is in essence directly subordinate to the life-interest of the pure will, which strives toward the good and demands of the intellect a more precise and full elucidation of true goodness as opposed to everything that seems to be or is considered good without in fact being so.[19]

Solovyov's social vision was progressive, his religion ecumenical, but he held out against technological social progress as a secular religion. One of his twentieth-century disciples, Semyon Frank, quoted him as justifying the gap he was filling in Russian intellectual life with the deduction that 'Nothing exists except matter and energy: man is a hairless monkey; therefore everyone must lay down his life for his friends.'[20]

Solovyov contended, as did Western philosophers from Descartes to Kant, that it was rational to believe in God because it gave man what he needed in his essence. Solovyov's foundational argument was that if we want the good – which we naturally do – and the highest good emanates from God, what choice could be more rational than faith? We will make this choice and be saved. The good life is in our grasp. Salvation is what we really mean by progress.

A task for philosophy was to encourage awareness of the good by elucidating love and creativity, or man's capacity to *make* the world a fit place to believe in. Philosophy was a homemaker on a cosmic scale, with creativity, which makes art and brings God alive, as its chief tool and source of hope. Since creativity is evident within us all, hope that we can build a spiritually more hospitable world is justified. The attention Kant and Schelling paid to imagination encouraged Solovyov to explore the workings of hope: hope treated as a spiritual asset; hope vested in man's creative capacity to re-enchant the modern soul.

Solovyov wrote a number of books. *The Crisis in Western Philosophy* (1874) attacked misplaced faith in science, *The Justification of the Good* (1897) revived the metaphysics Feuerbach had discarded. It accepted that, even if religious faith had to be abandoned as such, still the good could stand as an unassailable higher value. Solovyov's function in a Utilitarian environment was an attractive one. In British philosophical history G. E. Moore – the nearest equivalent to a British beautiful soul – and in our own time Iris Murdoch, have been kindred figures, standing out against their time to defend the good as a non-natural entity, not open to scientific scrutiny but furnishing a universal moral standard. No philosopher who dismissed Iris Murdoch would take Solovyov seriously either.[21] But one has to take Solovyov seriously in his Russian historical context because he upheld the need for moral individuals in a good society. In a pioneering step for Russian religious idealism he put the value of the individual into a religious framework which for the first time protected it; and he shaped all the other values of the beautiful soul, not least symbolic art, into a metaphysical system that would be much imitated by future generations so long as they were free.

Solovyov supplemented his technical philosophy with essays on the poetry he admired, on art and aesthetics generally and on *The Meaning of Love* (1892–4). He also developed, in *Philosophical Principles of Integral Knowledge* (1877) and *A Critique of Abstract Principles* (1880), the ideal of a different kind of knowledge from the scientific. The move harked back to Khomiakov. At stake was a relationship with the world oriented towards meaning rather than utility. Solovyov was searching, he said, for a positive philosophy of the kind 'which, starting out from beyond the bounds of general possibilities, recognizes essential being (*deistvitel'no-sushshee*) and at the same time gives higher principles for life'.[22]

4

The Populists

Populism was not at war with moral idealism. The instinct to teach the people was part of the social character of every *intelligent*. But the political tendencies which developed in Russia from the mid-1860s required immediate mass action impossible to organize *ex cathedra*.[1] The age witnessed peaceful social protest – *narodnichestvo* – but also on its fringe the sudden advent of terrorist violence spearheaded by an organization known as the People's Will, *Narodnaya Volya*. It was shaped by increasing disillusion with the 1861 abolition of serfdom, which justified Chernyshevsky's protest retrospectively. After 1861 the state was paying compensation to the landowners, whilst leaving the people without land. When Alexander II further offended liberal sentiment by brutally suppressing the Polish Uprising of 1863, the future opponent of all statecraft, the nobleman, anarchist and theorist of mutual aid Pyotr Kropotkin (1842–1921) left the army in protest and began to work underground for the political enlightenment of the peasantry.[2] Another semi-soldier, a professor of mathematics in a military academy, Pyotr Lavrov, moved closer to becoming an activist outsider as the decade progressed. The first watershed of Populism was an unsuccessful attempt on the tsar's life in 1866, by a student called Dmitry Karakozov.

Mikhail Bakunin (1814–76), who began his intellectual life as a student of Idealism and presented himself as a beautiful soul, represented one aspect of the increasingly shrill call for violent change among a minority of the 1860s intelligentsia. He had enjoyed a model Russian philosophical upbringing, influenced by Vellansky, Galich and Venevitinov, and went later to study among the Germans, sharing lodgings with Turgenev in Berlin.[3] In 1838 he translated Hegel's 'Gymnasial Speeches' into Russian with an introduction in which he stressed how appropriate Hegel's concept of alienation – the waste of beautiful souls detached from society – was to his Russian generation. Bakunin felt this waste personally and more than most: he passionately wanted to belong to some whole, some faith, some community, some sphere of Absolute Reason, greater than himself. A hijacked phrase from Hegel, 'reconciliation with reality', became his fantasy goal. In 1847 he wrote in a letter that he was awaiting 'my fiancée, revolution'. He devoted the next thirty years to her.[4]

His activist life across Europe, which included extradition to Russia, exile to Siberia, and a dashing escape to Liverpool via Japan, was a living illustration of the need for philosophy to drive Russia forward – to provide a justification for action. Bakunin's own life was the message and it asked a thoroughly philosophical question about what makes people act – reason or passion. In a Hegelian mode Bakunin would have claimed the motivation was reason, but in this text from 1868 it was passion that he tried to ignite in others.

What we demand is the proclamation anew of this great principle of the French Revolution: that every man must have the material and moral means to develop all his humanity, a principle which, according to us, is to be translated into the following problem: to organize society in such a fashion that every individual, man or woman, coming into life, shall find as nearly as possible equal means for the development of his or her different faculties and for their utilization by his or her labour; to organize a society which, rendering for every individual, whoever he may be, the exploitation of anybody else impossible, permits each to participate in social wealth – which in reality is never produced other than by labour – only in so far as he has contributed to produce it by his own labour.[5]

Action was one branch of Bakunin's interest; the other, demonstrated in this passage from *Federalism, Socialism and Anti-Theologism*, was to overcome alienation. Alienation was a social evil made possible by a privileged few who, being in possession of capital, could milk the lives of the many who lacked it and thus leave them without any necessary connection to the world except as other men's tools.[6] The evil of alienation gave him his political programme. Bakunin was Marxian, and with his writing on alienation he was a living reminder of where the legend of the beautiful soul had reached in his lifetime. The Romantic idea that the good man developed all his faculties to become happy had metamorphosed into a programme for universal social reform. The good society was such that *all* men and women could become beautiful souls. The crucial shift in German thinking on alienation – and it was a thoroughly German topic – came with the way Feuerbach and then Marx read Hegel. Hegel was already critical of the beautiful soul for not playing an active part in society. The beautiful soul was an asocial, unworldly and inadequate person who needed to overcome a life limited by reflection.[7] Feuerbach accepted that the inwardly directed personality was problematic but, rejecting the need for individuals to become more self-critical, he handed over the whole problem of incomplete and unhappy souls to social science. Bakunin found himself caught up in an argument hardly the most appropriate for solving backward Russia's most urgent problems, but to which he brought a typically Russian twist. For him, the only chance for a population of beautiful souls was to abolish the state. His message for unfulfilled Russian souls was not social integration, nor the benefits of welfare materialism, but anarchism.

The anarchist political theory for which he became famous Europe-wide typically borrowed a Western argument to assert an old Russian need – to get rid of the aristocracy. As an anarchist Bakunin believed that the state was 'an alien, anti-social force that must be destroyed in order to liberate the social instinct deeply embedded in the human personality'.[8] He was a typical Russian outsider: extreme, disorganized, emotional and excessive, but possibly with his heart in the right place on behalf of unfulfilled souls. Not averse to the use of violence to secure his political vision, he clashed famously with Marx, who personally disliked him and had him expelled from the socialist First International in 1872.[9] Though not a philosopher, like any member of the intelligentsia Bakunin could name the sources of his belief: he was a materialist, an atheist and a positivist, inspired by Feuerbach, Comte, Proudhon and Marx.[10] His vision of the liberated natural human condition partly rested on a romantic view of the Russian peasant commune, but was evidently also driven by that dark personal psychology which made him long to lose himself in 'the people'.[11] Andrzej Walicki observes that Bakunin associated himself with the peasant bandits of Russian history, the murderous folk heroes Pugachov and Stenka Razin.[12] Popular history persuaded him that the Russian peasantry was the multiple of these folk bandits, a viable political force ready to rise in rebellion. The English scholar Aileen Kelly has most recently emphasized Bakunin's tolerance of other men's violence, coupled with bungled attempts at conspiracy himself. He exemplified the terrorist as impotent voyeur. The contemporary bandits he admired were Pyotr Tkachev, chief theorist of the Jacobin trend in Russian Populism, who in an outspoken moment called for the extermination of anyone over twenty-five, and the convicted murderer Sergei Nechaev, the man on whom Dostoevsky modelled the gratuitously violent figure of Pyotr Verkhovensky in *The Devils*.[13]

The mainstream Populism movement remained remarkably untainted by violence. It was a spontaneous outpouring of conscience at the enduring gap between the educated few and the poor and ignorant masses. In 1872–4 thousands of students and activists voluntarily dispersed themselves as *narodniki* to teach the people literacy and their political rights. The situation was unwittingly exacerbated when the government ordered thousands of students home from Europe in 1874, fearing their minds were being contaminated by revolutionary propaganda abroad.[14]

The activists were too idealistic to take in the reality of the situation, which was defined by the sheer viciousness of the peasants. The much idealized 'people' were slow to respond to the students and quick to denounce them to the police. Some 770 students were arrested in the first two months of 1874, when one *intelligent* pictured his own efforts as 'like fish beating against ice'.[15] But the Populist crusade failed in a way reminiscent of the Decembrists' protest, which turned it into a moral triumph. Most memorable was the flow of sympathy which motivated the *narodniki* to act. Their courage and charity entered the history of the intelligentsia and became part of the good Russian identity. When the young Pavel Akselrod was a Populist he called on fellow *narodniki* to abandon both their education and their families. The echo of Christ's call to the apostles was unmistakable in this exhortation for the good man to venture forth, discarding all practical considerations, to work for a more just world.[16]

The spectacle of the Populists' self-belief was moving and exemplary. The name for their action in Russian, *khozhdenie v narod*, sounded like a religious mission. Nothing would be the same in Russia emotionally after the manifestations of the early 1870s, and, finally, after Alexander's successful assassination in 1881. Although it was destined to clash in theoretical means and goals with Marxism, the feeling behind Populism directly helped establish what a better twentieth-century Russia should be. It was a romantic and 'alternative' lifestyle movement akin to Slavophile communalism and the simple Christian community preached by Lev Tolstoy. Its adherents believed that the Russian problem would sooner or later be solved, only not as Chernyshevsky thought by catching up with the West, but by establishing a different system. Hope reached back to Herzen's enthusiasm for the *obshchina*, the communal foundation of peasant socialism, and also to Khomiakov's indigenous forms of Russian spiritual community, and was attuned to Kropotkin's anarchist ideal of mutual aid. But like other new waves to date in the creation of the Russian revolutionary outlook, because of the limited results of peaceful campaigning, Populism modified the qualities of the intelligentsia more than it changed society. The intelligentsia could still do nothing, get nowhere, so long as it refrained from violence. Populism tried hard to close the gap between the common people and the intelligentsia, but as a reform movement it lacked any other engine beside the human heart.

It was also potentially self-defeating in that it risked destroying the qualities of its own volunteers. Bakunin called on Russian students to leave the universities and go out and teach 'the people' Western socialism. In truth he thought the intelligentsia should not even teach but learn: learn from the peasants what their real Russian, not Western, needs were. Tolstoy expressed an enduring version of the peaceful Populist impulse when he taught the simple folk on his estate, dressed in their clothes and tried to live the plainest of lives. How, on this model, could a modern Russia ever come into being?

In the end Populism was about self-sacrifice. When Pyotr Lavrov (1823–1900) in *The Historical Letters* (1868–9) wrote its message into philosophy he, like Bakunin, gave a new twist to the long-admired habit of the intelligentsia for moral self-scrutiny inherited from Herzen and Turgenev. He used it to raise the stakes of social commitment by saying that beautiful souls who had worked on their knowledge and refined their sense of justice were actually to blame for Russia's ills, because their privileges rested on mass deprivation. To atone, all educated men were bound to work singlemindedly for the transformation of Russia into a just society. In the past a few individuals had developed to extraordinary heights in non-egalitarian societies. But for progress to take place in a modern society, 'a majority of society must be placed in a position where its development is possible'.[17]

The *Historical Letters* linked individual moral worth to general human progress in a pioneering moment for modern political and ethical thought. Lavrov's crucial pronouncement came in his fourth 'Letter':

> Mankind has paid dearly so that a few thinkers sitting in their studies could discuss its progress.[18]

The intelligentsia heard from Lavrov that they should take action now to build a better society or remain as if under an existential curse.

> We are responsible for the sins of our fathers only to the extent that we continue these sins and profit by them, without attempting to rectify their consequences.[19]

Far from Moscow, in exile, as he was writing his major work, Lavrov set down his view that there were still very few people in Russia who felt the burden of inequality and therefore understood the immediate task:

> The majority of persons... either... set up idols in place of truth and justice, or they limit themselves to truth and justice in thought but not in life, or they do not want to see what an insignificant minority enjoys the advantages of the progress of civilization.[20]

His answer was to make a few see, to make them feel guilty, and to hope that their guilt would make them act.

Does guilt prompted by privileged social origins actually make people act? Once the idea was created, once it became part of received modern values, the answer is surely yes, although the familiarity of the content of the idea doesn't make it any clearer whether, say, a decision not to send one's children to private schools is action sparked by a rational idea or a passion. Probably both ingredients are present. Often the passions rationalize themselves. Herzen decided it was an impulse nurtured by experience and that tradition motivated moral action. Lavrov supported his different moral theory by going back to Kant.

Kant said that the moral way to act was to follow the categorical imperative. The moral agent should act in such a way that the maxim for his action could become a universal law. The difficulty for Kant, which Lavrov inherited, was the extent to which the agent was free to choose the good if the right action was to obey a law. Kant insisted on freedom. His ethical space was empty, waiting for human actions to give it a content. Yet not quite empty, because the vacuum contained a signpost. Plekhanov among the next generation of Russians would put the matter well when he said Kant's ethics were a matter of the train and the railway track existing but the traveller needing to buy a ticket.[21] Kant drew on his Christian background when he suggested human beings were predisposed to choose the good.

Lavrov inherited this faith in a priori human goodness from Kant, and, as with Solovyov, who had it from Christian as well as philosophical sources, it became the major plank of his philosophy. Fully conscious, educated men and women surely could see the unfairness of their advantages and must want to make good the difference between themselves and others. Social reform was their moral and political duty, but surely also what they would freely choose. Lavrov politicized the beautiful soul in a new radical attempt to meet Russia's needs.

As the title suggests, Lavrov's other main topic in the *Letters* was history and here again he ran into difficulties over freedom. On the one hand he was a 'subjective sociologist' who believed history was made by the free contributions of free individuals; on the other he felt, on his reading of Hegel, that history was determined. Yet in this case the logical incompatibility of his two views was the mark of their truth. Many, perhaps most people feel that we have to believe ourselves free otherwise our good actions would be crippled, despite a suspicion that we are proceeding along predetermined lines.

Like nearly all Russian philosophers, Lavrov's interesting thoughts were mostly sparked by his reading of Western theories. First Hegel persuaded him that it was history, not science, which was the true guide to progress; second, against the influence of Hegel's view of history, at least as it was commonly perceived, Feuerbach reminded Lavrov of the importance of keeping the autonomous and active human subject centre-stage; while his third theme linked the finest deontological ethic of modern Western times to the old service mentality of the *dvoryanstvo*. Above all the Kantian move was brilliant and original because it allowed Lavrov to strengthen at a stroke an ethical habit of mind already deeply ingrained in the Russian intelligentsia. Hitherto its moral commitment had arisen freely from experience. Now such action was a metaphysical requirement.[22]

Lavrov was a civilized man, who wanted to give back to Russian thought some of that spiritual and moral and poetic texture which Chernyshevsky had thinned out. So he emphasized history, and the free man's contribution to culture and institutions. Against the absurd Bakuninist tendency to think the intelligentsia's way forward was to give up its education and conjoin with the wisdom of the people, Lavrov insisted that Russia needed educated men at the ideological helm. Education was the progress of self-consciousness. Freedom was its product. History showed 'by what logical process the aspiration for betterment and justice [gives] rise to protest and conservatism, reaction and progress'.[23]

Lavrov was a moderate, even wise writer, who endured a mild Russian fate. The period of internal exile in 1867–8, which gave him the chance to meet interesting intellectual companions and write the *Historical Letters*, was followed by escape in 1870 to Paris, prompted in part by an invitation from Herzen. In passing, one of the absurdities of tsarist Russia was that a backwater like Vologda, 250 miles north-east of Moscow, where so many suspect but not criminal intellectuals were sent to keep them out of the way, became, in all its plainness and relative isolation (though it was on the railway line), a breeding-ground for new ideas. Still Lavrov had to leave, if he wanted an active political life. He lived in Paris and, when the French periodically cracked down on Marxist revolutionaries, he crossed the Channel to London.

In European exile the French had some reason to watch him because he became more and more radical, publishing an underground journal *Vperyod!* [*Forwards!*] and finding himself caught between Marx and Bakunin, Marxists and Bakuninists. He witnessed the Paris Commune and like other exiled Russians with socialist hopes found the West disappointing. Gradually he came to accept that moral commitment alone was not enough to secure progress. It needed the kick-start of violence. Even in the *Historical Letters* he wrote that 'very often it is only through temporary agitation and disorder, only through revolution, that one can buy a better guarantee of order and tranquillity for the majority in future'.[24] His Bakuninist side spoke of the need for exemplary leaders, for deeds not words, for unity, for fighting tactics.

> Vigorous, fanatical men are needed, who will risk everything and are prepared to sacrifice everything . . . Martyrs are needed, whose legend will far outgrow their true worth and their actual service.[25]

'In the last analysis Lavrov was not a Marxist. He was a socialist with anarchistic leanings.' The tragedy for which he paved the way rested on the fact that the urgent need to overthrow tsarism finally exhausted all the theoretical arguments available.[26]

A striking feature of Lavrov's personal psychology was his propensity to guilt. A friend detected something wrong in the way he assumed blame for acts he hadn't committed. His exile to Vologda followed Karakozov's attempt on the tsar's life. Lavrov had no connection with the crime other than being an adviser to men with anti-tsarist views, but his friend recalled how he had waited to be arrested. His readiness to assume personal guilt coloured his ethics. In turn those ethics helped train the perpetrators of the 1917 Revolution.[27]

It would be a help to that revolution that, by Lavrov's day, in both Russian and Western thought, it was becoming difficult to insist on individual moral responsibility for desirable social change. Some people looked to the forces of history, from Hegel to Marx; others rested their hopes on specific social groups as Lavrov did on the intelligentsia and Lenin would on the Party. Joseph Proudhon (1809–65) was an important non-Marxist spokesman for group action who concentrated the minds of Lavrov and others on an active role for the intelligentsia. Working in the French utopian socialist tradition pioneered by Saint-Simon and Fourier, Proudhon said that philosophy should provide the norms to make possible a society organized on the principles of justice. The intelligentsia must fill society with the right ideas. A cherished idea of Proudhon's was voluntarism, which already had an embedded following in Russia. He was also a spokesman for the sublime Russian value of uncoerced cooperation.[28]

Nevertheless, thanks to his own contradictions, it was Lavrov who continued to insist that the individual morally determined contribution to history mattered. The idea behind 'subjective sociology' was 'that social processes, unlike natural ones, are partly determined by subjective desires and ideas which animate people because they are thought to be right, not necessarily because they are expected to triumph.'[29] These words from the *Historical Letters* were a sharp attack on the Marxist view of history as an impersonal and objective process. 'Subjective sociology' came into being because the climate of positivism was hardening the Marxist vision of Hegelian progress into a science, a development which would do a decent Russia no favours. Lavrov saw the difference between Hegel's idealism and Marx's materialism in terms of the freedom Hegel allowed. History was a dialectical process, by which individuals engaged with the world they created. 'Protest and conservatism, reaction and progress' were the alternating results. But the process was not distinct from the individuals who made it.

The further the nineteenth century advanced, however, the more 'objectivism' gained the upper hand. The Absolute Reason of Hegel, if not carefully read, the scientific positivism of Comte, and the dialectical materialism of Marx and Engels all threatened freedom and individualism by deeming them subjective aberrations from the historical law. If dialectical materialism really was objective, rational and based upon empirical evidence, then who by himself, by herself, could resist its laws without seeming perverse?

Nikolai Mikhailovsky (1842–1904), the other Russian thinker associated with 'subjective sociology', was the last of the civilized 'subjectivist' utopians in Russia before the Revolution swept their distinctiveness aside. He was a libertarian who argued against a determinist view of scientific progress. From his landmark 1869 essay 'What is Progress?' to his continuing work in the 1890s he consistently upheld the struggle for individuality.

A problem in his theory was that individuality had to be conceived without conflict. In his 1870 essay on 'Darwin's Theory and Social Science', he insisted, as ever in the utopian vein, on human cooperation, not competition. His target was a philosophy very few people outside Britain seem ever to have admired, the Social Darwinism of Herbert Spencer. Seen through later nineteenth-century Russian eyes Spencer's view that competition increased social productivity was only another unattractive aspect of capitalism and a renewed reason for rejecting, not individuals, but, if it could be distinguished, the individualistic way of life. Spencer may have been right that human beings are not as naturally cooperative as social idealists would like them to be. But for two good reasons few Russians went in for such Hobbesian realism, or pessimism. One was the much-loved Russian communal tradition a matter both of habit and law. The other was that the social coherence of Russia was too weak to admit the principle of conflict. The slowly modernizing country was too obviously divided for responsible men to give in to destructive thinking.

Mikhailovsky was a 'new man' in so far as he was no friend of metaphysics. He had absorbed the same post-Hegelian lessons as had Feuerbach and Marx, and he accepted the Marxian argument, set out by Engels, that Christianity and German Idealism had helped to keep societies divided and ruled by the educated and propertied classes. Religion was what Marx said it was, 'the opium of the people', and should disappear from the good society. But Mikhailovsky reverted to Romanticism when, against Spencer, he argued that the division of labour harmed a man's soul. Here he felt as strongly as Rousseau did, and with a lot more industrialization to combat, and as strongly as the wild Bakunin did, that progress should produce 'the integral individual'.[30] How could a man be a whole man if he worked in appalling factory conditions? Mikhailovsky had the condition of an actual factory in the town of Tula in mind, which he illuminated with a quotation from Schiller.[31] The social harm done by mass industrialization was hardly Russia's problem in 1869. But with Mikhailovsky once again Russia rehearsed that crucial shift in the history of ideas from the fulfilled individual to the society enabling mass fulfilment. In caring for the common man the intelligentsia accepted, as an extra weapon in their unworldly armoury, the Western argument that every last man and woman, not just privileged individuals, should have the chance to grow into a full human being.

The potential alienation of the Russian worker moved Mikhailovsky to neither anarchism nor Marxism, precisely because it wasn't the urgent question. Mikhailovsky remained with Populism because it looked like the way to resist a Western-style industrial future. Why should Russia follow the Marxist prescription and pass through a stage of capitalism, even temporarily sacrificing its humanity, in order to secure a socialist revolution? The aim of Populism was to mend the division between intelligentsia and people, not to court new divisions of labour. Alienation, said Mikhailovsky, was like love-sickness. Negatively it confirmed the overwhelming Populist emotion: frustrated love of the people.[32] Marxism aimed to create a world in which the integral individual and the unexploited worker could flourish. But since communal Russia already had a native peasant socialism of greater emotional appeal why should it change?

Mikhailovsky didn't idealize Russia's peasants. He thought them self-interested and reactionary and in need of a dose of Western progress. But he hankered after medieval-style social unity because harmonious togetherness was better than emotional isolation. Typical of the richer and more humane Russian thinkers, and in many ways close to the religious thinkers, he allowed Western reasoning to lead him to Russian ethical exceptionalism.[33]

That in turn led to his own most interesting contribution to philosophy, which came via a sociological distinction between the type and the level of societies. The West had a higher material level of culture, Mikhailovsky said, but it was not of a superior type. Why therefore should a marvellous soulful place like Russia want to catch up with a world whose moral and political ideals were defined by petty bourgeois comforts? The claim had the making of a legend. That Russia was a civilization of a higher moral type passed into its self-understanding.[34]

Russia certainly was different. Its very difference led Mikhailovsky to distinguish between two types of truth.

> To look reality and its reflection – *pravda* as truth, objective *pravda* – fearlessly in the eye while at the same time preserving *pravda* as justice, subjective *pravda* – such has been the task of my whole life.[35]

Mikhailovsky split the modern philosophical atom when he said there was not one truth but two kinds: factual and emotional. He released vast emotional energy that Russia could invest in being different from the West by virtue of its two truths. Subjective truth was the sum of those Proudhonian norms to be created by the intelligentsia in the name of justice. It was about the truth of values in people's minds, as opposed to the facts which science can measure. A later philosopher, Nikolai Berdyaev, would speak of *pravda* to describe emotional truth, and *istina*, from *est'*, the verb 'to be', for the truth of facts.[36]

5

The Impact of Marx

Bakunin laid one of the textual foundations for the shift to Marxism when he translated *The Communist Manifesto* into Russian in 1869. The other paper landmark was A. F. Danielson's translation of *Das Kapital*. Danielson stepped in after Bakunin's quarrel with Marx and produced the first version in any foreign language of Marx's crucial German text. When it appeared in 1872 *Kapital* immediately split Russian opinion. Russia was famously not the industrialized country which Marx said was the necessary springboard for proletarian revolution and the transition to socialism. But perhaps if one looked at it in a certain light? Striking a chord with Russian impatience, Marx persuaded a new generation of Russian thinkers to have second thoughts. Georgy Plekhanov (1856–1918) became convinced that Russia was now industrializing and therefore could follow the orthodox Marxist path. He became Marx's most devoted Russian admirer.[1]

Plekhanov was the son of a landowner who studied history and economics. He became a Populist but broke with the *Narodnaya Volya* movement over the issue of terrorism. He was only twenty-four when his revolutionary activities forced him abroad. Subsequently all the great moments of his career – the rejection of Populism in favour of Marxism, the acceptance of a capitalist path for Russia, and the quarrel with Lenin over the latter's deviation from Marxism's laws – took place over the thirty-seven years he spent outside Russia. In the history of revolutionary thought Plekhanov was the first thinker seriously to apply Marxist analysis to the Russian condition and thus to put the longing for change into a new framework. For a short while he shared Bakunin's anarchist-Populist hope that long-term peasant dissatisfaction might finally combust. No political means to change was acceptable because all politics was exploitative. Yet by the year of his flight from Russia Plekhanov had left Bakunin behind and was showing 'the rationalistic bent' that turned him towards Marxism.[2]

He admired the Hegelian-Marxist idea of an underlying orderliness of history. By 1884 he had set out the tenets of Russian Marxism in 'Socialism and Political Struggle', and the following year, 'Our Differences'. Lenin later said that the first of these essays had a significance for Russia comparable with *The Communist Manifesto* in the West.[3] Plekhanov broke with Populism's anti-Westernism by declaring that capitalism was a natural stage of development through which Russia had to pass. Its best hope was to speed up its capitalist development in order to make the eventual transition to socialism. The proletariat would lead the way instead of the disappointing peasantry.

If capitalism had penetrated Russia, then at last the country was becoming Europeanized; a century late but no less welcome for that. Plekhanov went back to the French Revolution in European history to see Russia's position in a new perspective. The French Revolution was the key event Russia had to replicate in order finally to move ahead of the West. A bourgeois revolution would consolidate capitalism from which Russia would proceed to socialism.[4]

Plekhanov's Marxism entailed exactly what the classical version spelled out: the belief that there were objective laws governing the development of society which could not be changed at will.[5] Those 'laws' bolstered the political faith of his generation. And those living abroad – out of touch with the actual condition of their country – were especially comforted by them. Plekhanov insisted on necessity, inevitability and objectivity too often not to betray doubt. The activists of the 1890s focused their vision for Russia by delivering themselves up to theory.[6]

It wasn't a new Russian experience. Seeking the best foundation for social hope, the Romantics chose between the 'subjective' idealism of Schelling and Fichte and the 'objective' idealism of Hegel. Plekhanov was so inspired by Belinsky's objective Hegelian phase that he took him as his immediate predecessor. Not quite a generation before Plekhanov early Populism weighed the 'subjective sociology' of Lavrov and Mikhailovsky against positivism and historical determinism. Each time the objective option gave the impression of a firmer foundation on which the Russian future could be pinned; a scaffolding to hold the country together; and a set of arguments, appealing to laws and higher patterns and even facts, by which to defend it. To depend on subjective good will and enterprise was a frail hope by comparison. Yet objective theories could easily lose touch with real people and places and build castles in the air.

When *On the Question of the Development of the Monistic View of History* (1894) appeared, Lenin hailed Plekhanov as the inspiration of the upcoming generation of Russian Marxists. By 1896 Russia had a vital Social Democratic movement that promised to achieve what no other force in Russia had done: a revolutionary working-class movement.[7] Plekhanov was to date the greatest revolutionary organizer Russia had known.

He made the decisive shift towards seeing economic relations as the basis of, and complete answer to, Russia's future. 'Marxism was a complete and integral body of theory embracing all the main questions of philosophy' and nothing needed to be discussed outside the framework it supplied.[8] He bequeathed to the coming Marxist utopia the dominance of the Party, the unblinking adherence to Marxist dogma and the very term 'dialectical materialism'. He more or less invented socialist realism in art, with a critical vocabulary that turned art and philosophy alike into a struggle for the real over the ideal. His admiration for the banal

Chernyshevsky and for Belinsky at his most formulaic helped create the mould in which Soviet taste was formed.

Plekhanov's loyalty to classical Marxism proved his downfall. Because revolutionary consciousness would arise in its own time out of class-determined material circumstances, so he insisted that revolution in Russia would have to wait until the people matured.[9] Lenin impatiently challenged this view. The Russian working class could not attain to socialist consciousness by itself and would have to be corralled. This deviation from the classical line gave Lenin's Bolshevik Party the advantage in activist politics from the year of its foundation, 1903, and Plekhanov was forced onto the sidelines.[10]

Sometimes, still under the influence of his Populist youth, Plekhanov looked like a good Marxist for the wrong reasons. For instance, his sense of Russia's cultural superiority protected him from the 'heresy' of the German socialist Eduard Bernstein. Bernstein said Marxism was a moral choice with nothing historically inevitable about it. Plekhanov demurred not only because he thought the movement would collapse without its dialectical-materialist pacemaker, but because Bernstein was turning Marxism into a bourgeois pursuit of petty material comforts for all. As trade unions in Germany improved working conditions, Bernstein said revolution was no longer necessary. Bernstein's revisionism dismayed Plekhanov as it was found to dismay all Russian activists seeking the overthrow of the autocracy. But Plekhanov also had the feeling Bernstein was taking the aristocratic romance out of Marxism. Russia could not retain its sense of cultural superiority over the West if it went down the revisionist path.[11]

A late personal worry of Plekhanov's was the lack of morality in Marxism. Here ironically he did – only not consciously – agree with Bernstein. Bernstein believed that Marxism had to be supplemented with Kantian ethics to provide a guide to the good life. Marxism talked about the class origins of morality, but it had no individual ethical content. It did not offer sustenance to the good man's own soul, as Kant did with his scrupulous attention to motive and his sense of the absolute good to be enacted.[12] Plekhanov rejected Kantian morality as 'bourgeois' but his views to the effect that 'freedom means being conscious of necessity' brought him straight back to Kant.

After a lifetime abroad, the most sincere Marxist who ever lived returned to Russia after the February 1917 Revolution. Disappointed, he lived eleven months more, just long enough to see the Bolsheviks seize power by force and to be horrified because in his view the Russian people were not ready.[13] If history really was a power which made use of individuals for its pre-ordained purposes, as Hegel and Marx conjured with it, then Russian Marxism surely used Plekhanov, whose temperament was gradualist despite his choice of the cause of revolution. A patriot who at his request was buried alongside Belinsky, Plekhanov has often been called a tragic figure.[14]

Yet in Plekhanov's day, pre-Lenin, was not the entire intelligentsia tragic? The best part of a century had passed, many good moral ideas had been discussed, but nothing had managed to bring tsarism to its knees. Belinsky, Herzen, Chernyshevsky, Bakunin, Lavrov, Mikhailovsky: they all failed. For more than three generations Russia had longed for social and political change conducive to a harmonious, undivided, communal society, and the only result was three generations of an extraordinary piling of dream upon dream. Marxism would mean something different. It would mean not only hope but political organization, coupled with a philosophy of historical inevitability. With Leninist coerciveness and opportunism to nudge the inevitability along, a Marxist intelligentsia would finally have a convincing formula for action. Come the Revolution the activists could turn round to the moralists and say: look, your hopes have at last been achieved. We've laid the foundation for the good Russia you always longed for. But the activists and the moralists were mostly two aspects of the same man, desperately torn over ends and means. Marxism was never going to be an easy legacy.

Until the Bolshevik victory in October 1917, Marxism still meant many different things in Russia. The *Bogostroiteli* or 'Godbuilders' like Alexander Bogdanov (1873–1928) and Anatoly Lunacharsky (1875–1933) claimed to be Marxists but took exception to the strident atheist message Lenin promoted and warned against shunning the social benefits of Christian belief. They were aware of Comte's spectacular vision of the institution of worship in a post-Christian state, and of Feuerbach's call in *The Essence of Christianity* (1841) for society to make use of hitherto religiously directed energies. Lunacharsky, a mild man with no great force of personality, a Marxist who still respected human beings more than theories, ventured that the secular good Russian society could obviously profit from feelings like altruism and modesty. Lenin ridiculed him as the powerless kind of Marxist who 'mutinied on his knees'.[15] As for Bogdanov, widely acclaimed by his contemporaries as a brilliant and original thinker, a mixture of brilliance and lack of political strategy was the problem. When Bogdanov published an unacceptable version of Marxist philosophy Lenin banished him from the Party.

Lenin's most powerful ideological enemies, however, were difficult to muzzle. They were the 'Legal Marxists' – liberals by another name.

6

The Silver Age

The high-calibre liberal generation which emerged from the universities in the 1890s marked a unique, fleeting age in Russia. The émigré philologist Roman Jakobson would later look back on that decade as the summit of old-Russian cultural achievement.[1] The 'Legal Marxism' of Nikolai Berdyaev, Semyon Frank, Sergei Bulgakov and the lawyer and political activist Pyotr Struve described no movement or coordinated action, only that they weren't underground writers like Lenin and Plekhanov, who were living and conspiring against tsarism abroad. The Legal Marxists looked forward to the end of autocracy and its replacement with liberal democracy. Russia's immediate future looked more like a long period of drawing closer to the capitalist West: a relatively congenial prospect. They became Marxists as students because that was the mood of the universities and because no liberal theory was available.[2] Men of deep culture, who upheld spiritual and individualist values for Russia, mainly in a religious context, they never expected their Marxist beliefs to be tested. In their writings on art, creativity and a civilized way forward for Russia they welcomed the legacy of Khomiakov and Herzen, Lavrov and Mikhailovsky, Leontiev and Solovyov, Tolstoy and Dostoevsky, and expected it to live on.

By 1901 they were deserting the Marxist camp for newly recovered versions of metaphysical idealism. Berdyaev published *Subjectivism and Individualism in Social Philosophy*, with a book-length introduction by Struve, and Bulgakov made his heretical mark with *From Marxism to Idealism* (1903). Two collections of essays followed, *Problems of Idealism* (1903) and *Landmarks* (1909), containing essays by Berdyaev, Frank, Bulgakov and others. The editor of *Landmarks*, the literary critic Mikhail Gershenzon, stressed in the shared outlook of its contributors 'the theoretical and practical pre-eminence of spiritual life over the external forms of community', and 'the sense that the individual's inner life is the sole creative force of human existence and that it, and not any self-sufficient principle of a political order, is the only firm basis for any social construction'.[3]

Nikolai Berdyaev (1874–1948) was born into a noble family in Kiev and always thought of himself as a Russian country gentleman. His maternal grandmother was French and he spoke French and German from childhood. He studied philosophy in Kiev though it is unclear with what success, since he admitted to being unable to pass exams because of a failure to summarize and memorize. He wrote in his autobiography, *Dream and Reality* (1950), by far the best introduction to his thought, that 'I am one of the "conscience-stricken, repentant noblemen" even though at one time I was opposed to and actively combated their influence in Russian culture.'[4] His politics were socialist, but not accompanied by the Utilitarian and materialist attitudes characteristic of Russian socialism before him and Soviet Communism later. In that small respect he resembled Herzen. In many of his books he fought Communism in Russia as a moral evil much as Nietzsche battled against herd mentality and cultural levelling in the West. Extreme reluctance to be pinned down and certain limitations to his talent made Berdyaev vague, although in the end vagueness was part of his message. He belonged in a mystical-anarchist tradition of thinkers from Angelus Silesius to Jakob Boehme, and Russian visionaries, who believed that the human grasp of the world was necessarily incomplete. Berdyaev cited St Symeon the New Theologian

(949–1022) as one of his models.[5] Symeon sensed the inaccessible divine light as 'fire uncreated and invisible, without beginning and immaterial' and he was an opponent of the institutional as opposed to the spiritual church.[6] The sacredness of the incomplete – the deferred – was as much Berdyaev's message in 1915 as it would be Derrida's in 1975. Berdyaev's mystical-theological vocabulary from the early twentieth century does not mean his thinking has no counterpart, even relevance, in the present day. The Russian Silver Age threw up interesting prefigurations of Western postmodernism which have still to be evaluated.

Like Hegel, Berdyaev enjoyed conflict in thought but not in the world. Unlike Hegel he was a natural disciple of German inwardness without feeling the need for the beautiful soul to be emancipated in social reality. The reflected life was the primary value for Berdyaev as it was for Plato and Aristotle. It was the means by which the individual defined himself and his moral space.

> The world within me is indeed much more real than the extraneous world without. Some have often reproached me with inability to acknowledge the movement from within outward – achievement, realization, success, victory . . . It is true that I have no liking for the victors and the successful: they seem to me to pursue the course of mere adaptation to a world which is situated in evil and is largely evil. I do not . . . believe in the possibility of true realization on the level of an alienated, *objectified* [my italics] universe: tragedy has struck too deep at the heart of the world.[7]

Berdyaev coined the term 'objectification' to depict a world in which no spiritual values were present. 'Spiritual' entailed that belief in good as a real non-natural presence in the world which Solovyov and nearly all the Russian religious philosophers after him endorsed. Consistently over more than forty years, from his essays in *Landmarks* to his many books decrying the secularization and disenchantment of the modern world,

Berdyaev insisted that 'objective processes *abstract* and disrupt existence. They substitute society for community, general principles for communion.'[8]

Berdyaev built up his philosophy by transforming religious ideas and arguments into arguments about knowledge and being, just as the German Idealists did a century before. Objectification was thus the opposite of the Orthodox idea of theosis. Theosis meant a loving reciprocity between thought and creation. It meant joining God in a bond of love – man's deification through his participation in spiritual reality.[9]

Berdyaev, who had a Catholic mother but was brought up in the Orthodox faith, took from the Eastern Church a vision of immanent community between the mind of man and all being beyond him. He pictured man as at home in the world through faith but lapsed from this happy state through his own reflectiveness and the rebarbative condition of the world. Creative work was needed to keep the inspirited view alive. 'Nature must be humanized, liberated, made alive and inspired by man . . . Man must give back spirit to the stones, reveal the living nature of stones, in order to free himself from their stony, oppressing power.'[10] To make the creative choice was to create freedom. *The Meaning of the Creative Act* (1914), from which this imperative came, though a long, rambling, unsatisfactory work, was unparalleled in the religious-philosophical habits of the Russian mind it disclosed.

In the mid-twentieth century Berdyaev acquired an international reputation as a Christian existentialist. Living in exile in France from 1922 until his death in 1948 he became well known as an opponent of Communism and a unique philosopher of culture. Many Western philosophers would decline any professional interest in a man who, though a contemporary of Russell and Wittgenstein, defined his subject in 1914 as 'not a science but an art . . . [because] . . . the philosopher's intuition presupposes genius, which is a universal perception of things.'[11] Analytical philosophy defined its desire to be scientific expressly by abandoning Romantic imagination and forging an alliance with logic and mathematics. But Berdyaev's value lies in an attempt to derive knowledge not from an analytical divorce between mind and object, rather from a sympathetic coalescence. He needs to be stripped of an unconvincing attempt to rank himself alongside Plato and Kant and to be appreciated for his sense that knowledge and ethics have to be created for the good of mankind. The Russian Christian answer to Nietzsche, Berdyaev believed in the spiritual benefits of culturally nourished individual imagination. He was terribly necessary in Russia.

Semyon Frank (1877–1950), the product of a mixture of nationalities and religious backgrounds, was like Berdyaev a philosopher in the mould of Solovyov, but more systematic and of a quieter, more scholarly temperament. Born into a Jewish professional family, he was given the basics of a Jewish religious education by his grandfather after his father died. His mother, an educated and talented German Jew whose parents only moved to Russia in her lifetime, remarried a Russian *intelligent* when Semyon was fourteen. He adopted his stepfather's interests in Populism and socialism and grew up bilingual. After university in Moscow, where he studied economics and styled himself a Marxist, he went in 1899 to study in Berlin. Finally in 1912 he converted to Christianity. He taught in Moscow and Saratov until he was expelled from Russia for his religious views in 1922.[12]

Frank gave up his early Marxism because he felt morality based on man's social being was limited. Key aspects of the moral life do not derive from membership of any community. They concern the integrity of the individual, which in turn relates to a man's relationship with himself or with his God. Only the individual can make exceptions and only the individual can really act from principle, because only an individual can hold beliefs. He wrote a number of books, attempting to construct a philosophical system in the old style of Spinoza. Each proceeded from the point of view of the pre-Hegelian idealist and mystical philosopher that Frank was. His greatest mentor as a thinker was Goethe, who suggested how the gulf between mind and world, idealism and materialism, which was never a happy spectacle to the Russian philosophical mind, could be overcome in a mixture of empirical observation supplemented by a leap of imagination. As a descendant of the beautiful souls Frank also wrote literary criticism in which he expressed his vision of the good life.

Sergei Bulgakov (1871–1944), no relation of the contemporary writer Mikhail Bulgakov, was, unlike his fellow giants of alternative philosophy in the age of Lenin, neither an aristocrat nor even a minor gentry figure, and certainly not cosmopolitan. His circumstances were undilutedly Russian. He was born to a poor, disharmonious family whose members had belonged to the clergy for six generations. This 'between ranks' origin, which he shared with Belinsky and Chernyshevsky, made him a typical member of the revolutionary intelligentsia. He went on to study economics at Moscow University alongside Frank. Oscillating between religious faith and Marxism, he became an economist before finally finding his way back to the Church. As a Populist economist Bulgakov saw no reason why Russia should develop a capitalist economy to become socialist. His most interesting contribution to philosophy was a theory of work and allegiance to the soil. His 'Sophic economy' aimed to solve the problem of alienation in a religious context, at the same time as it stressed the uniqueness of Russian agriculture measured against universal Marxist theory. 'Agriculture' could be read both literally and as a synomym for Russia itself.[13]

A man born almost fifty years earlier than Berdyaev, Frank and Bulgakov, but who was best known in the 1890s, must also be considered for his formative influence on the intelligentsia before totalitarianism took hold. Nikolai Fyodorov (1828–1903) was the illegitimate son of a prince, who became famous for his ascetic life. Tolstoy and others came to pay tribute to him. His most famous book, *The Common Task*, finished in 1902 and published posthumously, was a mystical philosophy of community. Like Bulgakov, Fyodorov explored the philosophical significance of work and set conditions for a philosophy appropriate to the working man. This man knew the world through his hands and through shared labour, rather than through cerebration, and provided Fyodorov with the means to an interesting refutation of Kant's ethics.

The range of these men's philosophies is too complex to develop here. Their values overlapped with the work of the Symbolist poets and critics who hugely enriched Russian culture in the last twenty years of the Russian Empire. The distinction between the poetic essay and the philosophical essay was one few Russians cared to make. Their political attitudes were diverse. Berdyaev always insisted he was a socialist. Before the Revolution he was twice exiled for taking an active part in revolutionary circles. Banishment to Vologda he found so much to his taste that he stayed on voluntarily. Mostly the consecutive generations of idealists, from those born in the 1820s to those born in the 1890s, decried the social harm done by tsarism while not wishing to see the Russian social fabric destroyed. Pyotr Struve, more of an economist, traversed the spectrum from real Marxism to increasingly right-wing liberalism and ended up fighting with the White Army in the civil war (1917–20). In between he passed through a period of Left liberalism and both before and after the Revolution his politics forced him to live abroad. In Paris Berdyaev moved in Christian socialist circles. His fellow Paris exile Bulgakov was less successful at surviving forcible uprooting and he pined for the old Russia of the tsars and the Church.

Russian philosophers – I shall still insist on calling them what they were in their own context – travelled and studied abroad with a new vigour in the years immediately before the Revolution. The neo-Kantianism which predominated in the German universities was as much a source of fascination and inspiration as German Idealism had been a century before. The phenomenology of Edmund Husserl was taken up by Aleksei Losev (1893–1988) and Gustav Shpet (1879–1937). The religious philosopher Father Pavel Florensky (1882–1943) also produced work of great interest. The religious-mystical-spiritual philosophers and the phenomenologists, however, left their mark on the intelligentsia so fleetingly that many Russians today have never heard their names. Florensky and Shpet died in Stalin's camps and, apart from Losev, who lived out an inconspicuous life in the Soviet Union, all the others were forcibly removed abroad by government decree in 1922.

The official ousting of Berdyaev, Frank and Bulgakov and of the lesser known Nikolai Lossky (1870–1965) and Fyodor Stepun (1884–1965) from their native land, and the attempt to expunge them from the historical record, followed directly from Lenin's view that anyone who was not a materialist, anyone who expressed a religious or mystical belief, was conservative and reactionary from a Marxist point of view. Lenin branded as dangerous idealists all thinkers who did not accept that material conditions determined reality. Against Lenin's materialism the idealists of the 1890s developed forms of individualism in a religious framework which were uniquely valuable in a country where the integrity of personality and the sacredness of the inner life were so readily belittled. These thoughts were however best expressed by poets, personalities and priests in a way appropriate to those callings. The metaphysical idealism which took off in the universities was obsolete in its own time. It was retrograde pseudo-philosophy, the unhappy casualty of a century of repression. Lossky, who wrote excellent memoirs of the time and led the field in St Petersburg, saw himself as a neo-Leibnizian trying to restore the seventeenth-century bond between reason and faith. In the most ferocious words he ever wrote, Isaiah Berlin called Lossky and his colleagues 'a knock-kneed collection of provincial practitioners decked out to resemble an intellectual renaissance'. Lossky's eventual *History of Russian Philosophy* (1953) persuaded Berlin and thus the entire anglophone world that Russia had no philosophers, only magi of the steppes.[14]

Yet for their accent on the value of persons alone the work of these men was not meaningless. In its native context, if it failed to train minds perhaps it could cultivate peaceful souls who respected each other and the world beyond them. Perhaps it could wean Russia off a century-long tendency to value philosophy as a springboard to immediate practical action and show how it might be contemplative; also relieve it of emotionalism.

Still the problem for Berlin was that precisely this emotionalism which a Western philosopher would normally disdain was what was valuable in Russia. Turgid academicism was all the more hateful for seeming to divert attention from this true heritage, of which Belinsky was typical.

> It is ideas and beliefs in this sense, as they are manifested in the lives and works of human beings – what is sometimes vaguely called ideology – that perpetually excited Belinsky to enthusiasm or anxiety or loathing, and kept him in a state sometimes amounting to a kind of moral frenzy. He believed what he believed very passionately, and sacrificed his entire nature to it . . . The questions which tormented him . . . were . . . about the proper relation of the individual to himself and to other individuals, to society, about the springs of human action and feeling, about the ends of life, but in particular about the imaginative work of the artist, and his moral purpose.[15]

What has mattered as philosophy in Russia has been what it is to hold an idea; what hope is attached; what personal and social investment has been made; not what follows logically from taking a certain position.[16]

The biggest compliment Lenin paid to the world under which he was about to draw a line was that he bothered to present his own vision in philosophical terms. *Materialism and Empiriocriticism* (1908) denied genuine philosophy the chance to exist, abused its practitioners and put a virulent ideology in its place. It was a shallow, improper book, concocted as an ideological weapon in an unholy nine months. At the same time it was a serious reply to prolific attempts to make metaphysical thought prevail in Russia.

Lenin, born Vladimir Ilyich Ulyanov, was part of the world he tried to destroy, an *intelligent* of the Silver Age. His family owned land. They had German-Jewish ancestry. They read the Russian classics aloud at home, and his parents' generation – Lenin's father was a schools inspector until his early death – respected the tsar. The Ulyanov sons had a university education. But everything changed in that family when the elder brother, Alexander, was sentenced to death for conspiring to take the life of Alexander III. The family were shunned and had to move from their home town.[17] Vladimir Ilyich was soon exiled to Siberia for his own political agitation, and his mother and sisters accompanied him.

For Lenin the significance of his brother's execution can hardly be overestimated. It authorized the execution of the past. In power he would banish his own early years by making public discussion and publication of ideas he disagreed with impossible. With force he banned the intelligentsia's favourite activity: philosophical dispute. Under Lenin's successors, the voices of dissident thinkers in Russia – the *inakomyslyashchie* of the twentieth century were literally 'those who thought differently' – would become almost impossible to hear. They spoke in muffled and disguised voices, while the banished philosophers worked abroad, out of touch.

Yet the life of the intelligentsia, and thus in its own way Russian philosophy, continued in a way that Lenin did not manage to break. The Revolution was a crisis, but not an end. Totalitarianism functioned like a funnel into which all the wealth of the nineteenth century was poured and frozen. Only a trickle of the rich culture was officially defrosted and allowed to flow on. The cone held Russia's heritage – not just a theory of revolution but a moral philosophy of being. It contained the entire Western philosophy of hope Russified, as well as the indelible desire for Russia to form a unique, non-Western, community.

PART II

The Making of Russian Philosophy

7

The Moral Map

The scope of Russian philosophy suggests itself in pictures and discussions of good individuals and their role in society. It resembles a map in which the key features are moral and movable – very much an unstable landscape. Individualists and individuals, selfish and selfless people, primitive and complex selves, and souls-in-God: just where do these pieces fit in the utopia of modern Russia? Historians of philosophy do not normally find themselves doing virtual jigsaws, but in the Russian case they seem inevitable. The few arguments that exist come in fragments – in stories and dialogues, often also with a political message. But the philosophical quest is primarily a moral search for the right way to live. Shall I be an individual? Or shall I give up my soul to the community of men, or dissolve it in the universal flow of things? To read Russian philosophy is rather like following an alternative *Pilgrim's Progress*.

One of the first nineteenth-century moralists was the neglected Schellingist Odoevsky, who rejected any way of living, any social or economic system, which encouraged individuals to calculate and pursue their own interests. The butt of his attack was moral and economic Utilitarianism as it was flourishing in England and America in his day. From a Russian viewpoint, the principle of self-interest seemed deeply foreign, both geographically and in spirit. In *Russian Nights* Odoevsky spoke of Britain as 'the birthplace of moral accountancy'. He denounced 'the crude materialism of Adam Smith' and glossed Thomas Malthus as a philosopher 'who concentrated in himself all the crimes and errors of his epoch and squeezed out of them laws for society, strict, and dressed up in mathematical form'. Benjamin Franklin he rejected as a 'philosopher-manufacturer', and 'the real Tartuffe of our age'. Such men were greedy egoists.[1]

Russian Nights was that unique Russian Romantic novel, not a work of genius but modern way ahead of its time, which asked: 'What should Russia do?' 'How should its people live?' Odoevsky provided a series of poetic encouragements and warnings, with the underlying message that Russia should be bold, morally imaginative and communal – indeed, as little like the contemporary West as possible. One story, 'Town without a Name', illustrated the terrible fate awaiting selfish individuals living in a Western-style system of institutionalized self-interest.

The time arrived which had been foretold by nineteenth-century philosophers: the human race multiplied; the proportionate relation between what human beings need and what nature supplies was lost. Slowly but constantly the human race approached disaster. Driven by indigence, the inhabitants of the towns fled to the fields, the fields turned into villages, the villages to towns, and the towns imperceptibly enlarged their borders; in vain man tried to use all the knowledge acquired by the sweat of brows through the centuries, in vain he joined to the contrivances of art that mighty activity born of mortal necessity. Long ago the sandy Arabian steppes had been turned into fertile pastures; long ago the ice of the north was covered with a layer of soil; by incredible efforts artificial heat brought to life the kingdom of eternal cold, but it was all in vain; centuries passed, and animal life crowded out vegetable life, the frontiers of the towns merged, and the whole surface of the earth from one pole to the other turned into one vast populated city, into which were transferred all luxuries, all illnesses, all refinement, all debauchery, all the activity of the former towns; but beyond the luxurious cosmopolis reigned terrible poverty and the means of communication, which had been perfected, carried into all corners of the globe only news of terrible outbreaks of hunger and sickness; the buildings still stood tall; a few rows of corn lit by artificial sunshine and irrigated with artificial water brought forth a plentiful harvest, but it disappeared before it could be picked; everywhere, at every step, on the canals, the rivers, in the air, people surged, everything was teeming with life, but life was destroying itself. In vain people begged each other for the means to resist the universal disaster. Old people remembered the past and blamed luxury and the decline of morals for everything. The young called upon strength of mind, will and imagination to help; the wisest looked for ways of prolonging human life without food, and no one laughed at them.[2]

In this wretched Benthamite colony somewhere in America rampant self-interest had bled nature dry. No longer able to feed itself, society had collapsed into violence and anarchy. Newbenthamtown, as we might call it, was always an ugly, excessive place to live when it was flourishing, because its people were egotistical and oblivious to the needs of others, but in decline it was murderous. Because its citizens lacked the moral impulse to be unselfish, there was no criterion for restraint in a time of practical hardship. The population in Newbenthamtown was encouraged to maximize consumption, but precisely when real need struck self-interest became a crime. So what of this universal principle of self-interest now, Odoevsky's story demanded. If you pursue your need for bread and firewood when both are short, you can hardly be increasing the prosperity of the majority. But if you are a Utilitarian, if you have been raised in such a moral environment, what practice will you have had at being a different kind of person? If the Utilitarian West can hardly save itself, perhaps Russia still can.

'Town without a Name' was thin anti-Western propaganda before the propaganda machine was invented. It seriously under-represented the complexity of human behaviour and made a typical Russian mistake by falsely assuming that the competitive economic principle had its absolutely inflexible and necessary counterpart in interpersonal indifference and a brutal struggle for survival. But it had a moral heart of some significance in the history of Russian thought because it suggested that to practise self-interest, even if it did lead to good economic results, was unequivocally wrong. What mattered in a better world were people of moral imagination, who could see that love mattered more than self-interest. To hypothetical Utilitarian questions like 'why should I aim to be morally fit in the longer term, when in the short term I can at least be rich?' and 'why am I wrong to treat life as a simple calculus for personal gain?', Odoevsky's answer was that since as human beings we have moral imagination at our disposal, and moral imagination is a good thing, we should use it. Moral imagination would then show us that egoism is a poor guide to the good life. Odoevsky's logic was persuasive.

In case the reader didn't quite get the point, however, another story in *Russian Nights*, 'The Avenger', featured an 'Invisible Hand' which smote men down if they did not use their moral imagination. The term was originally Adam Smith's for the self-regulating market mechanism, and by putting it to a moral-mystical use Odoevsky showed how readily Russia would take economic individualism as its moral enemy. *Russian Nights* was evidence of how Smith's economic philosophy in *The Wealth of Nations* prompted an immediate opposite flight of imagination in Russia. Smith brought on a moral panic in Odoevsky. It made him punitive.

'The Last Suicide' was yet another Odoevsky story in *Russian Nights*, in which a loveless man decided to kill himself after realizing the poverty of a lifetime's petty calculation. It was childishly punitive. It failed to foresee occasions where prudence might shape a loving decision or where a thoroughly good person might neither seek nor receive love. But somewhere between a dislike of moral Utilitarianism and a contempt for selfish individuals a good idea occurred to Odoevsky about how to live. Newbenthamtown showed by default the need, in a better world, for moral personality based on voluntary restraint.

Almost two hundred years later Alexander Solzhenitsyn would seek to persuade a Western audience that Russian philosophy virtually began with a dislike of Bentham. The Russian moral antipathy to Utilitarianism has been remarkably consistent.[3] In his stories Odoevsky was in fact grounding that typical distinction Khomiakov and Solovyov and Mikhailovsky and many other Russian thinkers would make, that Russia was morally superior to the West, and showing why. Less prosperous, technologically less advanced, admittedly, but Russian culture was morally of a higher type because it was interested in something other than crude statements of 'I want' and 'this is mine'. These are the distinctions which shape Russian philosophical history. As early as Odoevsky the country's desire not to be Western turned into a vision of itself as a mystical world economy running on selflessness.

In defence of Bentham, the Russian *infâme*, his Utilitarian ethics were based on law, not on individual moral conscience. Bentham was looking for a way to maximize individual freedom within a legal framework beneficial to the majority. This sophisticated conception would have been alien to Russian thinkers who lived in an unconstitutional and arbitrary political culture where either personal morality mattered or nothing.[4] In defence of Smith, *The Wealth of Nations* was an economic treatise and its author expressed a more complex ethics in his *Theory of Moral Sentiments*. Nevertheless Odoevsky's Russian criticism of these pragmatic British and American ways revealed a typical Russian mind at work. Smith's laissez-faire economics expressed inveterate Western rational optimism in the latest material and freedom-seeking terms. Odoevsky disagreed with this rationalism because as a Russian religious traditionalist he thought the ethical life could not be the product of reason but must have as its origin a dream of mystical-moral community. The idea was vague, but it accurately reflected conditions in a country where the intelligentsia had little else to do but dream.

In 'Town without a Name' Odoevsky stepped into the Anglo-French debate of the preceding two generations over economic freedom, the wealth of nations, and the situation of the poor. He saw free trade and its associated philosophical positions as entirely to blame for the misery of poverty and the ruin of nature. The debate in Britain led to the eventual repeal of the Corn Laws in 1846 but Odoevsky took the opposite view that the state should intervene in economic matters because only the state could regulate fair supplies for all. A little restraint imposed from on high would surely be a good thing if it helped men share. Smith's novelty was to decry state intervention in the market. Laws and regulations and taxation were to be minimized. 'The unlimited, unrestrained freedom of the corn trade, as it is the only effectual preventative of the miseries of a famine, so it is the best palliative of the inconveniences of a dearth.' In *The Wealth of Nations* Smith repeated five times his belief that the freedom of the corn trade was actually the best policy for the poor.[5] But 'Town without a Name' expressed Odoevsky's disagreement with Smith by evoking a world of moral shallowness. Culture should produce moral dreamers, he emphasized. Moral quality mattered more than economic efficiency.

The reflection of such issues in early nineteenth-century Russian literature and criticism shows how the invention of Utilitarianism first caused Russia to look in the philosophical mirror at its own ethical face, where it could discern traits of selflessness and mystical moral being. These had their immediate counterpart in distaste for an economically competitive way of life which seemed the antithesis of moral imagination. The negative revelations provided by Utilitarianism were as great as anything Hegel would ever say to Russia about the destiny of nations. The Western mirror revealed that what Russians instinctively admired was unselfishness and community. In an ideal Russia, thanks to the Orthodox religion and the mystical heritage, those values would be embedded in a ground of being which made them not so much daily choices as a natural way of life.

As *Russian Nights* appeared in 1844, Khomiakov and Kireevsky were ready with their religiously informed explanation of why egoism wasn't only a moral error but also and more fundamentally a form of wrong knowledge. A selfish man was not only unvirtuous, he couldn't know the very truth of existence if he was self-centred. Egoism was an epistemic crime as well as a moral one, these first Russian philosophers showed. On these foundations the pursuit of a moral philosophy of being came to define Russian philosophy and guide Russian culture.

Selflessness had its political and economic entailments, but fundamentally it described the right relationship between man and his world: how he sought truth in that world. With all its extensive ramifications the ideal of selflessness – of a human singularity defined by love not self-interest – grew from two sources. One was traditional Russian community. The other was that reaction against the West which Odoevsky demonstrated but which in fact predated Utilitarianism and referred directly back to the French Revolution. The conservative Russian response to 1789 was to decry Enlightenment reason as immoral. This sense of outrage at the Revolution was felt by the French Catholic Church and conservative Russia adopted its stance. Moral Russia thus prolonged European religious loathing of the perceived ways of reason for many decades – indeed, until its own revolution in 1917 and after. The context provided by late eighteenth-century England and France has remained vitally important to understanding anti-Western Russia ever since, because it linked reason and atheism with economic free-thinking. The eighteenth-century political Right associated Smith's and Condorcet's new science of political economy with everything that led to the overthrow of traditional values. Smith said that the weight of the superstitions and traditions of the past should not block men's true freedom to develop and determine a rational, habitable, vibrant world through free economic activity. But to his religious opponents either side of the Channel he spoke with a forked tongue on behalf of 'the sect of Enlightenment'. Lamennais – Chaadaev's source of inspiration – denounced the *philosophes*, including Smith, as 'apostles of impiety' who wanted to found a new religion founded on reason, and to forge a criminal combination of cosmic uncertainty with the triumph of individual will. The new way of thinking was a 'monstrous chaos of incoherent ideas [which] imagines that one can do everything with money'.[6]

In fact laissez-faire had little to do with the Jacobins, whose economics were interventionist, but enough anti-rationalists in Britain and France linked them together as two consequences of rationalism, and the repeated error made the connection stick. Odoevsky then helped carry to Russia a view of the world which linked conservative moralism with a dislike of the free market and the individualism it entailed. Rationalism in moral philosophy, liberalism in economics and the extinguishing of political and social hierarchies: a filthy individualistic high tide was sweeping in from the West, and Odoevsky's task was to establish the moral bridgehead against it.

Odoevsky's position was such a characteristic one for Russia over the next 150 years that it helps explain a much later confusion in Western perceptions of Russian and Soviet values. It was surely because Russia entered the European debate on economic and moral values late – Odoevsky picked up the Anglo-French debate of the 1780s only after 1836 – that henceforth Russian 'Left' and 'Right' would rarely coincide with a European sense of how the political-moral spectrum divided after the French Revolution. This is why a history of what opposition to self-interest has meant in Russia is so important. The model of the free West, expressed at its most free as a market economy, was rejected in Russia because it seemed to bring with it a lifestyle centred on individual self-assertion. The 'system' made individuals selfish and their rationalism made them lose sight of the true meaning of life.

The next man to join the selfishness debate was Herzen. The rise of Western socialism was the immediate influence on his early thinking. With its neo-Christian ideals of cooperation, socialism reinforced the Russian virtue of an unselfish existence at the same time as both Russia and the West were transferring their moral-religious ideals to the political domain. The ideal of unselfishness, though embedded in Orthodoxy, was thus really brought home to the semi-Western Herzen by his reading of French utopian socialism. Saint-Simon's and Fourier's utopian communities persuaded him he should dislike egoism and egoists and deny them a place in a decent society. The young socialist learned that moral virtue was political virtue. To be politically concerned with social welfare, to believe men were born to cooperate and not to compete, defined what unselfishness was. Herzen, aged twenty-four and a progressive thinker, believed all these things when he wrote a story about how he could only like a man whose life was focused on the common good, not on private interest.

The story concerned the friendship of Goethe and Schiller, and already by the time Herzen wrote down his version of it this chapter from German literary history had acquired the force of cultural myth in Russian minds. Herzen's story has no great merit as literature, but his desire to tell it, in the end twice over, is part of Russian philosophical history. The basis in fact was that Goethe remained aloof from the French Revolution, whereas Schiller, for all that the Jacobin slide into violence appalled him, remained passionately attached to the ideals of liberty, equality and fraternity. Herzen wrote up a first fictional comment on this friendship in 1836, under the title 'First Meeting'. It showed a young Russian dazzled by Goethe's calm and lofty genius but appalled by the political implications of his egoism. Finally the Russian burst out: 'I cannot love this man.' Schiller, concerned for the welfare of the greatest number, was the more attractive moral figure because of his unselfishness.[7]

Yet Herzen, who was a genuine free thinker, found it difficult to retain this doctrinaire view, because he didn't like the kind of society which might result from its being widely held. In a new version of the Goethe/Schiller encounter called 'One Man's Notes' and finished in 1841, only five years later, he made clear that to be a warm, unselfish and sympathetic person concerned with general welfare might not benefit society more, and probably less, than a great artist might. The artist might be a model of spiritual self-sufficiency and promote a fresh understanding of life. Indeed, Goethe was such a man, an example of one whose selfish devotion to his work could do more for society than his commitment and good nature.[8] Herzen was saying that the benevolent activist's view of the world therefore, the more so if it was dogmatic, was too simple as moral philosophy, for surely any intelligent person could see that it was not only the direct consequences of moral actions which could lead to improved states of human affairs. Unreflected goodness might be deeply attractive, but any outlook which simplified good to such an extent, and required blind, selfless service to it, was mistaken.

Herzen's nuanced position was rare among his peers. As his American biographer Martin Malia remarked, after reading Schiller's philosophical writings as a young man Herzen was never able to conceive of human greatness without moral integrity and cultivated intellect. He clung on to the branches of a Socratic-Aristotelian heritage which failed to put down roots in Russia. He was destined to be swept away in the current of the Utilitarian 'new men' and later by Populism, but before he went he was able to express his fear that the idea of the good man in Russia risked becoming a puritanical cult. His response to the world of Odoevsky was already a caveat. Beware of making the standard of the good man too primitive.

The risk was that this habit of subordinating all cultural and political values to a vision of moral being – a kind of mystical Utilitarianism in which all goods are communal – would make Russia a non-Western nation, or one at best on the Western fringe. A key to Herzen's own development as a Westernizer was the way he came to reject the obsession with unselfishness and plead for the opposite in Russia. The ideal of unselfishness, and the mysticism which hovered around it, had to be relinquished if Russia was properly to become a rich and diverse modern culture, rather than the faraway home of a clumsy and eccentric puritanism.

In *The Historical Letters* Lavrov asked Herzen to think again. He demanded selfless commitment to the political cause, if Russia was to make progress. By easing up on moral and political accusations of selfishness Herzen wanted to encourage a liberal society in Russia in which all kinds of men and women, different, but not necessarily immoral, could find their place. But Lavrov insisted on a political commitment for the moral man which would entail a self-sacrifice from which all other values would follow. The good man in Russia would have to denounce the society that gave him that self-conscious 'self'. He would have to denounce in himself a kind of selfishness over which he had no control and of which he had never been the agent, namely the very circumstances of his birth. 'A member of a small group within the minority, who finds pleasure in his own development, in the search for truth, and in the realization of justice, would say to himself: each of the material comforts which I enjoy, each thought which I have had the leisure to acquire or to develop, has been bought with the blood, sufferings, or toil of millions.'[9]

Lavrov told Herzen: Look, given the mess that Russia is, you can't define moral truth in terms that suit you privately as an educated man. The political cause has to come first. Fine not to talk about the mystical ground of moral being, fine not to be an old-fashioned type like Odoevsky, but the only adequate moral theory in Russia must be one which creates model campaigners for the cause. All educated Russians must be willing to serve their country and eradicate injustice. It's not enough in Russia to hold a point of view. Any moral philosophy has also to be a philosophy of political action. We educated men have to sacrifice something. We have to give up the time we would spend reflecting and make this vast world of ours better. 'I cannot correct the past, and however high the cost of my cultivation I cannot repudiate it; it constitutes the very ideal which arouses me to action. [Yet] only a weak and uncultivated person collapses under his responsibilities and flees from evil to the Thebaid or to the grave. Evil must be corrected *vitally*. I shall relieve myself of the bloody cost of my own development if I utilize this same development to diminish evil in the present and in the future. If I am a cultivated person I am obliged to do this.'[10]

To be prepared to 'correct evil vitally' became Lavrov's definition of the good man in Russia. The need for action against injustice made a moral goal out of the willingness to act as such, regardless of motive. To act was in itself good, and action should not be inhibited by consideration of any but ideal results. Lavrov taught a socialized Russian version of what Nietzsche would call Will to Power – a kind of self-overcoming for reflective men who might otherwise be tempted not to pursue social goals actively. 'Evil must be corrected vitally . . . I am obliged to do this. But for me this obligation is very light, since it coincides exactly with what constitutes pleasure for me: by seeking and disseminating greater truth, by coming to understand what social order is most just and striving to realize it, I am increasing my own pleasure and at the same time doing everything I can for the suffering majority in the present and in the future. And so my task is limited to one simple rule: live according to the ideal which you yourself have set up as the idea of a *cultivated* man.'[11] Russian Will to Power was a mixture of Utilitarian and Kantian exhortations to the good man to commit himself to the cause.

Lavrov appealed to the moral imagination of educated men in Russia, but in case they wavered he observed that a quasi-Kantian categorical imperative bound them not to be selfish. As reflective human beings they had no choice but to work for the political good. What kind of individuals or selves did Lavrov's moral philosophy implicitly work with? He was a Western-style thinker influenced by Kant and Hegel and he certainly had individuals in mind as responsible moral agents. The educated men who were his starting-point were selves conscious of their capacity to reflect singly on the world. But the political demands Lavrov made on individuals turned them into what I will call 'morally commandeered individuals'. They were selves required to give up their selfhood for the cause.

More than any Russian philosopher before him Lavrov was primarily concerned with political action. He tended to sacrifice the Western moral values he admired to that end. The result led him into difficulties over how much unfettered individualism was required for a country to make progress – or how much could be allowed. Hegel had the argument for progress. He envisaged a complex ideal society in which an unlimited and growing number of fulfilled individuals would play a fully integrated part in the social product. They would play their part by developing as rational beings. Hegel described how the rational man matured. Simple community was his first home – his family and immediate locality. But as he grew older and more reflective he distanced himself from his origins and considered his place in a wider world. The accomplished man for Hegel – what a Greek philosopher would have called a just or excellent man – was therefore neither a happy yokel nor an introspective loner. He was a complex modern individual, whose task was to know a world beyond his native sphere. A Hegelian rational man constantly extended his life outwardly, away from his inner concerns. To this process there was no limit. This was the meaning of the obscure lines on the opening pages of this book.

> The power of the mind is only as great as its expression, and its depth only as deep as it dares to extend itself in its exposition and lose itself.[12]

The vocabulary was Cartesian. It proceeded from the division of the world into mind and matter, *res cogitans* and *res extensa*. Hegel's achievement was to set the Cartesian pursuit of knowledge into an evolving historical context. For Hegel, knowledge was progress and progress was knowledge. Knowledge made the shift from simple community to complex society possible. It allowed simple souls to become selves. Free, reflective individuals emerged as a general force in history for the first time, as Hegel set 'I think, I am' into a context which became 'I think, I become'.

Hegel's good arguments persuaded Stankevich and Herzen that a good modern society was bound to encourage individuals to pursue unlimited knowledge. Stankevich, that beautiful soul who studied in Berlin and died so young, declared in 1835 that he found Hegel's sense of life as an intellectual and spiritual *process* to be the essence of modern philosophy. He admired and hoped to make his own a philosophy which 'founded on vast knowledge, shows man the goal of life and the way to this goal and opens up his mind'.

> I want to know to what degree man has developed his thinking, and having found that out, I want to show people their merits and their calling, I want to summon them towards the good, I want to inspire all the other sciences with a single idea . . . I am a believer, but I want always to protect and strengthen my faith with my mind. I was delighted to find some of my favourite ideas in Hegel. It wasn't the delight of vanity, no, I was happy that a man of such great intellect, having undergone all the painful ordeals which the mind must undergo, was not estranged from these beliefs.[13]

In *The Phenomenology of Spirit*, a book Stankevich apparently knew and Herzen explicitly admired, Hegel described what it was like to be knowingly-in-the-world. He told stories about how individuals develop mentally, psychologically, culturally – stories that have ever since reminded literary critics of the *Bildungsroman*, the most successful form of the German novel in the nineteenth century. *Bildungsromane* were about individuals making their way in the world: novels which compared simple beginnings with complex ends. In a similar spirit Hegel's philosophy of growth expressed faith in progress, so long as individuals responded actively to the challenge of an increasingly complex world.

Russia should modernize and grow through the free input of individual effort and invention into the rational-historical process, Lavrov agreed. But could the free individual really do enough? Hegel's historicism meant that individuals in pursuit of knowledge were necessarily enlarging the quantity of reason in society and making it a more enlightened place, but Lavrov felt that in Russia the pursuit of knowledge alone was not enough to secure the modern future. The moral goal had to be explicit because of Russia's peculiarly oppressive political circumstances. The engine of change, even if history set it in motion, had to be fuelled by individuals willing consciously to act in moral concert. To that extent, for the sake of effective action, something of their individual freedom to pursue diverse ends had to be reined in. There would be a dialectical give-and-take between necessity and invention – an exchange of interests as if necessity and invention were two businessmen – but it would need to be morally supervised. I suggested the term just now of 'morally commandeered individuals' – not quite free moral agents.

Lavrov was torn between his belief in Hegelian-style free individuals and the needs of Russian society. As a Westernizer, he could live with competitive individuality if he could offset it with infallible moral commitment. But many, perhaps most, Russian thinkers who preceded and followed him found they disliked individualism as such. Progress had to be moral progress. At the very least Hegel would have to be adapted.

Hegel's picture of an individualistic, combative world in which persons and nations developed by defining themselves against others, featured a constant jockeying for power. Just as in Smith's world men exchanged goods for profit, so in Hegel's individuals – but also the very power of thought – traded ambitions for the chance to realize them. Individuals collided with nature and society in a constant bid for

domination and the chance to expand their domain. Hegel's was a vision
of the growing West as an engine of reason. Stankevich and Herzen
approved and Lavrov half-did. The beautiful souls accepted the general
moral benefit of unbridled individual knowledge-seeking. Lavrov's more
equivocal position was finely poised between recognizing that a civilized
Russia needed individualistic Western ethics – and thus a choice of ways
of seeing – and accepting that achieving the moral cause at whatever cost
was paramount.

The thoroughly negative Russian position on Hegel was the
Slavophile one. Khomiakov and his fellow Slavophiles felt instantly that
Hegel's competitive world, so passionate about its own fulfilment, and
with its central detail of individuals grappling for advantage one over
another, was unsuitable for Russia. The West stood for competition and
energy and conflict, but a moral Russia stood for community and peace.
The subtlest tension in Russian philosophy emerges from the encounter
with Hegel, between reined-in selves, either voluntary or morally
commandeered from without, and the non-existent selves the Slavophiles
idealized – simple souls untouched by the lure of progress. As Herzen's
liberalism fell by the wayside Russia retained two philosophical options
on progress, both of which justified imposing moral constraints on
knowledge-seeking. The Lavrovian option envisaged, in not so many
words, a mildly to modestly repressed society in which Hegelian
individuals gave up some of their freedom and allowed themselves to be
morally commandeered. The other ideal, established by Slavophilism,
revelled in a revamped version of a traditional community of selfless
souls: Hegel minus both freedom and progress. Each of these potential
futures for Russia had its distinctive moral colouring visible in the way it
treated individuals: either as constrained selves for political reasons or as
non-existent selves for moral reasons.

What could the justification be for rejecting selfhood in favour of a
simple soulful existence? Traditional Russia was in no doubt. A year

before Khomiakov's death Hegel's tales of individuals maturing in Western society through their own rational strivings were answered by a picture of a much more congenial Russian world. Ivan Goncharov's novel *Oblomov* (1959) was an anti-*Bildungsroman* in all but name. All its energies were harnessed to mocking the Hegelian *mythos* and refuting the *logos* behind it. A work of accidental genius, with nothing else written by Goncharov approaching it, it illustrated the fundamental Russian choice of non-selfhood as the basis of ideal community. It poked superior fun at the futility of individualistic competitiveness.

'A sleepy labouring towards meaning' is the way one critic has described the existence of Ilya Ilyich Oblomov, the easy-going Russian nobleman who takes a hundred pages to get out of bed, and can never quite make the effort to marry the lovely modern Olga. Young, active and demanding, Olga is a model of aspiration and passion. Oblomov belongs psychologically – and also epistemically – to a different world. Goncharov reached back to the alternative Russian knowledge picture Khomiakov and Kireevsky set out. I. I. Oblomov embodied consubstantial, 'integral' knowledge for souls rather than aggressive-divisive knowledge for individuals.

The modern philosopher's question and the essence of Western individualism for Hegel – the difference between individual consciousness and what exists outside it – never occurs to Oblomov. His bond with nature is undynamic and unproblematic. No troubling energy sparks across from his individualized being to a separate entity called the 'outside world'. No external object, assumed to be 'the world', needs to be worked on, moulded, grasped and labelled. The distinction between thinking matter and extended matter is almost non-existent in his pre-Cartesian world.

Hegel pitched the inner man against the outer world of nature and society. But in the vision of the old-world Russian there were no such epistemic gaps to be bridged or suffered. The peaceful way in which Oblomov absorbed knowledge placed him at the centre of an emotional and epistemological idyll. His character suggested an impossible picture for classical Western philosophy, namely that there wasn't a problem – thought and matter combined in a bear hug. Because Oblomov wanted power neither over nature nor over other men, his political existence followed a parallel pacific, non-Western pattern. A feudal lord, but an aristocrat and a Russian, Oblomov ran his estate as a master, but without slaves. He was a lord, but explicitly without bondsmen. In the brief period when he did serve the state as a civil servant he behaved as a father to his subordinates. His social and political relations were either relations of kinship or they didn't exist.[14]

One hint that the novel may have been a deliberate answer to Hegel was a counter-Oblomovian character, a half-German called Stolz, who competed with the Russian for happiness, success and Olga's hand. Stolz's German surname meant 'pride', and with his Russian mother and German father he was a new type in society and the cause in 1859 of much Russian thought about industry and modernity. Olga eventually married Stolz who, as a token of Western-style progress in Russia, was fully engaged in running his estate more efficiently. He rose early, worked, disciplined himself and pursued goals. He was active and ambitious. Yet the subtle symbolism of the novel showed Stolz to be living in an unreal world which only existed as the creation of his own will and desire. Stolz was a mild version of the man-God – the individual in Russian nineteenth-century philosophical mythology whose desire for self-fulfilment was a bid to take God's place. The term was defined by Solovyov, against the pattern of Western aspiration defined by Hegel and Feuerbach. The Hegelian Stolz was not a monstrous example of a man-God, but Goncharov made his achievement – Western-style happiness as reward for hard work – morally unconvincing.

The life of 'Plato of Oblomovka' has a soft, rounded quality and a feminine serenity. Oblomov is naive, a child, content with being, dwelling in nature construed as a tame garden. Neither dependent nor independent, and never doubting his natural place in nature and his own community, he rejects the notion of life as a struggle. He is not a thinker. He rejects the very notion of thought as reflection. Were you to look into his bedroom you would see that

> instead of reflecting objects, [those mirrors] could better have served as tablets on which reminder notes could be written in the dust.[15]

A man who doesn't go in for (self-)reflection is one who has no use for reason. Oblomov does not engage with the world through reason. His reality is immediate and undifferentiated, and by the same token he does not see modern competitive Western society as the right goal for a good Russia.

This communal and often religious psychology, typical of Russian conservatism, may be why Bakunin, when he entered a dialogue with Hegel, passed over the pictures of conflict in that foreign philosophy and looked to the goal of self-delivery beyond. No metaphysical wheeler-dealer in love with the process of self-assertion, he longed for the final handshake; his last deal with life as an individual. Bakunin approached Hegel as if the German philosopher were a soul doctor rather than a philosopher of competition. Bakunin was troubled by reflectiveness. He complained that exposure to Western individualism had caused an unnaturally large critical self to grow in him. He ached to get rid of this savage growth – reason as a gratuitous piece of weaponry attached to his personal being – in order to live in peace with the world.

Bakunin's biographer Aileen Kelly described the strange resolution for which Bakunin sought a prescription from Hegel:

> Through a titanic feat of will he would achieve self-fulfilment as a higher nature and would simultaneously lose himself in the Absolute by serving as the instrument of its eternal purposes.[16]

Bakunin spoke repeatedly of his desire to destroy the individual personality which the modern world had urged him to create.

> One must wholly annihilate one's personal ego, annihilate everything that forms its life, its hopes and its personal beliefs. One must love and breath only for the Absolute, through the Absolute ... happiness ... is possible only through total self-oblivion, total self-denial.[17]

He brought Fichte into the dialogue to assure himself that 'the more [man] dissolves himself in [the divine world] the more he becomes man; the more he identifies his will with the will of God the more he becomes free'. And then he asked Christ to affirm that he had made the right philosophical choice, for was not Christ the ultimate example of the man whose divinity was confirmed through dissolution of his material ego?[18]

Bakunin's psychology suggests his natural role in life would have been as a religious servant or officiary of a mystical sect. As an individual uneasy with the burden of autonomous selfhood he longed for the Day of Judgement. He was an hysterical child, a bearer of the kind of excessive emotionalism that the historian Georgy Florovsky said ruined the medieval Russian Church and which many observers used to notice about Russian society when it was Communist. Bakunin, ahead of all later devotees to the absolute moral cause, saw in 'philosophy' or 'reason' the chance to lose himself. He was probably too emotional to be a good example of the Lavrovian commandeered individual but he was certainly a candidate whose writing helps us appreciate his anti-individualistic motivation from within.[19]

Dostoevsky was another extremist who only spoke up on the question of self-fulfilment in order to opt for self-abandon:

> The highest use a man can make of his individuality, of the

completed development of his I, would be to destroy this I, and to return it entirely to all and to each inseparably and supremely. And this is the greatest happiness. In this way the law of *I* merges with the law of humanity and both are one and I and all (which appear to be two opposed extremes) are both mutually destroyed, while at the same time they attain the higher goal of their own individual development on this basis. This is the paradise of Christ. All history, both of humanity and of every separate part of it, is only the growth, the struggle, the yearning for, and the attainment of this goal.[20]

Hegel's view of a history made by free individuals was all but explicitly rejected here as Dostoevsky chose in preference the Orthodox ideal of kenosis. A man's highest moral task was to empty himself to receive God. Dostoevsky advocated 'destroying this I' to save humanity.[21] He enacted what one historian, identifying a fundamental attitude to life, has called the *doleo*. *Doleo, ergo sumus* – I suffer, therefore we are – is, according to Daniel Rancour-Laferrière's fine appreciation of the moment, the Russian emotional truth. Dostoevsky sought to apologize to God for being an individual.[22]

But now imagine, if you will, a worldly Russian, not a fanatic. Here is a man who is neither child, fool nor saint, who has nevertheless decided that the right way to live is as part of a simple community. An educated and potentially ambitious man, he accepts that his goal involves a degree of self-renunciation. The St Petersburg-born German writer Lou Salomé (1861–1937), or perhaps she might be called the German-domiciled Russian writer on the strength of her insights, could have been any sympathetic Western traveller to Russia, at almost any period since the mid-nineteenth century, when she met Nikolai Alexandrovich 'Kolya' Tolstoy. This titled, landed figure – not related to the writer Lev Tolstoy – impressed her as a man who somehow embodied a typical Russian attitude which belonged to the aristocracy. This memoir dated from her visit to Russia in 1900.

The originality and solidity of the Tolstoys remains for me an unforgettable impression, the strongest after the discovery of liberalism and of the disinterest of the emancipators of the people in Moscow. I will often come back to the plenitude of this experience to enjoy it and to enrich myself. For the lord of the manor who retains his faith without losing anything of his individual power is quite different from the religious peasant, who has less need to develop his individuality. A nobleman like Kolya represents in himself a drama perhaps, while the peasant remains a serene hymn. It's not a matter of the familar drama known to the rebel pitted against tradition and the reactionary, the champion of tradition against the tempests which threaten it (a spectacle of which liberals and noblemen in Germany offer an example). The drama [here] is born of the conviction that critical existence removes too many fruitful elements and that the right thing to do is to imitate the peasant who bows to the supreme law. The nobleman's pride therefore becomes humility and the force of his individuality, impatiently seeking an outlet, is no more than an accent placed on the demands of tradition.

To be Russian means to understand and legitimize the fruitful possibilities which are inscribed in the harmony of each life. The Russian does not criticize, he simply nourishes himself on the good things life offers . . .

He lets himself be carried along naively by life, fortified by the capacity for assimilation which is his natural strength. Maybe his vast soul, which has to complete so many syntheses in itself, to absorb so many contrasts, perhaps involuntarily this soul experiences its centre of gravity and its unity in tradition and in religious faith. That would be the most profound and most instinctive motivation, the gesture by which in full virile consciousness he sacrifices his individuality to a totality which is greater than himself. It would explain how the summit of his strength as a man resides for him in his humility and not in arrogance. Russians who give way to the critical spirit most often lack strength of being. For this force is so powerful that its weight can bring a man to his knees.[23]

Lou Salomé's description of Kolya Tolstoy was a remarkable parable, a testament to how much she had absorbed of the Russian world, and how aware she was, consciously and subliminally, that Russian distinctiveness was built upon its difference from the German sense of individuals and selves. Her evocation of Kolya – a kind of real-life, serious counterpart to Oblomov – became a virtual lesson in how men and women potentially critical of their country could stay loyal; and what their motives and their satisfaction would be in stepping back from Western-style individualism. She explained how, despite the urge to steer his life along a more individual course, Kolya would hold back for the sake of the community; how his self-restraint would not seem false to himself or to others; how his beliefs rooted in the communal life would on the contrary reward him with personal strength and happiness.[24]

The aristocratic Russian conservative ethos was not essentially different from the communal ethos of the peasantry, but more complex because of the factor of education. As Westernizers, Herzen and Stankevich and Lavrov faced the question of how an educated man could fit into the backward peasant land he came from. Herzen's friend, Ivan Turgenev, asked himself the question over and over again in his stories. The Westernizers' answer was two-fold: accept it and at the same time change it for the better. Kolya Tolstoy though showed how, with a different grasp of Russia's needs, an educated individual might retain his place in a non-Westernized motherland. He would submerge himself in daily life – in that continuity of being which Russians call *bytie*. *Bytie* is objective existence, reality, being, a standard which remains when all the superficialities of culture and whims of human thought have passed.

'He sacrifices his individuality to a totality which is greater than himself... his strength as a man resides for him in his humility.' This attitude begins to show how the term I applied to Lavrov's pre-revolutionary ideal of commitment to the cause, 'commandeered individuals', might be only one side of a coin which would have voluntary self-limitation on its other face. Voluntary self-limitation would certainly affect how a man felt about his educational advantages. Seeking above all to belong to the community, he would want to eschew his power over the uneducated and replace it with sympathy. In this process the moral value of knowledge would be severely dented, but as a true Populist he would accept that. Typically he would say '*I* know about Descartes and Hegel, and *I* even value the freedom of mind they teach, but *you*, my Russian brother, you do not know about Descartes and Hegel and about freedom and responsibility, and that makes me unhappy for the whole of society which hasn't given you the chance to know, and therefore *I* must put my knowledge aside and act in solidarity with you.'

In Russia, Khomiakov and Lavrov both felt the validity of this reasoning, as did Pisarev, another educated man locked out of communal belonging and ready to resort to drastic social engineering to get himself let in.

If the generality and not only the select are to study and reflect and wish to do so, it would be good to expel from science everything that can be understood only by the few and can never become common knowledge... Abstractions can be interesting and intelligible only to the abnormally developed and insignificant minority.[25]

The Russian complex of communal belonging, the potential tragedy behind these words, was, as Lou Salomé said of Kolya Tolstoy's choice of a way of life, a drama, but not a German one. It was not the Hegelian drama of individual selves forging their way to successful self-expression against all the competition of others and the resistance of the status quo. It reflected rather the drama of Russia's torn soul. Nineteenth-century Russia wanted so much from the West but only on condition of not sacrificing its own moral authenticity. The Russian hope was for a high degree of civilization but on morally acceptable terms. The fact – never solved before the Revolution – that civilization in Russia was a minority privilege, and only increased the social gap the intelligentsia existed to close, dramatized the hope of national fulfilment and made it a painful issue in every educated individual. In the end the intelligentsia had the choice of loyalty *either* to Russia, *or* to the quality of what the West had to offer; to lead a fulfilling life based on educated discrimination or to be Russian. This was the context in which Populists such as Akselrod and Bakunin and Pisarev came to feel that Western intellectual standards should be lowered for the Russian people's sake. They themselves had been nurtured on high standards, so that as individuals they could talk of Descartes and Hegel and Plato, but to wish such an education on the common people was almost tantamount to ill-will. That there should be no social gap in Russia mattered above all.

The Russians used German philosophical devices to build up their picture of the ideally fulfilling community of souls because – and this was the condition of all Russian philosophizing – German discourse provided the most suitable foundations. The Germans, with their own relatively late arrival as a political and cultural entity in modern Europe, and their national unity for the best part of a century mostly in the mind, had experienced some similar needs to the Russian. The simple Russian communal idea, for instance, corresponded to what the German Romantics, inspired by a seminal debate between Goethe and Schiller, had called 'the naive'. The naive was part of a mythological vision of where, at the end of the eighteenth century, the German mind had arrived in the history of the world. The idea of the naive was intended to mark what the critical, modern, self-conscious mind had lost – the spontaneity of the Ancient Greeks – and what it hoped to regain for happiness' sake. The Hungarian Marxist Georg Lukács, who as a literary critic was steeped in the classical German world, once called it a paradise of resurrected naivety; the chance to live as happily as a child again.[26]

When the Russians faced up to the idea of becoming a modern country, they did so conscious of the fact that they were choosing naivety as a quality they, unlike the intellectual Germans, had never lost. They chose a myth of simplicity connected with the community and nominated 'the people' as their guide. As Khomiakov saw it, whereas the Germans had long left Greek naivety behind, but hoped to resurrect it on a higher cultural level, the Russians had never relinquished their naive state, and hoped they never would. They wanted simple knowledge, the equivalent of not leaving the family and the village.

Their philosophy needed a parallel foundational story to the one Hegel had given the Germans. So Khomiakov and his friend created a *mythos* of the collective life of souls upheld by integral, non-divisive knowledge. What the Greek vision was for the Germans, the peasant *obshchina* became for the Russians. Just like the German, the Russian holistic model was philosophically fertile, because it proposed a way to express man's simplest relationship with nature, and therefore the conditions which fell to souls, not individuals, as knowledge-seekers. The *obshchina* is usually discussed in the factual form in which it presents itself in the revolutionary tradition, namely that it was a free co-operative association of peasants which periodically distributed the agricultural land to be tilled, and whose decisions bound all its members. But the *obshchina* was also a philosophical myth, which expressed exactly that unreflected belonging to a community and that spontaneous enforcing of collective rules and interests which Schiller and Hegel and others admired in Ancient Greece.

The difference between the German and Russian situations vis-à-vis naivety was that the Germans felt intellectually too advanced for their own good, while the conservative Russians were proud of their opposite condition, because it left them spiritually intact. Those different starting-points reflected their national cultural needs. If Russia was the last European home of the whole man, whose knowledge reflected the condition of his undivided soul, this meant in effect that the good man in Russia, the moral man, had no need of Rousseau or Schiller to guide him back to nature.

What Russia did need, however, was to modernize and humanize its economy despite its desire not to change traditional society. So, where the Germans thought they might resurrect naivety, the Russians thought they could celebrate never having lost it by pointing to the *obshchina* as the way forward. The *obshchina* meant projecting Russian socialism as an ideal also into the future. By extension, just as Russia chose not to go down the Hegelian-individualistic path to self-fulfilment, so too it would not need to follow the prescription of the Hegelian Marx and take the Western, i.e. capitalist, path to socialism; nor would it need commandeered moral individuals to bring about progress through revolution when Russian socialism might remain in harmony with simple souls.

According to this founding Russian spiritual myth of naivety, the contact souls had with the world was consubstantial and loving and intuitive, not individualistic and confrontational. The economic extension of the myth was the idyll of peasant cooperation. The Russian ideal, the native way to happiness, never invited men to become individuals and think for themselves; it actively discouraged that independence. In compensation it invited them to belong, and feel secure, and to protect themselves from a damaged, disintegrated, aggressive West. Right up to 1991, Russia remained with its willed naivety; its deliberate choice of backwardness. But of course the passing of time was problematic. In a country which, despite the myth, *had* become modern some time early in the twentieth century, did not wish to be treated as one vast peasant community and did contain individuals who thought for themselves, the choice to retain a false naivety was the cause of intellectual agony.

In *The First Circle* (1968) the novelist, historian and Russian thinker Alexander Solzhenitsyn (1918–) sent one of his many thoughtful characters, Gleb Nerzhin, a mathematician and prisoner in the special prison of Mavrino, on a spiritual journey to examine the relative truth about individuals and souls. All the highly qualified political prisoners compelled to work in Mavrino – a prison cum technological research establishment – reflected on how their compulsory membership of a commandeered community affected their view of Russian intellectual history. His friends defined Nerzhin as the Populist among them who wanted to befriend the common people. 'Nerzhin's friendship with the handyman Spiridon was indulgently referred to by Rubin and Sologdin as an attempt to "go among the people" in search of the same great home-spun truths which had been sought in vain by Gogol, Nekrasov, Herzen, the Slavophiles, the Populists, Leo Tolstoy.'[27] Rubin's criticisms followed from his being a convinced Marxist-Leninist, while as an individualist Sologdin was probably speaking for views Solzhenitsyn himself held in those days, before he went into Western exile and became disillusioned with the Western liberal achievement. A different Solzhenitsyn was writing in 1968, balancing the hope which at the time he felt the West represented with the sympathy he felt for his fellow Russians. Neither Rubin nor Sologdin agreed with Nerzhin, but as fellow Russians they knew the form of hope and consolation he had sought from his own community.

Neither Rubin nor Sologdin needed this homespun truth themselves because each of them already had his own ultimate truth.

Rubin knew perfectly well that 'the people' was an artificial construct, an unjustified generalization, and that every people is divided into *classes*, which even change their nature in the course of time.

To see the key to an understanding of life among the peasants was quite futile, because only the proletariat was consistently revolutionary in its outlook – the future belonged to it and only its collectivism and selflessness could give it a higher meaning.

For Sologdin, on the other hand, the people was just a general term for all those dull, drab, uncouth individuals who were totally absorbed in their joyless daily round. The great temple of the human spirit could not be built on such foundations. Only outstanding individuals, shining forth like lonely stars in the dark firmament of our existence, could embody the higher meaning of life.

Both he and Rubin were sure that Nerzhin would get over his present mood and come to think better of it.

In fact Nerzhin had already been through many extreme phases in the evolution of his ideas.

With its anguished concern for the peasants, Russian nineteenth-century literature had created for him, as for all its other readers, the image of a venerable grey-haired People which embodied wisdom, moral purity and greatness.

But this had been something remote, existing in books, somewhere in the villages, fields and byways of the nineteenth century. When the heavens unfolded on the twentieth century, these places had long ago ceased to exist in Russia.[28]

The story went on that Gleb Nerzhin had grown up in 'something called the Soviet Union', which valued science above all and nurtured a scientific elite. 'The People at that time still only existed in books, and, as he then saw it, nobody mattered unless he was highly educated and had an all-round knowledge of history, science and art. It seemed obvious to him that unless you were numbered among that elite you were a miserable failure.' Then the war broke out and with the country plunged into a moral emergency, Nerzhin was impractical. The common people laughed at him. But he found a decent role for himself, and their respect, by giving political lectures. He was evidently a Lavrovian soul, an organizer, an educated man committed to making a good Russia flourish. But then he was arrested and in circumstances which made him depend on the loyalty and friendship of his old colleagues, Soviet beautiful souls, he felt let down and renounced all intellectual sophistication.

And so he came back full circle to the fashionable idea of the previous century about 'going to the people'.

But, unlike his intellectual forebears of the nineteenth-century nobility, Nerzhin didn't have to put on simple dress and laboriously seek a way to the People – he was thrown down among them in the shabby quilted trousers and jacket of a prisoner and made to do his work-quota side by side with them. He thus lived their life not as a social superior who had deigned to come among them, but as an equal not easily distinguished from them.

If Nerzhin now learnt to drive a nail home without bending it ... it was not to prove himself in the eyes of the ordinary people, but to earn his soggy hunk of daily bread.

But finally he attained wisdom:

The brutal education of camp life had destroyed yet another of his illusions: he understood that ... the People possessed no advantage, no great, homespun wisdom ... these people were in no way superior to him. They did not stand up to hunger and thirst any better than he ... they were no more resourceful ... The only solution left, Nerzhin now felt, was simply to be oneself ...

It was only character that mattered, and this was something that everybody had to forge for himself, by constant effort over the years.

Only thus could one make oneself into a human being and hence be regarded as a tiny part of one's people.[29]

In two panoramic novels, *The First Circle* and *Cancer Ward*, both written in the mid-1960s and published in the West in 1968, Solzhenitsyn, Russia's greatest contemporary intellectual historian of the mid-twentieth century, drew a line under the myth of a simple community of souls. The notion had been rubbish. The individual's voluntary self-limitation to remain part of the community was worthless. The only right way to live was for individuals to develop freely and assume moral responsibility for themselves. These things were nevertheless excruciatingly painful for a Russian to admit, because they entailed calling all he had grown up to love worthless. Most of us cannot manage so much.

Looking back from two thirds of the way through the twentieth century, community had often seemed like the right idea for Russia. In philosophy it was a search for a moral way of being which would act as the foundation for truth. It meant that if the ethic was right then the knowledge it afforded was true. The good man, the just or excellent Russian, naturally saw the world as it rightly was. This myth justified simple knowledge for selfless souls, but also in the sophisticated intellectual spheres where commandeered individuals functioned it exercised its epistemic magic, leading them to believe by an inverse process of reasoning that if knowledge was total and true then all individuals would accept it and it would become a new basis for moral community on a higher level. Under the influence of the right choice of moral community Russia came to believe that science would turn out in its moral favour. Russia would bypass the need for individualism without sacrificing scientific progress. One way to argue this view was to take a different approach to Hegel and thus to his successor Marx. This would not stress Hegel's requirement for free individuals to play their part in progress, but focus on the impersonal idea of rational progress as necessary truth on the march. On this reading of Hegel/Marx science couldn't be stopped. All individuals had to do was understand it, and accept that finally it would create a morally coherent community on a higher level. Russia accepted that Hegel – and Marx after him – offered a moral-ontological foundation for being. They explained *bytie* as a kind of irresistible science implicit in history.

Odoevsky was in at the beginning of the discovery of what German Idealism could do for a morally integrated Russia. It could provide an idea or a science to give meaning to the lives of all the souls in its sphere of influence.

> My youth unfolded at a time when metaphysics was as much the general atmosphere as the political sciences are now. We believed in the possibility of an absolute theory by means of which it would be possible to plot (but we used a Russianized form of the foreign word construct) all the phenomena of nature, in the same way as people now believe in the possibility of a social form which would entirely satisfy all the needs of mankind . . .
>
> Then all of nature, the whole life of mankind appeared to us fairly clear, and we somewhat looked down upon those physicists and chemists and utilitarians who rummaged about in crude matter.[30]

Half a century after Odoevsky's death Marxist-Leninism would aim to reconstruct Russia on such a metaphysical-scientific-moral foundation.

But the souls who had their place in *bytie* were suspicious of the rational project. Hegelian reason created individuals and selves by devaluing souls. Khomiakov insisted 'reason' could only be the name of a force which protected simple Russian life from the products of complex thought.

> I gave the name faith to that faculty of reason which apprehends actual (real) data and makes them available for analysis and

awareness by the understanding. Only in this area do the data still have the fullness of their character and the marks of their origin. In this area, which precedes logical consciousness and which is filled with a living consciousness that does not need demonstrations and arguments, man realizes what belongs to his intellectual world and what to the external world. Here by the touchstone of his free will, man perceives what in his (objective) world is produced by his creative (subjective) activity and what is independent of it.[31]

The greater part of Russian moral attention was directed indefinitely from the mid-nineteenth century against *false* foundations proposed as guides to the good life in Russia. Solovyov spoke of 'false wholenesses', Berdyaev of false community.[32] In his golden year of 1841 Belinsky was horrified to see that reason or science associated with Hegel was being used to draw men's eyes away from real life and excuse any present barbarity meted out on anonymous souls.

Heartfelt thanks, Yegor Fyodorych [Georg Friedrich Hegel], I bow to your philosopher's cap; but with every respect for your all-embracing philosophical philistinism, I have the honour to inform you that even if I succeeded in climbing to the topmost step of the ladder of progress, even there I would ask you to account for all the victims of the conditions of life and of history, for all the victims of coincidence, superstition, the Inquisition of Philip II and so on and so on; otherwise [if you can't] I shall throw myself head first from that top step. I don't want happiness, even for nothing, if I cannot be peaceful with regard to each of my brothers in blood – bone of my bone and flesh of my flesh.[33]

Belinsky's moral point was that reason ignored souls. He stood for a Russian moral awareness which sought to protect non-assertive, non-individualized souls from authority. The awareness was of brothers against external authority. Whether that authority was political or rational was all the same. Souls were human life in its most basic form. From its earliest years Life was a force in Russian philosophy locked into a quarrel with Reason for these moral reasons. In truth Life could barely be spoken about. It was a mystical entity, the truth of which was either disclosed in immediate, personal experience or art, or had to be taken on trust. But on it the moral affirmation of the nation depended.

Lev Tolstoy (1828–1910) confessed that on one occasion he was drawn to the answers of reason as Kant set them down in his *Critique of Pure Reason*; but then another part of him on another occasion read Kant's second critique, on the workings of reason in the practical life, and he was glad with all the joy of the artist and the anarchist in him that man was free. Andrzej Walicki observed of that moment of insight on Tolstoy's part in 1887: 'Reason denies life, Tolstoy writes, but is itself the child of life. Life is all.' It is how millions of human beings live, without doubting that their unreflected experience is meaningful.[34]

Isaiah Berlin would take up the argument for Tolstoy.

It is the very present sense of [a] framework . . . as something 'inexorable', universal, pervasive, not alterable by us, not in our power (in the sense of 'power' in which the progress of scientific knowledge has given us power over nature), that is at the root of Tolstoy's determinism . . . Tolstoy knows that the truth is there and not 'here' – not in the regions susceptible to observation . . . of which he is so much the greatest master of our time; but he has not himself seen it face to face; . . . he . . . has not a vision of the whole; he is not . . . a hedgehog, and what he sees is not the one, but . . . with . . . a lucidity which maddens him, the many.[35]

Tolstoy, wrote Berlin in an elaborately embroidered essay, was both a hedgehog and a fox. As a hedgehog he wanted to believe in the existence of a single higher order of Reason, but what he actually saw as a fox was the multiplicity, the myriad possibilities of Life.

According to Lev Shestov, Tolstoy once expressed his distrust of a rational reality as a place where he couldn't be good. Odoevsky held this Russian view of the Utilitarian West. What Tolstoy and Odoevsky plausibly felt was that Utilitarian reason, which reduced reality to quantities and concepts, defined a world which shut out the real source of morality. Tolstoy silently set God, the Unattainable, against science, and suggested that the future of a *good* world depended on understanding the difference. 'The truth has always been the truth, but I didn't recognize it because, had I admitted that two and two make four, I would have had to recognize that I wasn't good. But to feel that I was good was for me more important and more necessary than two and two make four.'[36] Tolstoy and Odoevsky both made the point that a man needs the right spiritual environment to be good. That Tolstoy couldn't be good in a morally uninspired world was also why Odoevsky couldn't be good in 'the birth-place of moral accountancy'. The need in Russia was not so much for simple as for moral community, which was bound to support itself with some form of religion or mysticism.

Dostoevsky had Shatov ask Stavrogin that question in *The Devils*, which set the problem of a moral philosophy of being directly in a religious context:

If it were mathematically proved to you that the truth was outside Christ, you would remain with Christ rather than the truth? Did you say that?[37]

Eight years later 'The Legend of the Grand Inquisitor', the parable at the heart of *The Brothers Karamazov*, dramatized the choice between the truth of Christ and Reason. Dostoevsky took Belinsky's 1841 rejection of Hegel as his starting-point. The disappointed Western rationalist Ivan Karamazov threatened to 'send back the ticket to Utopia' if Reason allowed a single child to suffer; if the truth of Life had to be suppressed, then the cost of Reason was too high.

Sergei Bulgakov lectured to a university audience in Kiev in 1901 on 'Ivan Karamazov as a Philosophical Type' and in that lecture, published in 1903 as part of his book *From Marxism to Idealism*, he wrote:

> Ivan Karamazov is a Russian *intelligent* from head to toe, with his attachment to universal questions, with his tendency to protracted discussions, with constant self-analysis, with his sick, tortured conscience ... Ivan Karamazov is a true Russian precisely in that he is wholly preoccupied with the ethical problem; the indifference of this strong philosophical mind to all other problems of philosophy – for example the theory of knowledge – is striking.[38]

Bulgakov, who in fact did as most Russians did and treated knowledge as a matter of ethics, captivated his audience:

> The young professor ... addressed a set of questions so original and forceful that they could not fail to astonish ... The lecture's main achievement was to move the moral problem, the question of ethics, so long banned from explicit public discussion, to the forefront. The Karamazov lecture posed the vexed questions of good and evil.[39]

An irritated, godless version of Dostoevsky's thesis could be found in his own novella of twenty years earlier, *The Underground Man*, in which the protagonist, insisting on the freedom to be perverse, heaped invective on the false wisdom of 2+2=4. The parable of the Grand Inquisitor was more powerful because it allowed Reason or Utilitarianism to fight back. For Dostoevsky, Utilitarianism's social-moral form was socialism, which established a world of certain values to make men happy. The motive of socialism was the happiness and security of the many. Those who tried to step outside its confines would be punished. Socialism was a new form of Inquisition. Yet its charitable motive meant that Christ, who in the story appeared to the Grand Inquisitor and kissed his forehead, could not quite dismiss socialism as evil. For Dostoevsky, however, socialism remained the false moral ground, an untrue way of being. It put the calculations of social science in place of moral truth. Life, the reality of Christ's love, had to be preserved from this gross modern depredation made in the name of progress.

Lev Shestov (1866–1938), who emigrated before the Revolution and continued his work in difficult conditions in France, announced that the battle to keep Reason at bay, and to free Life, was the task of Russian philosophy. Consciously treading in Dostoevsky's and Belinsky's footsteps, Shestov began at last to interpret a century of pictures and fragments. Philosophy was to be 'a cultivation of the impossible'.[40] It should be about spiritual gain. Reason, which puts the world to use, takes things away from us. 'Infinite interestedness is the beginning of faith.'[41] Philosophy is faith not in the rational but in the impossible. Hegel claimed that 'truth can only be sought in one's reason and what reason does not accept is not true'.[42] But rationalism overlooked the omnipotence of God, by virtue of which no historical fact or scientific law was irreversible or eternally necessary.[43] Rational knowledge was a constraint on living life, which was as God designed it and contained no negation. 'Constraining knowledge is an abomination of desolation, the source of original sin.'[44] The struggle of philosophy is to see beyond the negativity that men's minds bring into the world. 'The struggle of faith: an insane struggle for the possible [which rationalists call impossible]. The truths provided by [rational] knowledge are vanquished by human suffering.'[45]

Shestov invented a Dionysian Christ in his essay *Athens and Jerusalem* (1938) to lead men away from Reason. Like Nietzsche's Zarathustra this saviour would revolutionize the human soul and keep it responsive to irrational Life. He would act against the 'imprisoning' rational tradition which the modern world inherited from the post-Socratic Greeks. Reason was associated in Russia with an alien order imposed from above. Life and human souls would always be found elsewhere, in defiance of the power of Reason, so long as Life could survive.

But was reason, which would be imposed on Russia for most of the twentieth century in the form of a single official and incontestable truth, really so harmful? Did it not provide the only realistic modern foundation for that moral-communal being which Russia craved, once the myth of the people was left behind? This would be one way of looking at Soviet Communism as an actual moral achievement. To his own surprise the Solzhenitsyn of 1968 found that he could see that argument. According to *The First Circle*, conditions at Mavrino, where the imprisoned brain-workers pursued scientific projects to benefit the state, had an unexpectedly almost ideal outcome.

The men floating in this ark were detached and their thoughts could wander unfettered. They were not hungry and not full. They were not happy and therefore not disturbed by the prospect of forfeiting happiness. Their heads were not full of trivial worries about their jobs, office intrigue or anxieties about their promotion, their shoulders unbowed by cares about housing, fuel, food and clothing for their children. Love, man's age-old source of pleasure and suffering, was powerless to touch them with its agony or its expectation. Their terms of imprisonment were so long that none of them had started to think of the time when they would be released. Men of outstanding intellect, education and experience, who were normally too devoted to their families to have enough of themselves to spare for friendship, were here wholly given over to their friends. From this ark, serenely ploughing its way through the darkness, it was easy for them to survey, as from a great height, the whole tortuous, errant flow of history; yet at the same time, like people completely immersed in it, they could see every pebble in its depths.

On these Sunday evenings the physical, material world never intruded. A spirit of manly friendship and philosophy hovered over the sail-shaped vault of the ceiling. Was this perhaps that state of bliss which all the philosophers of antiquity tried in vain to define and describe?[46]

Mavrino did not represent the usual conditions of Soviet life for millions of anonymous souls, but under its auspices certain conditions had been brought to bear which had symbolic value for individuals. The intelligentsia had wrestled for a century and a half to define the good life and here was a plausible result. Mavrino was a morally commandeered community in the service of science. It required of developed individuals, in exchange for satisfying their basic needs, that they lead selfless lives in intellectual community. It required brainwork beneficial to the motherland but otherwise left them free. Under these conditions the commandeered men channelled all their emotions into friendship, and as they did so they realized that their Soviet conditions were in some sense ideal. They led lives devoted to brotherhood and knowledge. Prison purged them of all the personal and assertive aspects of the individual pursuit of truth and turned them into selfless seekers. They led the rarefied lives of an elite. They glimpsed the wisdom which might come to a Platonic Guardian after years of discipline and searching, namely the meaning of existence and their place in it. In that privileged detention they felt themselves in the presence of the great and timeless ideal of reined-in individualism in pursuit of absolute truth. The irony was only that the Soviet system had perfected a Western vision of what reason could achieve. Russia had caught up with and overtaken the West in this one way. It had achieved *almost* an ideal moral foundation of being for Russia, but not quite.

The title of Solzhenitsyn's novel explained that 'not quite'. According to Dante, the 'First Circle of Hell' was the place in the Inferno closest to Paradise. In the Fourth Canto Dante called it 'a blaze of light enclosed in a hemisphere of darkness' and described how he walked there with Virgil. 'Thus we went on as far as the light, talking of things which were fitting for that place and of which it is well now to be silent.' There was light in that near-heaven but also a limit to the light. Mavrino stood for what men could achieve through a combination of technical knowledge and self-discipline; almost everything; except mastery of the darkness beyond.

When Russian thinkers from Odoevsky and Khomiakov to Shestov insisted that no human construction could contain God's world, that for the world to be truly good there had to be an ultimate ground of moral being, beyond human access, this is what they meant. Hope for Russia, hope for mankind, the promise of light, could never be constructed artificially but had to be in accordance with the cosmic design. An artificial world on Plato's model, however brilliant and successful, had finally to be revealed as a sham. Absolute truth lay ineffably beyond, and therefore, although this ideal Russian place was so close to Paradise, it remained Hell.

The Russian scene of philosophizing was dominated by the political struggle of the nineteenth century and the political reality of the twentieth. Yet clearly its nature was moral before it was political. It was interested in individuals, selves and souls in various combinations as makers and movers of the good society. The Enlightenment ideal of the good life as liberally governed, legally protected and individually free generated four aims in Russia, all of them fuelled by moral idealism:

1) To serve the people by ridding Russia of tsarism
2) To close the gap between the intelligentsia and the people and make Russia a harmonious and integrated society
3) To avoid the defects of Western socio-economic life, such as acquisitiveness, selfishness and excessive individualism

4) To find an alternative way to flourish as an educated society capable of making a contribution to world history in modern times.

To meet these goals Russia required the service of selfless and non-individualistic human beings, either morally commandeered individuals or simple souls, and a way had to be found to secure scientific progress without developing more assertive forms of individualism. From before the middle of the nineteenth century it was clear that reason could not be the basis for the moral life in Russia because of the suspicion individualism attracted – as in life, so in knowledge. Russia was destined to be a place of alternative morality. Its distinctiveness from the West would be difficult to sustain, given world progress. It would be moved to preserve its special moral-ontological domain artificially. To understand the philosophical tensions of the nineteenth century – the upheavals which threw up the features on the moral map – is to understand how the moral agony of the Soviet period came about. It is not to justify it, but to appreciate that although in one sense it was a lie, in a moral sense to its own people it was not.

8

Rejecting the View from Descartes

Kostoglotov: 'There was this philosopher Descartes. He said, "Suspect everything".'

'But that's nothing to do with our way of life,' Rusanov reminded him, raising a finger in admonition.

'No, of course it isn't,' said Kostoglotov, utterly amazed by the objection. 'All I mean is we shouldn't behave like rabbits and put our complete trust in doctors.'[1]

The exchange, in Solzhenitsyn's novel *Cancer Ward* (1968), between Rusanov (the Russophile) and Kostoglotov (the man who has swallowed a bone) was a moment of powerful concision. In what these men thought of the motherland – and the symbolism of their names – lay an entire history of Russian philosophy in miniature. In the early nineteenth century a significant portion of Russian thinkers rejected reason because they felt Russia's destiny was different from Europe's. They rejected Hegel but to more profound effect they rejected Descartes. Two centuries of counter-rationalism followed, as Russian philosophy sailed out on a poetic crusade to save life from cogitation.

The first Russian attacks on Descartes came from the early nineteenth-century religious philosophers. They attacked the Cartesian view of knowledge as incompatible with a moral way of life. To Khomiakov, the Cartesian *cogito* beginning with the premise 'I think, I am' could never give a true picture of reality. Khomiakov and Kireevsky were not sophisticated epistemologists but social idealists who worried that the philosophy of the *cogito* would lead to a spiritually impoverished life. Repeatedly over the next century they exemplified the way the question of impartial, tested knowledge in Russia would come in a poor second to the right way of being.

To Descartes they preferred Pascal. Descartes for the West, Pascal for Russia. Pascal, famous for his 'wager' on the advantages of belief in God, found Descartes absurd. Speaking with the wisdom of the heart, he called the founder of modern scientific method a Don Quixote.[2] Cervantes' novel showed a good-hearted fool imposing himself on a reality which resisted him. The enterprises Quixote undertook as helpful to others were ridiculously misplaced. Descartes' rational excursions similarly left the full truth of life untouched.

The difference between Pascal and Descartes could be seen clearly in their interpretation of the role of doubt. Descartes' pursuit of certain knowledge began with self-doubt. He was sceptical about whether the evidence of his senses amounted to the truth. Although he hardly doubted the world had meaning, he believed the world's meaningfulness needed to be established on new terms for the modern age. He willed himself to submit his faith to the test of science. Could God's world be justified rationally? Could it be known by reason? Descartes felt his own work was proof that it could. Pascal by contrast risked belief without proof. He made a non-rational, proto-existential leap into meaning from a position of absolute unknowing. Perhaps God existed, perhaps He did not. Possibly belief was absurd. But since reason alone could not provide spiritual meaning and purpose, the potential absurdity of faith had to be weighed against its benefits.

The readiness of Russian thinkers to associate themselves with Pascal was noticed some years ago by the Jesuit historian of philosophy, Father Frederick Copleston:

> Apprehension of the truth which can guide us in life is a function not of any one isolated power or faculty, whether logical reasoning or imagination or any other, but of the whole human spirit, the human being considered as a unity. Pascal had a glimpse of this when he underlined the limitations of reason in his famous statement that 'the heart has its reasons which the reason does not understand'. According to Kireevsky, 'the thoughts of Pascal could have been a thoughtful embryo for this new philosophy of the West', the reference being to a philosophy on lines suggested by Port-Royal and by Fénelon. But this was not how things were to work out.[3]

Under an anti-Cartesian aegis, not always named as such, prominent Russian thinkers rejected reason in favour of intuition and moral being. Kireevsky and Khomiakov established a preference to which all the major religious idealists after them adhered. With the decision against Descartes a first alternative Russian philosophy got under way.

For Solovyov the non-rational Pascalian tradition would be a bulwark against scientific positivism. For Berdyaev it would be a way to attack the scientific rationalism of Marx. In an age when it was fashionable to talk of the collapse of the West, Berdyaev's contemporary Shestov would see himself siding with Pascal against Western civilization as such. The West had taken a wrong turning in the seventeenth century when it elevated the Cartesian method over Pascal's leap of faith.[4]

> Only rare, lonely people, like Pascal, did not share the general joy and exultation, as if they sensed that the clear and distinct light or *lumen naturale* hides in itself a great threat and that the spirit of the age, possessing without exception the best minds of the day,

was the spirit of mendacity and evil, and not truth and goodness. But as I say Pascal stood outside history . . . Our history of Pascal as a philosopher is silent.[5]

Shestov's contemporary in exile, Ilya Lapshin, one of the Silver Age minor academic philosophers who specialized in Dostoevsky and after he fled Bolshevism settled to teach in Prague, was another early twentieth-century metaphysical idealist who insisted that modern philosophy began with Pascal.[6] Frank was eloquent in Pascal's favour, as was Boris Vysheslavtsev.[7] In fact, in each Russian age since the early nineteenth century there was a thinker to clear a path for Pascal and open the way for Russian mystical existentialism to grow.

The attraction in retrospect of both the image and the substance of Pascal seems obvious. Pascal was a dissident figure in the Western tradition, whom the institutional church expelled for heresy. His fate as an outsider over whom history was silent embodied what so many Russian *intelligenty* thought of Russia's own position in world culture. To derive a historical message from Pascal's fate made sense for a Russia inclined to take a chance and not to follow the West into godlessness. Pascal's essential message, his insistence on the value of faith over reason, needed no endorsement in a still primitively religious country. From Solovyov to Shestov and Berdyaev, Vysheslavtsev and Frank, Russian religous idealism would try to show how valid Pascal's wager was as the moral basis in a Christian but non-Western country. The very texture of Western life was thinned by the requirement to prove that spiritual values were worthwhile. Russia was a higher kind of civilization because it was ready to respond to God voluntarily and *creatively*. Berdyaev liked to quote the German mystic Angelus Silesius (1624–77) on man's willingness to enter into a bond of cognitive love with the world.

I know that without me God cannot live for a minute
If I become nothing, need will make Him lose His spirit.

The Creative Act set out this spiritual voluntarism as the right way to be. 'I still believe that God calls man to creative activity and to a creative answer to His love.'[8]

The 'creative act' reflected Kant's idea that human beings were born free but positively inclined to build a meaningful moral world. Indirectly it was also a gesture in favour of Pascal because of Kant's difference from Descartes. For Kant perceived two kinds of reason. Against the pure kind, which could not go beyond the reach of its own tools, had to be weighed practical or moral reason to which men's minds had absolute access. When the German counter-rational tradition seized its opportunity to build on Kant's ethics, and on a similar loophole in Kant's aesthetics, a century of Romantic and neo-Romantic – neo-Kantian – German and Russian thought was the result. The message of the German Romantic heritage was that beauty, creativity and the moral leap of faith led the way to the truth.[9]

Shestov, more of a mystical thinker than a religious idealist, associated himself personally with Pascal's 'loneliness' and with the failure of posterity to appreciate Pascal's contra-rational achievement. Pascal helped Shestov to see that to criticize Descartes would be the way to ground his own thought. In *Discourse on Method* (1637) and the *Meditations on First Philosophy* (1641) Descartes had suggested that knowledge could be tested according to whether it allowed us to form clear and distinct ideas of reality. The 'method' of 1637 was a procedure which, by examining every reason why we should doubt the evidence of our senses, finally established grounds for scientific certainty. Anti-Cartesians from Pascal to Shestov rejected this approach to truth. They were not anti-science, but they did not think a method suited to the natural sciences could also measure a reality including the human spirit. This larger notion of reality was crucial to their case. Science could be objective, but reality and objectivity were not the same thing. Reality exhausted what was objectively knowable. Not everything beyond the grasp of science was simply waiting for man's final explanation; nor was it an illusion; but it was more than men could grasp with their finite human means.

Descartes' Russian detractors wanted to include in truth the dimensions of feeling and imagination, just what Descartes said had to be excluded if knowledge was to be reliable. They wanted truth to be in some measure personal. They wanted to preserve a place within reality for the unknowable. The result for literature was superb but by the same proportion the cultivation of reason suffered. Descartes and Kant, like most philosophers, were not enemies of imagination in its own sphere. Their point was a judicious segregation of the faculties. Also if they saw reason as a hypothesis and a tool, they certainly never saw it as a weapon. The Russian idealists were too anxious to defend life-as-it-is-fully-lived against the perceived weapon. Out of cultural inexperience they were unable to suspend judgement and let the scientific hypothesis operate and ground a rational culture, not to interfere with faith but to sit alongside it. The Russian position looks today mostly like an unhappy choice for society, though a possible source of inspiration for individuals.

The Russian case against the too broad encroachment of science on reality acquired immediate political relevance when it was coupled with conservative reaction against the 'rationalist' French Revolution. Later it broadened its philosophical targets to include positivism, probably the greatest threat to religious belief in the nineteenth century. Positivism was an exaggerated and monolithic faith in science influentially espoused by Comte, Feuerbach and Marx. Russian idealism became known in the twentieth century as a conservative and reactionary point of view because of this heritage of science playing its part on the political Left. What we can see now is that its main aim was to defend the integrity of individual souls and the integrity of nature against the threat from constraining concepts which might, like dialectical materialism, anyway turn out to be false. As for the Western academic world which regarded Russian religious idealism as beyond the pale, it is worth remembering that the West had its own parallel untrammelled faith in reason up to the 1960s and a rather marked socialist sympathy for the Soviet Union. These two factors encouraged the treatment of Russian religious and mystical thought as obscure and reactionary, which led in turn to a very partial view of Russia. For anyone who cared to look beneath the religious surface, the rejection of Descartes in the first real Russian philosophy would eventually explain more about the Communist phenomenon than any attempt to treat Communism as a manifestation of reason. It was the clue to understanding Russia's choice of an anti-Western path.

Central to Russian idealist philosophy was its ability to pick out the *moral* problem which Western rationalism presented for anti-Cartesians. A Cartesian rationalist had to be a cognitive individualist because by definition the *cogito* concerned how 'I' think and judge. The Russian objection was simple: how can the truth depend on one man? Surely truth is shared and evident to all, or it is not worth pursuing. The Russian idealist way was to reject truth dependent on individual discrimination, and to pour scorn on the moral and social value of a theory which would isolate subjects in their own perceptions. How could truth rest on a theory whose immediate secondary implication was interpersonal obscurity? How could the world be harmonious if what was going on in your mind with respect to that world was quite different to mine?

Not all these points were immediately raised, and especially not in the form Western philosophers know as the problem of 'other minds'. But they were implicit in a general feeling that Cartesian reason could not get at real, living truth. Tolstoy exemplified Russian idealist unease on this point. In the anti-Cartesian vein Isaiah Berlin perceived him to feel that 'clear, logical and scientific constructions – the well-defined, symmetrical patterns of human reason – seem smooth, thin, empty, "abstract" and totally ineffective as the means either of description or of analysis of anything that lives'.[10] Berdyaev wrote in 1904 that rationalism was 'the original sin of almost all European philosophy'.[11] Khomiakov, Solovyov, Berdyaev and Frank all made it their task to rescue the isolated Cartesian subject. According to friendlier epistemology, true knowledge would not result from a hostile confrontation between ego and world, but from a loving coition between cognizing subject and cognized object.[12] Distinguished by their imaginative variations on a theme, all these thinkers were linked by their insistence on a living truth beyond the grasp of science. Solovyov imagined an erotic cosmos in which human and divine knowledge interpenetrated.[13]

Isaiah Berlin was himself a Russian-style anti-Cartesian. His true philosophical identity was mainly concealed in his writing, leaving the impression of a thinker uneasily caught between the nineteenth and the twentieth century, but his sense of how important the Russian anti-Cartesian tradition was answers the otherwise still open question asked by his biographer Michael Ignatieff, as to why this Russian-born, Oxford-employed man of reason made so many mental journeys into the non-rational.[14] All of Berlin's sustained writing was devoted to figures of the Counter-Enlightenment – Vico (1688–1744), Hamann (1730–88), Herder (1744–1803), and Joseph de Maistre (1753–1821). Maistre, the Jesuit Sardinian ambassador to St Petersburg for most of the last twenty years before his death, called in strident terms for Russia to resist the French revolutionary spirit and remain a modern Inquisition of an unparalleled kind.[15] Berlin introduced these Blakean knowledge-poets on the Enlightenment's outer rim to a rationalist and sceptical Anglo-American public where they were bound to strike an unusual note. Maistre's eloquent essays on the spiritual destructiveness of modern freedom seem to have substituted for Russian conservative and religious positions Berlin declined to investigate, although he wrote on most of the Westernizing thinkers. Why did he not work on Odoevsky and Khomiakov and Kireevsky and Shestov? As he said, the Western – just Western – representatives of the Counter-Enlightenment stated the anti-rational case most clearly.[16] I call them 'just Western' because, like the Riga-born Berlin himself, Herder and Hamann both came from the Baltic area of East Prussia, on the borderline between Russian and German cultural influence. These are not matters for philosophy proper, but it does concern history why a historian wrote as Berlin did. As a half-Russian thinker with one foot in the nineteenth century, Berlin seemed to pay tribute to his own origins in his essays on the Counter-Enlightenment at the same time as being ashamed of Russian provincialism and obscurity. The focus of his historical work is a good indication of how the European Counter-Enlightenment, though not a direct source for Russian anti-Cartesianism, explains the deeper connections behind the options Russia took up over two centuries.

The rejection of the scientific revolution spearheaded by Vico in Italy and Hamann in East Prussia became concentrated in the second half of the eighteenth century in a new German interpretation of Spinoza, which was compounded by an equal and opposite attack on Kant. Friedrich Jacobi attacked pure reason and insisted on the practical necessity of irrational belief. Hamann, Herder and Goethe (1749–1832) all at some time shared his views. Hamann represented the common Blakean feeling that men should think as whole beings, not with their logical minds alone. Jacobi coined the term 'nihilism' to describe the outcome of mere rationalism and insisted that reason be coupled with faith based on an intuition of the absolute good.[17]

The Counter-Enlightenment was fascinated with *Homo sapiens* as *Homo faber* – man as the maker who creates truth. In a passage cited by Berlin, Hamann once compared a man with only logic at his disposal to a man incapable of sexual love.[18] Noetic imagination incorporated love and poetry into thought on a grand scale. It brought meaning and spiritual satisfaction into life. To think was to use words – symbols lent by God – and to try to grasp the ineffable flow of truth, not to analyse. All generalizations involved falsehood and only creative genius could succeed where analysis failed. Before those ideas turned up in Odoevsky and Kireevsky they were to be found poetically expressed by Hamann.

The Romantics who nevertheless wanted to write philosophy rather than poetry elected Spinoza (1632–97) to be their Pascal in the new war against reason. In the Portuguese-born Jewish philosopher, another excommunicant and outsider, they admired the idea that God and nature were two aspects of one living substance; that knowledge was the intellectual love of God; that everything was in God, who caused everything in the world. Typically the anti-Cartesian way was led by a poet who was also a scientist. Goethe praised Spinoza as the philosopher who so loved this dynamic, living nature that he called for a new science of 'the pure phenomenon'. 'Participatory contemplation' or 'mental and spiritual participation' was required of the new kind of scientist who could see the ideal in the real.[19] This could be said in prose which praised the extraordinary delicacy and fascination of the created world:

> An organic being is so multi-faceted in its exterior and is so multifarious and inexhaustible in its interior that one cannot choose enough points of view to contemplate it; one cannot develop enough organs in oneself to analyse it without destroying it.[20]

Or in poetry. Man did not know where to begin to understand the miracle of nature.

> Nothing is within, nothing is without.
> For what is within, that is without.[21]

Unlike the model established by Descartes, the Goethean 'I' was not neutral in knowledge. It was loving and trusting. Its task was to extend itself out towards a world shaped and dynamized by the same God as had made man himself. Nature and man, the world without and the world within, were two aspects of the one Spinozan substance. Against any Cartesian who doubted why scientific scrutiny needed an admixture of sympathy to achieve its goal, Goethe stressed that for him good scientific results rested on the 'inner solidity' of his own nature. The quality of his attitude affected the quality of the scientific outcome.

My habit of seeing and reading all things as they are, letting the light of my eye be my faithful support [*meine Treue*], ridding myself of all pretension, make me happy, especially when everything is quiet. Every day a new and remarkable object, new, great, unusual images daily and a totality which one can think long and dream about without ever reaching in one's imagination . . . what gives me the deepest joy is the effect that I already feel in my soul: it is an inner solidity, with which the mind is stamped, as it were; seriousness without dryness and a composed being with joy. I think I can feel the blessed consequences of this flowing through my whole life.[22]

The phrase 'meine Treue' reflected homely loyalty, fidelity in marriage, good faith in dealings with others; but it was also the key to the observation of nature which Goethe made his own brand of science. It was a feeling of being at home in the world, which gave way to a method of understanding it, as a familiar object, and spiritually as kin.

In a more formal statement of his method Goethe called it, apparently in direct response to Descartes, 'active scepticism'. The scientist had to take a critical view of his data, yet also reach out emotionally to the world he was trying to understand.

An active scepticism: which is tirelessly concerned to overcome itself, in order to arrive through controlled experience at a reliable perception under certain conditions.[23]

Goethe's method, his equivalent of Vico's *nuova scienza*, was dialectical. It was based on a fluid interchange of what the perceiving subject hoped to find in the world and what in return the objective world had to offer. The interchange brought truth into being, for truth like a human relationship had to be made. The dialectical method was a way of getting at the dynamic potential of matter to become something true in conjunction with man. It was a constant elaboration of the relation between two aspects of the one divine and living substance.

A few years before his death in 1831 Hegel would write to Goethe that no man, no philosopher, had influenced his own work more than the great Weimar poet-scientist.

> ... when I survey the course of my intellectual development, I see you interwoven in it everywhere and fancy to call myself one of your sons; for my innermost being has received from you the nourishment and strength to withstand abstraction and has corrected its course by following the products of your imagination like torches.[24]

'The strength to withstand abstraction' must be one of the most ironic phrases a philosopher has ever written across the gulf between what he intended to write and what he was assumed by his subsequent readers to have written. Herzen was a rare reader who felt Hegel had delivered on his aim. 'I know no one else besides Goethe who so fully understood life and can express it as a concept ... At the end of [*The Phenomenology of Spirit*] you seem to enter a sea – such depth, such transparency – here are the juicy fruits of reality.'[25]

How did Hegel come to believe he could 'withstand abstraction'? How did he think that his system stood for Life and not, in the vilified Russian sense, Reason? The question brings with it the pathos of two centuries of intellectual disaster for Russia. What persuaded Hegel was the idea of a non-Cartesian method of getting at the truth: Goethe's 'active scepticism'. It led Hegel to believe that a combined method of emotional investment and reflection would constantly discover real new truths in the material world. These would not be mere abstractions, not mere fantasies of the human mind, but real phenomena, tangible examples of the ideal. The dialectical method was possible because the best kind of human mind, the Goethean kind, empowered by faith –

Treue – was anchored in the same substance as nature. The two were one. Nature and mind were engaged in a shared creativity. Nature's method of making itself known was dialectical because of the way it reached out to man to make that knowledge happen. As Hegel made Goethe's method the key to a new understanding, not only of nature but also of history, it became possible to believe that the truth was not only what we find in the world but what we make out of it to suit our dreams of happiness – and this process too, according to Hegel, could be called the way of reason.

The Russian anti-Cartesians would not discover Goethe until Solovyov showed them the path, and they did not really absorb a poetic Hegel until – irony of ironies – Marx showed them how in a new political context. Instead, Khomiakov's generation began with the legacy of Spinoza and Jacobi and Goethe as it was absorbed by Schelling. As a result, the relatively obscure Schelling became a major figure in Russian thought.

Friedrich Schelling (1775–1854) was born in Württemberg and studied at the Tübingen seminary with Hegel, his occasional pupil, and Friedrich Hölderlin, the poet of the lost glories of Ancient Greece. The era was legendary. The work these friends did, developing ideas from Kant on poetic grounds, transformed religious idealism into a theory of knowledge and a vision of the future. They departed from the Counter-Enlightenment not so much in what they believed as in how they presented it. They reappropriated the word 'reason' and the ambition to write systematic philosophy while underneath they remained poets and theologians. They were, if one wanted to label them, post-Kantian neo-Spinozans.

Kant argued that the great rationalists – Descartes, Leibniz and Spinoza – were wrong to think full knowledge of the truth was possible. His objection to Descartes was that 'the-thing-in-itself' is unknowable to the human mind, because our mental equipment sets conditions. We claim to know facts about the world, but what we actually know are our own creations. Since the human mind also creates time and space we can't get behind those creations and see them in any other context. The human mind is knowable but not reality itself.

But Kant, the Romantics found, could be reinterpreted. Art and personality were ways out of the rational bind, and Kant admitted as much. For was not moral knowledge absolutely within our human reach provided we were willing to act on it? Human beings were free to create an ideal moral world. That was Kant's gift to the Romantics: absolute knowledge as creativity, a kind of super-faculty of unlimited mental freedom. Art too gave an insight into that higher truth because it was another reflection of freedom. The future of the world now depended on creativity and imagination.

Johann Gottlieb Fichte (1762–1814) developed the first Absolute Idealism in the 1790s. The Absolute I in each of us creates the world by 'positing' or creating it as a knowable object. The world continually comes into being because human thought creates objects for itself. We form simple transitive sentences of the subject-verb-object type and reality is made. Fichtean creation-perception is thinking or writing as sheer human power. Thought is originary. The world makes sense because human subjects continually perceive/make/act upon/speak about it. It is perfectly knowable because it has the same character as, indeed is part of and a complement to, the human mind. Just as the biblical God of 'in the beginning was the Word' created and filled Spinoza's world, so thinking, verbalizing man created Fichte's.

Schelling moved aside from Fichte to develop a philosophy based on the identity of mind and nature. He emphasized that nature's and mind's patterns ran in parallel and mutually elucidated each other. Natural science and cognitive philosophy, Newton (natural science) and Leibniz (rationalist metaphysics) should combine to form a new science to make this living truth clear. Schelling wanted to discover through natural science the kind of cosmic patterns which in Leibniz showed the mind of God and the minds of men working in synchrony. The parallel discovery in nature and mentality was possible because of 'a divine connectedness of knowledge' by which the human mind was married to the divine.[26] 'Intuition' – *Anschauung* – could see how the two realms interpenetrated. It used imagination and metaphor to find what it was seeking.

> We all have this wonderful secret capacity inside us to withdraw from the flux of time, from everything coming to us from outside, into our innermost, naked being, there to contemplate the eternal in us in the form of immutability. This intuition [*Anschauung*] is the innermost and most personal experience, upon which everything we know and believe of the supersensual world alone depends. It is this intuition which first convinces us that anything in the true sense is, whereas everything else merely appears to be.[27]

Intense self-reflection, *Anschauung*, opened up metaphysical experience. A man passed through the gateway to higher perception and would see nature revealed before his eyes as one vast self-powering process with the manufacture of the human mind as its greatest achievement.

> What is then that secret link which connects our minds to nature?
> Nature must become visible mind, mind must become invisible nature.[28]

Anschauung was the opposite of mechanical thinking. It was imagination, but more accurately it was moral imagination, because of the world it wanted to build. It was creative imagination, wanting to make a perfect work of art, and therefore also a form of *will*, insisting on bringing a meaningful, lovable world into being.

Philosophy was now not about the truth of facts. It was about every form of perfection the mind ever dreamed of. Descartes and after him Kant tried to keep all these imaginative and evaluative elements either out of philosophy or under strict control. The Romantics, however, reversed the containment of imagination dramatically by placing the greatest feat of Western imagination – the notion of Christ as simultaneously divine and human – at the centre of their philosophy. From this first Western idea of perfection all else proceeded. The mysteries of the Trinity and the Incarnation, timeless human hopes, were now repackaged as the triumph of metaphysics. Hölderlin's great poem 'Bread and Wine' contained the lines:

Miraculous is the favour of the Exalted,
And no one knows from where and what it bestows on one.
Thus it moves the world and the hoping soul of mankind,
No wise man even can grasp what it prepares, for so
The supreme God wills it, who loves you greatly, and therefore . . .[29]

Philosophy in the Schellingian mode was about how 'a moral person' would want the world to be:

The first idea is of course the idea of me myself, as an absolutely free being. With free, self-conscious being comes forth simultaneously a whole world out of nothing – the only true and thinkable creation out of nothing. Here I descend to the realms of physics: the question is this: how must the world be made for a moral being? I want to give wings again to our physics, which moves so slowly and cumbersomely from one experiment to the next.[30]

For Schelling, as it was for Fichte and as it would be for Hegel, the anti-Cartesian, anti-Kantian marriage of reason and mysticism they fabulated as young men laid the foundations for a new *German* science:

All German science has tended towards this goal from the beginning, that is it has striven to see the vitality of nature and its inner oneness with intellectual and divine being . . . The German nation strives with its whole nature towards religion, but religion which is bound up with knowledge and founded in science [*Wissenschaft*].[31]

It only remained for Schelling to add that like the devotees of the esoteric mysteries of the Ancients he had always seen his philosophy as conveying general truths but only to specially qualified minds. It needed men versed in the dense poetics of German Idealism – men of Greek excellence, *arete*, men like Plato's Guardians – to interpet the hopes for the future of mankind.[32]

Schelling's subjective Idealism gave Russian anti-Cartesian philosophy two great gifts: a world of kindred emotion and a quasi-philosophical structure. It also issued an invitation to the Russians to think of their achievement in national terms. If 'Russian' were substituted for 'German' in the passage just quoted, Schelling's words from 1811 would hold good for what the next century of Russian religious philosophers hoped they could do; what persuaded them they could call themselves philosophers.

All Russian science has tended towards this goal from the beginning, that is it has striven to see the vitality of nature and its inner oneness with intellectual and divine being . . . The Russian nation strives with its whole nature towards religion, but religion which is bound up with knowledge and founded in science.

The Russian idealists were anti-Cartesians. They wanted knowledge which joined people. But probably they were always more communal in their thoughts than the erotic-individualistic German Romantics dreaming of Hölderlin's Diotima. She was one man's lover, whereas the Russians wanted brotherly love. The 'I' -centredness of the *cogito* wouldn't do as a way of life, and as a philosophy of hope, because it encouraged interpersonal obscurity. The *lumen naturale* that shines on objects, if it is the light of truth, must also reveal clearly and distinctly what joins man to man – which is charity, not erotic love, despite Solovyov's vision of the divine Sophia.

The Russians were anti-Cartesians, and, just as the German Romantics turned their late anti-rationalist guns on Kant, so they now turned on Hegel, as they understood him. The *cogito* offered no prospect of unity and collective salvation. Nor could philosophy begin, as Hegel proposed, from 'things splitting in two'.[33]

Khomiakov spoke with the voice of a Russian Schelling:

Since [the whole philosophy of the Kantian school] has to deal only with concepts, it can never find within itself a criterion for the definition of the internal and the external, for it has to do only with what has been already apprehended and which, consequently, has already become internal.[34]

There had to be a different way of getting at the pre-logical truth. If reason were reconfigured as understanding from within, that might be the way forward. What had to be avoided was knowledge which set subject against object.

I gave the name faith to that faculty of reason which apprehends actual (real) data and makes them available for analysis and awareness by the understanding. Only in this area do the data still have the fullness of their character and the marks of their origin. In this area, which precedes logical consciousness and which is filled with a living consciousness that does not need demonstrations and arguments, man realizes what belongs to his intellectual world and what to the external world. Here by the touchstone of his free will, man perceives what in his (objective) world is produced by his creative (subjective) activity and what is independent of it.[35]

Knowledge should not be divisive, neither of men from men nor men from their world. Human beings and their surrounding world form a continuum. After perception has done its work something remains which

> ... is God's world, as Russian people say ... God's world has with us primarily the meaning of blessing or beneficence, but I think that it is not without an admixture of the concept of 'general' or 'universal'.[36]

God's world exists regardless of who perceives it. It is the being in which we are all embedded.

In a striking metaphor which challenged the whole Cartesian epistemic tradition, which depended on 'the subject seeing the object', and also attacked Kant and Hegel, Khomiakov spoke of the blind student of optics, whose knowledge of light was not his own.

> He knows the laws of a light which is inaccessible to him but he accepts them as phenomena on *faith in other men's senses* [my emphasis]. In all possible circumstances the object (or phenomenon or fact) is an object of belief; it is fully transformed into an object of consciousness only by the action of consciousness. The degree of consciousness never exceeds the limits, or more exactly does not change the character of the way in which the object was initially accepted (thus the blind student of optics will always know light only as an episode in another's life, not in his own).[37]

There could be no more eloquent statement of Russian disquiet with Western rationalism than Khomiakov's metaphor. It was coupled with a redoubled defence of the world against the aggression of concepts.

The Russian anti-rationalists travelled back through Schelling's own sources to medieval mysticism to further build their tradition. They attached themselves to mystics from Plotinus (205–70) to Meister Eckhart (1260–1327), Nicholas of Cusa (1401–64) and Jakob Boehme (1575–1624), although Berdyaev would make a sharp division between the first and second pairs, the former being once again too rational and insufficiently in touch with warm life in his view. Russia's most positive mystical inheritance, from Boehme, was full of 'everything concrete, pictorial, bound up with the face of Christ and the face of man, everything permeated by anthropological consciousness', Berdyaev said.[38] Seventy years earlier Odoevsky's intellectual sights took in Boehme, the English mystic John Pordage, the founder of the French Martinist sect Martinez de Pasqualis (1715?–79), and Pasqualis's pupil Louis-Claude de Saint-Martin (1743–1803). Mysticism in Russia was encouraged in the early nineteenth century by freemasonry, a force always feared by Russia's rulers. The Russian Masons had in Odoevsky's day recently published Saint-Martin's book *On Errors and Truth* and Boehme was another discovery of the period.[39]

The other source of nourishment for Russian religious and mystical thought was evidently Orthodoxy. Here was the arena where anti-Cartesian mysticism joined forces with a deep feeling for Russian community. A notion of nature as sacrosanct but infected by human sins heightened the anti-scientific outlook, as did the idea of kenosis.[40] The kenotic idea was one of the most prominent of Kievan Christianity, embracing the virtues of poverty, humility and love. It suggested, archetypally in John Chrysostom, that men should be equal to each other in what they are and in what they know. John Chrysostom was, in his going to the people, a defender of the poor, and a teacher of *agape*, Christian love.

Where the Russian Church powerfully affected Russian philosophy was in reinforcing what Schelling idealized as *Mitwissenschaft*, knowledge-with.[41] The doctrine had prevailed in Eastern and Western Christian churches since the fourth century. Christ was of one substance or consubstantial, *homoousios*, with the Father. The Nicene Creed, which forms part of the Eucharist service in the Anglican Church, and the Catholic Mass, is still a familiar sound in Western churches:

> I believe in one God the Father Almighty, maker of heaven and earth and of all things visible and invisible. And in one Lord Jesus Christ, the only begotten son of God, begotten of his father before all worlds, God of God, Light of Light, Very God of Very God, begotten not made, being *of one substance with the Father* [my italics]; by whom all things were made.

> *Credo in unum Deum, Patrem omnipotentem, factorem coeli et terrae, visibilium omnium et invisibilium. Et in unum Dominum Jesum Christum Filium Dei unigenitum, et ex Patre natum ante omnia saecula: Deum de Deo, lumen de lumine, Deum verum de Deo vero;* genitum non factum, consubstantialem Patri; *per quem omnia facta sunt.*

In Russian worship the doctrine of consubstantiality, the terms which can still be heard in the Latin text of the Creed, was accompanied by a stress on theosis or the idea that man could become part of the living divine substance.[42] What Khomiakov stressed much more than the individualistic German Schelling was that the capacity to see life as a whole, and see spiritual reality in the material, only came about when the individual was part of a loving community. Quite the opposite of Schelling's esoteric truth, Khomiakov's knowledge was only available to genuine members of a religious community, and an Orthodox one.

Solovyov's task was to systematize the anti-Cartesian bias in Russian philosophy. *The Crisis in Western Philosophy* (1874), with its subtitle 'Against the Positivists', suggested this had to be done because the scientific spirit was destroying Western philosophy. Though not Descartes' own doing, the Cartesian revolution had put science in place of metaphysics and left the world without the means to synthesize human knowledge at its broadest. It affected a painful divorce between science and religion. By reviving metaphysics Solovyov would try to stave off what the Polish philosopher Leszek Kolakowski has described as the great harm done by scientific positivism to a true rational culture. As it swept through Europe from the mid-nineteenth century, positivism impoverished the culture of reason with its narrowly instrumental definition.[43]

A key aspect of Solovyov's thinking was to adapt the doctrine of theosis to philosophical use. It was developed in the *Lectures on Godmanhood* (1878), which Tolstoy and Dostoevsky came to hear in St Petersburg. Another name for the topic was 'Christology', or the belief that the dual nature of Christ was also shared by man. The Godmanhood of Christ made ethical and spiritual life possible. In the time of Solovyov the target of anti-rationalism was no longer Descartes but Auguste Comte (1789–1857) and Feuerbach. Solovyov's Godmanhood was an attempt to refute these men's visions of a world saved by science. Comte suggested that science would supersede religion and metaphysics to become the definitive source of human wisdom. For Solovyov this alarming prospect warranted a deliberate step back in the history of philosophy.

Solovyov turned back to Kant to seek a way of broadening reason out again, just as the German Romantics did. The Russian seminarist reread Kant as if it were possible to see Plato's Ideal Forms in things-in-themselves and thus through intuition, like Schelling, to bypass all constraints on absolute knowledge. But, not wanting to end up promoting an individualistic man-God, he insisted on reinscribing his German Romantic philosophy of intuition within Russian faith. Art and moral instinct showed men that they were free to create their ideal world, but not that that ideal came into their heads of their own making. In one of the finest achievements of the Russian moral-religious tradition, Solovyov made it clear that humanity needed high forms of encouragement to be ethical and creative. In a series of works – *Beauty in Nature* (1889), *The Overall Meaning of Art* (1890) and *The Power of Love* (1892–94) – he suggested how the good in love, in beauty, nature and art, encouraged men to be fully human. 'Artistic activity in itself has no particular, allegedly higher object, but that it serves the general life-goal of humanity in its way and by its means.'[44]

Solovyov's philosophy of Christian being once more brought to the attention of Russian thought the moral problem Descartes left behind, of a gap between mind and world. Descartes in Russia raised worries not about the conditions of knowledge but about the condition of the heart of the knower. The 'I' of 'I know' would have right knowledge if it was an ego of morally good intentions. For most of his career Solovyov could hardly conceive of that good man without his having faith in God.

Solovyov established the first article of belief of Russian mystical philosophy: that there could be no separation of facts and values. Neither Descartes nor Kant could have accepted this. But for Russian idealism it was love, that great bridge of facts and values, which made possible knowledge of reality. Here was a late Russian answer to Spinoza's *amor intellectualis dei*, the intellectual love of God, newly overlaid with mystical and Christian enthusiasm. The ideal subject of Russian philosophy yearned not just for one special other, but for all community. Human beings, whose condition was to have fallen away from the divine, sensed the original unity that bound them and felt the power to rebuild it. The history of the world, with the first God-Man as its model and its goal, was the story of increasing human unity. But the religious terminology was not strictly necessary, and in his last years, said to have been marked by waning faith, Solovyov stripped away the Christian supports and spoke more generally of the good. *The Justification of the Good* (1897) made belief in the good its own justification. Addressing individuals, its author gave metaphysical reasons why human beings should actively cherish community and care for the natural world and refine their sensibilities through art. Solovyov often felt he was striving to unite the best of the Eastern and Western Churches in his philosophy. His was an interesting answer to Chaadaev fifty years on, a small attempt for Russia at a renaissance of individualism protected by faith.

Russian anti-Cartesian philosophy moved mainly along branchlines after Solovyov as the power of rationalism as an alternative way of being – although not of reason as a critical tool – grew and spread.

By the end of the nineteenth century only Shestov still measured his resistance to rationalism symbolically in terms of Descartes and Pascal. The rationalist enemy was positivism for Solovyov and Marxism for the men of the 1890s, as it would be for covert anti-rationalists and humanists for the next hundred years.

Berdyaev encouraged the turn-of-the-century intelligentsia to feel that mysticism was in its blood and that therefore it should resist Marxism. In 'Philosophical Truth and the Pravda of the Intelligentsia', one of his two contributions to the 1909 volume *Landmarks*, he suggested Russia's philosophical weaknesses were also her strength:

> Not without ground the intelligentsia takes a negative and suspicious attitude to abstract academicism, to the dissection of living truth (*istina*) ... in its demands for an integral (*tselostnyi*) relationship to the world and to life one can discern the features of unconscious religious feeling.[45]

Yet Berdyaev's generation had to face the difficulty that, although through mystical philosophy the Russian intelligentsia had become conscious of its spiritual assets, the same anti-Cartesianism had hampered its critical intellectual development. Russia could boast of nothing comparable to the Western rational achievement. In *Landmarks* Frank echoed Berdyaev but only to emphasize a position of unmitigated weakness:

> Theoretical aesthetic, religious values have no power over the heart of the Russian intelligentsia, which feels them dimly and without intensity.[46]

The emphasis in this passage fell on the word 'theoretical'. For the

Russian intelligentsia the pursuit of 'theoretical, scientific truth' and a 'disinterested striving for an adequate intellectual representation of the world' had no value, according to Frank.[47] Chaadaev had once put it even more bluntly when he accused his countrymen of not caring to distinguish between true and false. A rare nineteenth-century French writer who studied the Russian mind, Théophile Funck-Brentano, unsurprisingly found that these Russian self-critics were quite right. It was exactly the absence of Cartesian clear and distinct ideas which condemned Russia to a style of philosophy which utterly failed to embrace the real world because it couldn't distinguish between the concrete and the chimeric. In a curious and possibly conscious reply to Khomiakov, Funck-Brentano spoke of blind men trying to write a philosophy of colours.[48]

Cartesian rationalism was not anti-social; it proposed rationality as community. Descartes could easily be defended against the charge that he divided men where he should have united them. First, the 'I' of the *cogito* was an operational or instrumental ego, not a psychological ego. Cartesian rationality was a professional procedure, not a threat to belonging. Second, the *cogito* was not as 'subjective' as it was taken to be on a crude psychological reading, because in the pledge to think men committed themselves to behaving rationally and discarding opinions which did not conform to evidence. Reason was a choice, a club, a social place where men might feel at ease in the company of others who respected it. The evidence for the *cogito* not being subjective was the testable reality of the world, the world shared by men, nothing to do with God.

But emotional Russia did not want to join that Western club, for, if it did, it told itself, it would lose its one great asset, its sense of community.

There was a great poetic power in Russia's review of the philosophical alternatives to reason, but its rejection of the *cogito* did not leave it well placed on the world map of philosophy. It did not, for instance, recognize as a consequence the question of 'other minds', a foundational problem bequeathed to classical Western philosophy by Descartes. Paradoxically this has meant that Russia, for all its moral preoccupations, has scarcely reaped the ethical benefits of one of the great Western questions. The sense of how difficult it is to know what is beyond one's own mind is conducive to respect for other minds and, because it demands high standards of one's own, encourages humility towards the truth. The Cartesian individual, since he alone is responsible for truth, has a moral obligation not to fake his evidence. As a single human being he might happily abandon his lonely task, but he has a duty to reason to fulfil. This duty is social. Although we can only have access to the truth singly, the reason we use to get at it is not a private language. At worst, the Russian misapplication of ethical criteria to denigrate rational activity leads to no social value at all being placed on individual epistemic integrity.

It is interesting to see what a Western thinker thought of the moral value of Descartes, and the French Cartesian tradition, at a difficult time for his country. The situation was France just after the end of the Second World War and the philosopher was Jean-Paul Sartre, who had been imprisoned under the German Occupation. An intensely patriotic argument came over the later renegade in a 1946 introduction to Descartes' thought. He even repeated it in his famous essay of the same year, 'Existentialism and Humanism'. The claim was that Descartes simultaneously laid the foundation of modern science *and* the basis of modern democratic freedom with the *cogito*. Sartre writes so strongly on this point that it is difficult to understand how he could have become a Communist in sympathy with the Soviet Union, except on the basis of extreme ignorance. But even if he was hardly about to give up his Communism the war had made him aware of some intrinsic goodness in his own intellectual world. His resulting ruminations brilliantly illuminate the Russian weakness.

Thus in his description of divine freedom, Descartes ends by rejoining and explicating his primary intuition of his own freedom . . . We shall not reproach Descartes with having given to God that which reverts to us in our own right. Rather we shall admire him, for having, in a dictatorial age, laid the groundwork of democracy, for having followed to the very end the demands of the idea of *autonomy* and for having understood long before . . . Heidegger . . . that the sole foundation of being is freedom.[49]

For Sartre in the best hour of his career the guarantee of modern liberty lay in the institution of Cartesian inwardness. The *cogito* provided a moral foundation for responsible individualism and a free society. The true social meaning of the *cogito* was 'I think, therefore I am free'.

As for Russia's rejection of this tradition, Berdyaev's critics would say he was part of the problem. But he was clear-sighted about the choice of Pascal over Descartes. It meant that 'in its basic tendency, Russian philosophy continues the great philosophical tradition of the past, the Greek and the German; Plato's spirit and the spirit of classical German Idealism live on in it'.[50] For better, for worse, this Platonic-Pascalian inheritance was the face of modern Russia. Its problematic legacy was more poetic than critical, more moral than scientific. The philosophy it had was built on weak truth-seeking foundations but its interest in the spiritual rewards of hope was unparalleled.

9

The Contest of Good and Evil

To define Russian philosophy in terms of its plural traditions in the nineteenth century, and to trace the roots of those traditions in the longer history of Western thought and Russian community, would be to begin to understand Russia on its own terms, as a unique culture on the fringes of the West. It would be to understand that the Russian search for a moral philosophy of being affects and limits knowledge and that to limit and shape knowledge is morally justified. It would resemble Pascal's justification for belief in God. The risk of falsehood would be worth accepting if it brought spiritual rewards which the critical life could not equal. Happiness and a world saturated in moral meaning might justify averting one's gaze from sources of doubt. Russia's Pascalian endeavour over the last two hundred years, and particularly in the last century, would make sense to the degree that it revealed the desperate need for a principle or set of beliefs to hold the country together as one coherent community or society. It would be understood that Russia's philosophical and revolutionary traditions met in their shared belief that hope – often hope against reason and against the testimony of experience – could provide a framework for social, spiritual and political community; that would be the nexus for understanding the uniqueness – not to speak of the tragedy – of Russian culture.

A contemporary Russian philosopher has suggested that the need to hold society together has been the prime mover of Russian thought:

> The sense of philosophizing in Russia cannot be understood separately from the fact that this society is internally disorganized, periodically inclines towards localism, to disintegration, that it has reached the proportions of schism. For this reason the striving for synthesis, for wholeness in Russian philosophy can be considered as a reaction to the negative aspects of socio-cultural development, to the dangers of spiritual, organizational, economic, political and other forms of disintegration ... The practical pathos of Russian philosophy is directed at preventing the falling away of the part from the whole, which has an infinite number of forms: the falling away of man from God, of the people from authority, of the intelligentsia from the people, the individual from the collective, and so on.[1]

What needs to be understood is the immeasurable moral zeal and hope and readiness to assume faith implied by those words 'practical pathos'; and how the pathos of 'falling away' and the romance of re-enchantment found equal embodiment in the mystical-religious and 'rational' camps. From the first Schellingians to the last Communists, philosophy in Russia during its long tradition 1815–1991 aimed at integration. It tried to construct a coherent social whole and to provide the social glue to bind it. Around the beginning of the twentieth century the task of the Russian revolutionary intelligentsia *and* Russian moral philosophy was to make Russian society whole – perhaps for the first time – by finding the means to coherence.

But equally from the beginning of Russian philosophy, Life resisted rational schemes to harness it. In the eyes of a Russian Hegelian, Absolute Reason was slowly becoming a real social force in Russia; but patently, as Belinsky almost immediately realized, this was not the case. Not only was the truth of Life quite different from the truth of Reason, the philosophy of social construction was a threat to real, individual lives. The experience of philosophy as social construction therefore split the philosophical-political discourse into two contrary modes: the one constructive, the other anarchic. Russia was never in a Western, Cartesian sense a culture of reason, but in all its philosophical forms it was a culture of hope. Only that hope took two forms. The constructivists translated hope into order dependent on the active commitment of dedicated or morally commandeered individuals. They sought an idea or principle which would bring wholeness; whereas the anarchists saw hope in the mystical quality of life-as-it-was-lived – a kind of natural unity in being which protected the integrity of simple souls. The anarchists described in positive terms a falling-away from conceptual order and a way of resisting the prison of definitive meaning.

Anarchism supposes that the principal threat to the human spirit is not disorder but coercion by some external authority. In the political sphere that authority would be the state, but for Russian philosophy even before the Revolution the threat seemed to come from language and concepts. The Russian anarchist strain attacked the very tools which made philosophy possible as a rational enterprise. Russian philosophical anarchists were opposed to all forms of naming and fixing. They believed – to echo the Third Commandment – that philosophy should take no name in vain and that all names and concepts operational in society undermined two sacred values: the autonomy of the person and the integrity of the world. The anarchists were Counter-Rationalists and mystics, and although some would say that was the embattled form liberal individualism had to take in Russia, their position was extreme because no liberal political institutions corresponded to it.

Berdyaev spoke of the 'groundless ground' of the seventeenth-century mystical thinker Jakob Boehme. His 'groundlessness' reflected the need for the mind to remain open to a fluid and bottomless reality.[2] Berdyaev's own anarchism led to a denial of every description of his work which came his way, although in *Dream and Reality* (1950) he spoke of 'metaphysical anarchism' and 'moral lawlessness' with a consistency that made three propositions discernible:

1. that man should 'stand over against society'
2. that the only truth comes from man's relationship with God
3. that contradiction is always preferable to closure.[3]

He wrote:

> I believed, above all, that truth cannot be imprisoned in any social net . . . and that those who pursue the knowledge of truth step tiresomely and boldly out of neat prisons into worlds that have more to them than sociology or science could ever contain. My thought was thus left free to move in whatever direction it chose. I defended the freedom of philosophical knowledge in the context of religious orthodoxy.[4]

The Russian philosophical anarchism Berdyaev, Frank and Shestov elaborated might be defined as radical inwardness. It authorized the sovereign person to retreat inwards to be free from all worldly constraint. Frank believed that 'primary, immediate being-for-self is a reality in and through which man transcends the world of objective fact and discovers quite a new dimension of being; in that dimension he finds the ultimate depths of reality and has them directly in his own self'.[5] The Russian philosophical anarchists found a way of securing what Sartre in his explication of Descartes called the subject's 'primary intuition of his own freedom', while not giving up their adherence to mystical truth.[6]

What defined this inwardness as something other than radical individualism and an invitation to social chaos, however, was the religious context. To refer to God was to invoke the absolute and eternal truth of mystical personhood and to stress the relative unimportance of passing social truths. To believe in God was a way of being at ease with worldly disorder. Far from succumbing to that disorder, retreat from social-rational norms was a step towards truly shared and unlimited being. It was not the social loss Hegel would have called it. For Frank 'the inward path is not an escape from the common objective world into the closed-in sphere of subjectivity. The very reverse is the case. Only through penetrating into the primary reality do we find our true inner bond with the objective world. The path inwards . . . leads not to a dark enclosure, but on the contrary . . . The inner bond with primary reality frees us from the power of the world and enables us to take a creative part in it.'[7]

The Russian philosophical anarchists were liberal individualists in disguise to the extent that, in the few years until it was silenced, philosophical anarchism became the primary discourse of freedom in Russian culture. 'I have always believed that life in God is freedom, untrammelled flight, anarchy in the true sense of the word,' wrote Berdyaev. 'The real call of freedom is not to be thought of in moral or psychological but in metaphysical terms.'[8] Under pressure from the Hegelian tradition of social construction for most of the nineteenth century, any Russian philosopher wanting to defend the integrity of the individual had to emphasize the open-ended and mystical nature of truth. He had to insist that no rational concepts could arbitrarily reorder chaotic but still vital Russian life because none could be finally true.

Shestov's anarchism was all the more powerful for the way it suggested that precisely the long Russian experience of arbitrary state power was proof that no 'rational' culture of social construction was acceptable. Explicitly Shestov twinned Christ's agony in the Garden of Gethsemane with Dostoevsky's scarring experience in 1849, when, accused of political conspiracy, he and a group of fellow revolutionaries – as Dostoevsky was in his youth – were subjected to a mock execution. One of the group went mad with shock.[9] Shestov inscribed a century of Russian suffering into his anarchist philosophy. All the pain and martyrdom and waste of love and talent – from the destroyed philosophers

Radishchev, Galich and Chaadaev, to Gogol's creative and religious despair, to Chernyshevsky and Pisarev in prison, to Herzen banished, to Belinsky struggling to survive, to Turgenev's sorrow for an unproductive land, to the sudden late apprehension by Solovyov of the reality of evil, to terrorism and murder in the name of what Solovyov called 'false wholenesses' – all this extreme Russian experience Shestov absorbed into a philosophy which damned all human enterprise.

Human beings were responsible for bringing negativity into the world, he declared.[10] The attempt to conceptualize higher truth always resulted in distortions of truth being imposed on real human beings, comparable to physical and mental torture. Scientific method was a trap, and freedom could only be sought in an imagined state of being where no truths were certain, nothing was fixed, and uncertainty was the ultimate mystery to be respected. This was Russian philosophy's task – to accept and get past negativity and pain and see the emptiness as positive openness.

A generation or so earlier the individualistic, anti-Hegelian West had witnessed the protests of the German anarchist-individualist Max Stirner and of Nietzsche that rationalization was eating up social existence, that Life should be allowed to escape from the tyranny of abstractions, that the autonomy of the person must stand over against the social concept. Yet for several reasons anarchism was of unique importance in Russian philosophy. For if 'in essence Western anarchism is liberal indi-vidualism',[11] then its Russian philosophical counterpart probably was liberal individualism forced by cultural circumstances into an extreme form. Second, if Russian philosophical anarchism was 'flight', then it was not individualistic flight, because of that long religious tradition of theosis which put men in mutual touch with God in a realm of immanent being. And third, of at least equal importance with these two other points, mystical anarchism operated as the critical other half of Russian philosophy. It operated as a check on the excesses of social construction, just as social construction did on anarchism. Every attempt to formulate a way to make a rational society cohere in Russia was a victory over un-productive dreaming, but a Russian philosophy of anarchism was desperately needed from the moment that coherence turned into a prison. The two philosophical moments belonged in frustrating but ultimately salutary partnership.

One difficulty with anarchism, from the viewpoint of those who craved a better order of Russian society, and why it might be rejected, was that it gave no moral guidance. It was in that respect as incomplete as Utilitarianism in the West because it made all real values and motives a private matter. Dostoevsky was unsure about the virtue of groundlessness years before Berdyaev and Shestov conjured with it. He did not think it was psychologically possible to suspend the human desire for certainty and comfort indefinitely. This was one meaning, of the many contained by 'The Legend of the the Grand Inquisitor', which potentially came down on the Inquisitor's side. Dostoevsky asked his readers to consider the comforts of an institutionalized, repressive socialism which might yet make them happy, and to compare that attainable reality with the love of Christ, which was only a promise and a kiss. He asked them to consider whether they could live on the strength of an anarchistic kiss, without regressing to the domain of fixed values. Shestov opted for the kiss, but Dostoevsky himself was ambivalent. In his hands, in Odoevsky's, in Solovyov's and others, Russian philosophy occupied a position somewhere between social construction and anarchism, when it focused attention on moral personality. As moral individualists who believed that moral personality was the only way forward to the good society, these men introduced another nuance to the philosophical picture. Practising another beleaguered form of liberalism, their difficulty, however, was where moral standards should come from. Dostoevsky accepted the need for moral hope while rejecting every form in which it was available, apart from religious faith. The inadequacy of philosophical anarchism as a constructive moral force can therefore be said to have given rise to a very prevalent force in Russian thought, namely a concern with the metaphysics of morals.

In their fiction Odoevsky and Dostoevsky sought a transcendent source of moral value to put the current state of Russian society in perspective. Their metaphysics of morals began with a love of voluntarism which Dostoevsky associated with Kant. Odoevsky probably out of ignorance did not make the Kantian connection, but his encounter with Utilitarianism in *Russian Nights* showed just as readily as *Notes from Underground* what was wrong with a question like 'Why am I wrong to treat life as a simple calculus for personal gain?'. He came up with the very Kantian answer that, since as human beings we have moral imagination at our disposal, and moral imagination is a good thing, we should use it. Rational egoism can hardly be a guide to the good life if it ignores the greatest moral gift in our possession – the capacity to imagine the universal good. Yet, living later into the progressively atheistic nineteenth century than Odoevsky, Dostoevsky worried about nourishment for that imagination. In his fictional world his believers in the salvational power of beauty were privileged by their vision but also deluded, because, as it turned out, a beautiful world was revealed to them only because they were sick.[12]

More sober Russian thinkers either side of Dostoevsky concluded that moral personality needed positive encouragement from society. Unlike what Kant imagined to be the case, moral personality in Russia could not make its choices on the basis of inner freedom alone. Society needed to encourage moral values which enabled individuals to transcend that society's own limitations. It needed to encourage moral belief by referring its members to a higher moral law. In Odoevsky's collapsed Benthamite colony, people raised on self-interest could not cope in an emergency because they had lost the habit of voluntary restraint and mutual cooperation. The risk with a Utilitarian outlook was that moral personality would get out of practice. But the same deficiency could result from other types of society too.

Dostoevsky's friend Solovyov suggested art and religious belief would keep the good man on course and that the ethical state should encourage these cultural forms. Half a century later, as the metaphysics of morals lost ground in both Russia and the West, Frank, whose ontological anarchism was firmly wedded to a belief in God, judged that the moral life of Russian society – so precious to the traditional intelligentsia – couldn't survive without objective moral values.[13] Particularly in Russia moral personality needed the right cultural environment. The good man in Russia was a volunteer easily blown off course – by atheism, by subjectivism and by philosophical materialism.

There was always something mystical about the Russian value attached to moral personality. If the nineteenth-century West was under-pinned by an economic Utilitarianism, then the East – the Russian way – rested on a Utilitarianism of a mystical kind, whereby the self, saving its poetic soul, dissolved in the general good. In Odoevsky's ideal scheme individual good actions would add up to good community, but in a way that could not be identified in figures. The Russian ethical climate was, and has remained, predominantly Christian. But clearly that had to be, for if those objective ethical values Frank insisted upon were to have their social place, they could only occur in Russia as concepts of God and, borrowed from Kant, the good. Berdyaev was aiming at something like a Christian socialism for Russia. He said in defiance of both Eastern and Western atheist and materialist trends in his day, and in defiance of the lifeless social construct of Communism above all: don't equate moral values with the present fashion in social and political values. Moral values are aspects of moral personalities who are not afraid to invoke the time-less metaphysical values of God and the good. Moral personalities are not afraid to invoke absolute values because they are prepared to take a leap of faith: not to debate whether such values exist, but to accept the spiritual benefits of belief. Berdyaev was a Christian socialist and the first Russian Christian existentialist.

Russian philosophy as it emerged at the end of the nineteenth century usefully pitted against each other its contrasting tendencies towards social construction and mystical anarchism. Morally it was interested above all in volunteers for the good – men who had a sense that they were following a moral law, not improvising action in their own interest. But over the scene of philosophizing hung a blight which affected all attempts at social improvement and which finally encouraged not only waves of anarchism and mysticism but also despair. It was perhaps the cardinal emotional experience of the *intelligent* who cared to monitor his feelings honestly that while imaginative-speculative visions of the totally meaningful life loomed from studies of Hegel and Marx, and from pages of Kant and Schiller, critical Russian minds could only refer in real life to the false place where they lived; a place where those ideas were not at home. Dostoevsky talked about 'schillerism' and 'bookishness' to say what it was like to live in the dead shadow of Europe, among the waxwork copies of living ideas. The way Russian subjects were bound together under the rule of the tsars left a social vacuum where meaning should have stepped in, and where philosophy *promised* it would, but didn't. Russian reality could never match up to the constructive vision and the anarchist vision only made things worse. To experience a would-be great nation in endless social disarray was disorienting and morally undermining for constructivists and believers alike. It was like being laughed at by God. In the social chaos which reason itself in the end encouraged, Russia in the nineteenth century already had a taste of the postmodern and the end of philosophy.[14]

Hegel offered reason in God's place, and secular socialism promised the apparent inevitability of a just social order. But Dostoevsky, who died in 1881, left this world unconvinced. He saw the devil in the gap between aspiration and what might be made of it. Solovyov had a vision of Antichrist. Together these two friends were among the most prescient men in Europe about the evil lurking in the philosophy of hope.

In *The Devils* Shatov, 'the vacillator', struggled with atheism before killing himself. He went to live in America, which Dostoevsky considered the home of atheism, then returned to Russia, and still found no God. His hero Stavrogin, 'the cross-bearer', might have given meaning to the lives of those around him, but he too was uncertain of a God whose existence he tested with acts of desecration. Dostoevsky depicted a moral-intellectual life so highly charged, so frenetic and so consumed by self-doubt in his Russia that it suggested no man could bear to live there by reason alone. For order and calm to prevail there had to be God. But perhaps He didn't exist.

Evil has been almost completely ignored by classical Western philosophy, though it was clearly the meaning behind the last of Descartes' six considerations, in *The Meditations*, of what might obstruct the pursuit of truth. There might be a *malin génie* who deliberately mismatched our perceptions to what is the case. If the *malin génie* – the late, underworld successor to the God of the medieval theodicies – were to function as such, then instead of everything in the world being justified by the existence of God, no order would be knowable, and we couldn't even know that it wasn't knowable. Descartes tried but gave up imagining how things might be, if in fact our world was a metaphysical disaster – a catastrophe Walter Benjamin once called the result of a 'bad mood of God'.[15]

Russia never worked through the doubts about the reliability of the senses and the actual existence of an objective world that constituted Descartes' scientific method and his real secular achievement in Western eyes. Therefore when Russian doubt came as the sudden experience of the secular and the modern, imported from the West, the effect was not a patient revision of philosophical method but a spiritual catastrophe. For Dostoevsky the Russian form of the Cartesian doubt was a chaotic social and psychological apprehensiveness threatening to destroy each and every individual soul who could no longer believe in 'man', 'mankind', and a morally coherent universe.

Dostoevsky was filled with doubt. Doubt about the existence of God, but also doubt about the power of Enlightenment: really the fear of what would happen if man were left alone. After that mock execution and exile to Siberia his sense of disbelief in 'man' and of any nobility attached to that name grew with his experience of living in a 'House of the Dead'. He was struck by the overwhelming existential randomness of things. The self-lacerating solipsism of the narrator of *Notes from Underground* has been compared to what Hegel meant by Unhappy Consciousness. But what that nameless man went through was already Hegel stripped of the redeeming myth of Reason. The Underground Man belonged to a world in which there was no good Design, and no means to coherence. Because Russia was not the sceptical, atheistic West, not the worst place on earth, Dostoevsky could still turn towards Russian spirituality to try to escape from doubt. But mostly he failed to find what he needed. Meanwhile his actual experience of Russia from day to day only compounded his dilemma, because what he saw was not even the problems of reason as such but their parody. He saw in his mind's eye the mass alienation of 'small men' in Russia's semi-Europeanized cities. Along Nevsky Prospect he saw men who wore foreign ideas like ill-fitting suits of borrowed clothes and who therefore could not relate to each other authentically, or to themselves. Progress depended on education, but the handling of words and ideas by a mass of semi-educated people produced difficulties and temptations which classical philosophy never envisaged. Thus Dostoevsky's metaphysical doubt in God, which had to be a doubt about mankind as a universal truth and aspiration, expanded further into a doubt about actual men; about the very possibility of culture.

His concept of 'bookishness' – *knizhnost'* – was poor education raised to a degree of metaphysical horror. It made particular sense in Russia because it was the opposite of knowledge conceived under the mantle of *sobornost'*. What Dostoevsky saw was that in an unwitting, or devilishly inspired parody of the consubstantial knowledge ideal, Russia's main experience of 'culture' was to have no connection with truth at all. Education, a synonym for philosophy whenever it promised to make Russian society more cohesive, had so far resulted in the country's self-alienation on a massive scale.[16]

Hegel's Unhappy Consciousness dwelt in a man who could not escape himself because he had only words and ideas at his disposal, with no reality attached to them. A rational society must find such a man inadequate. Man's task is to get a grip, adjust, make progress. But life in Russia under Dostoevsky's gaze simply bred unlimited unhappy consciousnesses because it was itself unreal. Fakeness and imitativeness were its defining qualities. As a culture it was really only an absence. Its words didn't relate to anything real. The Underground Man staved off admission of this void by laughing at an intellectual world of which he was both a part and, for fiction's sake, a superior outsider: he was, thanks to fiction alone, a consciousness that could get out of the orbit of the species and see the *malin génie* at work. Thus, speaking intermittently through the Underground Man's monologue in what seemed to be his own voice, Dostoevsky addressed the End of Enlightenment.

His superficial target was Chernyshevsky, the Utilitarian Positivist who stood for a popular rationalism. Dostoevsky like Belinsky was implacably opposed to constructive systems of Reason pretending to order life, at the expense of real, diverse, irrational, perverse, human Being. He saw this happening with both socialism and capitalism. His positive cause was Life, full Life, but he needed that life to be good if he was to hold on to his faith. Thus his real worry, in philosophy, was Kant. In Kant, Dostoevsky found a noble faith in man's ability to determine the good and the beautiful. The effect of Kant's ethics amounted – as Tolstoy noticed – to a continuing faith in God, or, more exactly, in man's capacity to believe in 'man'. Only it was clear to Dostoevsky that this faith was no longer possible. The humanist culture around him, both East and West, was debased. He could neither discard Kant nor believe in him.

With *knizhnost'* Russian philosophy began to think in a very modern – and postmodern – way about the reception of ideas, and how they related to the minds thinking them. Words were unreliable, writing misled. There are several essays of the period 1860–62 in which Dostoevsky expressed his loathing of *knizhnost'* and specifically of a parroted version of German Idealism. In *Notes from Underground* he called this strip-cartoon version of the immediate Western high cultural heritage *shillerism* (in the Russian spelling) because for so long Schiller had been its figurehead. Ideas turned into their opposite, gave way to their doubles, with no guarantee of where the truth would come to rest. This fate befell ideas and also people. All identity had to struggle to maintain itself against corruption and parody. Hegel had said that all ideas enjoy two lives. They appear once in history as themselves and a second time as parody. The force of Dostoevsky's term *shillerism* was that intellectual Russia amounted to nothing more than a parody of German mentality.

What the Underground Man allows us to feel is the social and intellectual effect of all the fragmentation and senselessness Russian philosophy has feared since the French Revolution now coming true. The message is delivered through manipulation of the literary text. The Underground Man constantly discounts the truth of everything he has just stated. He anticipates the reader's likely response only to undermine or disown it. He derides the very medium on which he depends for his only satisfaction, namely the relationship between himself and the reader. As the original unreliable narrator his relation to the reader replicates his relation to the world at large. Nothing is certain in the text and no viewpoint fixed. Through the disabled culture of reading and writing which *Notes from Underground* presents, Dostoevsky conveys a vivid impression of what it means to be disinherited from all certainty. Faith in a stable humanity has collapsed. The questions which arise in its place are: what is it like to live a life which does not relate to anything we claim to believe in? What is it not to 'mean' the values on which we base that life? What is it to use words without 'meaning' them?

Tolstoy's only solution was not to let these 'post-educational' and post-Enlightenment problems arise. But Dostoevsky knew the form the disease of modernity was taking. For him the only feasible opposite of *knizhnost'* was *pochvennost'*, entailing a new return to the medieval sense of rooted community in Being. *Pochvennost'* was earth-ness or soil-belonging.

Ideally, in a civilization returned to earth-ness, learning would be from one man to another, orally. Knowledge would go forward in the form of the teaching of a Church Elder (*starets*) like Father Zosima. There would be no alienation because the priest would become the mind and the heart of his pupil. But Dostoevsky, having come back to Khomiakov and Kireevsky's position by a painful and circuitous route on which he sacrificed his innocence, was never wholly convinced by the close-to-the-native-soil solution, which would mean enclosing the whole of modern life in a monastery. Besides which secular confusion was his subject. It fascinated him. This is why his fiction is so comic and so wordily desperate at the same time. His universe is crammed with words. In the novels everyone is chattering, not noticing that he or she is trapped in un-meaning. Everything fine is parodied. Meaning is elusive. The devil is at work. Philosophy laughs silently.[17]

Dostoevsky's greatest contribution to philosophy was to examine how, with reference to Russia's experience of self-alienation, what would one day be called a postmodern culture would function. The moral pain of living in a world which did not respect freedom and dignity, combined with the anguish brought on by bungled education, delivered an experience of horror. The practice of serfdom in Russia meant that the tradition of moral repugnance was older and in the end deeper-rooted than the tradition of hope. Chaadaev spoke of the terrible stain or blot of serfdom. Russia's experience of malignity included the dehumanizing bureaucracy to which Gogol dedicated his stories, and the stagnant, provincial inertia of the society he depicted in *Dead Souls*. This malignity was about deliberate falsification, about not caring for truth and justice and good and evil, and about not respecting the individual and his labour, his dignity and his property. It was about the misuse of power up to a level which left such a shock of disorder that it shook the metaphysical foundations. The kind of good scheme of things which Descartes' proof of God guaranteed was already ripped apart in a world which neglected beauty, in which the Church was corrupt, and in which the tsar, the representative of God on earth, abused the trust of his people. Russian consciousness from the later nineteenth century began to store up an intense awareness of the world being thrust out of joint. It was intensely aware that the Russian mental world did not tick harmoniously, with its parts running in parallel, as Leibniz reassured the European eighteenth century was the case in the best of all possible worlds. Descartes' doubts could be heuristic and temporary in a mind which had equal faith in God and reason, but in a mind like Dostoevsky's, that knew Russia and feared its dislocation and emptiness, they were real doubts about the existence of goodness.

The power of spiritual community hovers over Dostoevsky's narratives, trying to restore the hurt fledgling individual to the fold. Community is the answer – not anarchism and not social construction – but where can community be found in an uncoerced form? All of Dostoevsky's attempted atheists are these tormented individuals who can't quite get away from belonging and faith and can't rest easy with the idea of being back either. Alienation begins as a foreign intellectual disease in Russia but becomes an intense everyday experience of self-alienation and inauthenticity. It is their own tradition in falsehood, their own lack of universal criteria, which produces deep alienation of intellect and spirit in honest Russian thinkers, and evokes a sense of nothingness as the result of generation after generation of misplaced, wasted striving, and of intellectual, social and cultural edifices grounded in the absence of virtue.

With Dostoevsky Russia went through the shock of social incoherence much earlier than what Spengler picked up on in his *Decline of the West*. The Western sense of *Untergang* following the Great War and the collapse of the old empires in Austria and Germany struck Heidegger after the Russian soul was already lost. And yet Dostoevsky never gave up hope of a Russian resurrection by which it would finally emerge as spiritually superior to the West, once it had conquered its doubt and transcended its own unreality.

The desire to construct the good society, mystical anarchism, profound social alienation and an inextinguishable feeling that traditional Russian community was the answer were the four great intellectual experiences which made Russian nineteenth-century philosophy a mixture of hope and catastrophe and a battleground for good and evil. A brilliant writer on Hegel and Marx thirty years ago suggested why. After Hegel had created the most perfect and detailed explanation of what rational life might be, both the Germans and the Russians needed an antidote of common sense to bring some flexibility and healthy scepticism into philosophical play. They needed a philosopher who never was, a German David Hume. Herzen felt it and moved towards a Humean position when he decided morality was a matter of impulse taught by traditions and institutions. The problem for Russia was that its only acceptable institutions were religious and deeply anti-individual and anti-progressive. Russian would-be Humeans, who included the later nineteenth-century, arch-conservative figure of Konstantin Pobedonostev, had to accept there was a void where the right kind of tradition would have been. Philosophically Russia needed an empiricist who believed that truth was a matter of vivid impressions, of which ideas in the mind stored only faded memories; that personalities were only bundles of impressions, not metaphysical entities, and that moral and social behaviour were assimilated as part of tradition rather than arrived at through the dis-criminations of reason.

All this a German Hume would have insisted upon, in the name of common sense. Instead, the philosopher who stepped into Hegel's shoes was the medical-materialist Feuerbach, who paved the way for disaster. For Feuerbach's materialism was not empiricism. The truth of his materialism could not be experienced. That a single substance, 'matter', underpinned the whole of life was itself a metaphysical idea, not an inference from what could be seen and felt. Because materialism was no more friendly to real experience than idealism was, German and Russian philosophical friends of experience, of life-as-it-is-lived, were pushed into anarchism, a more extreme position than they might otherwise have adopted. Because materialism was as much of a metaphysical theory as idealism, Russian mystical philosophy had to defend the integrity of the world and of persons against such enemies as 'sociology' and 'science' and 'progress'. This was a position held by Max Stirner and by Nietzsche, for the German part. The fact that materialism was no substitute for a healthy and sceptical empiricism was exactly why Russian philosophy was flooded with communal-religious anarchists defending Life against the evil of conceptual thought – and still the real experience of men, the real beyond-good-and-evil, was neglected.

The impulses to anarchism and social construction constantly rivalled each other, the latter trying to make Russia modern and dynamic, the former looking for ways to save the last source of satisfaction and dignity and sanity in the bond with nature; the one subordinating life to concepts, the other trying to rescue it like an ill-treated pet. These intellectual tensions made it difficult for Russia to become a flourishing modern secular society just as they made the Russian Silver Age one of the most brilliant in alternative philosophy anywhere in the world.

PART III

Against Idealism: Cure or Undoing?

10

Lenin and the View from No One

Philosophy is the childhood of the intellect and a culture that tries to skip it will never grow up.

Thomas Nagel, *The View from Nowhere*

Lenin entered the scene of philosophizing when Marxism and religious idealism were joined in open battle. For a remarkable period of twenty-five to thirty years – 1895–1925 – though latterly under increasing political pressure to desist, Russia practised its two traditions. Scientific positivism clashed with Solovyovan spirituality. Pursuing hope, the intelligentsia oscillated between the human (anarchic) and the abstract (constructivist) poles of mystical belief. When Berdyaev divided up the neo-Platonic and Christian mystics into those positively on the side of life and those whose mysticism vouchsafed the perfect idea, he unconsciously pictured the contemporary battle. All Russian philosophy except positivism was theology at heart. What mattered was to retain a set of beliefs protective of individual souls.

Lenin's project shouldn't automatically be counted among the negative mysticisms to which the romance of Communism belonged. His goal was a simple positivism – a concentrated focus on measurable facts.

He aimed to build a modern, secular, socially integrated country by getting rid of all the dreaming and uncertainty that passed for philosophy in Russia. A genius for power persuaded him that what Russia needed in its conquest of the twentieth century was least of all intellectual subtlety, mystical individualism and poetry. Russian culture was riddled with intellectual weakness, as Lenin's opponents, the authors of *Landmarks*, readily admitted. Lenin was a classic Russian *intelligent* to whom the writing of a philosophical treatise fell as a political necessity rather than a vocation. On one occasion he disavowed his role as a philosopher. On another he accepted that with Marx philosophy had become *praxis*, a matter of action rather than reflection, which suited him well.

If Russia was to pull itself together, almost literally, as a modern secular society, what it would need would be an anti-idealist philosophy of progress. The thrust of Lenin's thought was probably latent from the moment he studied Marxism, but what brought it into being was the occasion in 1906 when Bogdanov published his alternative version of Marxist philosophy for Russia. Bogdanov couldn't see what was politically necessary in Lenin's view. Meanwhile Lenin's liberal opponents were vociferously demanding that Russian culture be based on liberal individualism. Future *Landmarks* editor Mikhail Gershenzon was about to pay tribute to the West as the most successful culture in modern history: 'Self-assertion is a great force: it is that which makes the Western bourgeoisie a mighty unconscious instrument of the Divine work on earth.'[1] Lenin's definitive version of Marxist philosophy for Russia anticipated the liberal declaration. *Materialism and Empiriocriticism* was published in autumn 1908.

Lenin laid down a marker for the power of ideas in Russia when he conceded that what the Bolshevik party stood for in the political arena had to be reinforced with an appropriate philosophy. If he was to mend the country he would have to mend philosophy with it. He decided that philosophy as social construction had to succeed, and it had to be of such a kind as to rid Russia of its endemic intellectual dalliance. Philosophy had to create intellectual authority. What was right and proper for a member of that society to know and think would have to be defined so as to leave no individual-mystical-anarchic options.

What Lenin had to contend with in 1908 was in a way not dissimilar to the unproductive inwardness Hegel wanted to tackle in 1807. Russia was a politically crippled nation 'wasting itself in yearning'.

> The 'beautiful soul', lacking an actual existence, entangled in the contradiction between its pure self and the necessity of that self to externalize itself and change itself into an actual existence, and dwelling in the immediacy of . . . pure being or empty nothingness – this 'beautiful soul', then, being conscious of this contradiction in its unreconciled immediacy, is disordered to the point of madness, wastes itself in yearning and pines away in consumption. Thereby it does in fact surrender the being-for-itself to which it so stubbornly clings.[2]

It was hyper-emotional and politically underpowered. It had to move on from self-indulgent mysticism. Rejection of the introspective and religious beautiful soul was Feuerbach's point of departure in the first onslaught of 'positive' philosophy against idealism. It was the starting-point for Marx's own 'positive' philosophy in the Paris Manuscripts of 1844. Now it would spur Lenin on too.[3]

Idealism, as Engels explained it, meant an imbalanced society, dominated by an economic-intellectual elite, the bourgeoisie. Idealism meant education – and the material means to sustain it – confined to a narrow social group, which meant in turn that only a tiny proportion of the population had a taste of personal fulfilment and happiness. A modern society was a mass society in which by contrast every last man should have the chance to improve his material and educational lot and enter society in an active reciprocal bond. This shift in the balance of happiness and political power was what materialism promised. Materialism as a synonym for an integrated, egalitarian welfare society lent a certain legitimacy to what Lenin was about to do.

Hegelian Idealism, of a kind that transcended moments of soulful subjective weakness, was a robust philosophy of success. Hegelian individuals achieved success when they found a way of realizing their particular talents in society. Rational individuals by definition sought social emancipation. They put pressure on a progressive society to expand to accommodate their talents. Their competitiveness fuelled the engine of progress which reason in a higher form predetermined as the condition of modern nations. Modernization and success-seeking were therefore simultaneously voluntary matters for individuals and predetermined ones for enlightened states which gave individuals scope to develop. Those states, once they had reached a certain level of cultural development, could expect to grow ever more dynamic and rational.

Sixty years before Lenin, Herzen had seen how well Hegel's analysis of what impeded modern progress applied to Russia. The gap between the intelligentsia and the mass of society ruined the country. In his day Herzen still hoped for a liberal Russia which would lift this blight and allow able individuals to play a confident and autonomous role in a socially complex society. Lenin chose the Marxist route instead. It was beside the liberal dream an equal bid for modernization and success, but it took the emphasis away from individual emancipation according to effort and talent. Instead, it entrusted the modernization project to a class-determined engine. Lenin hooked Russia up to the Marxist train of history. The name of the train was hope. History, the ways of which Marxism claimed to be able to detect, was moving in favour of a proletarian state with 'historical materialist' values. With help from a dedicated political party, and a textbook like *Materialism and Empiriocriticism*, Russia was about to become a dynamic modern society with a materialist philosophy.

Marxism virtually defined political modernity as the shift from idealism to materialism. It was just the model for Lenin. The idea belonged to Engels, who set down much of Marxist theory. Engels believed that through the mediation of Feuerbach, the German working man had inherited Hegelian philosophy to his benefit, once Hegel's idealist formulation was reworked into a materialist vision.[4] That reworking was the task of Marxism, and its outcome was materialist because, instead of being concerned with maximizing reason in the world, it set itself the task of maximizing material well-being. Material well-being was the only basis on which all men could set out on that road to the personal wholeness and social emancipation which Hegel pictured. Marxism had to change the material conditions of the world in order for Hegel's vision to come true.[5] 'The cult of abstract man ... had to be replaced by the science of real men and of their historical development. This further development ... was inaugurated by Marx.'[6] 'The science of real men and their historical development' was a description of Marxism's potency. The rationality of history made that development inevitable. History, of which the class struggle was the human engine, was progress. The class struggle was the way the most insightful class, the proletariat and its spokesmen, acknowledged what history was about.

So armed, Lenin took up philosophy as a combative task. He took over one portion of philosophy's territory and declared civil war on the rest. Idealism was to be annihilated. But Marxism, with Marx and Engels already dead, somehow lacked arguments which would make it strong in a battle with three centuries of philosophical idealism.[7] Neither Marx nor Engels had attended to the battle Lenin needed to wage against Russian mystical anarchism. So Lenin, a representative of the most philosophical country in the world in that its very existence seemed to depend on ideas, stepped in to complete the theoretical task.[8]

Lenin reacted in a peculiarly Russian way when he realized that the clue to making Marxism work in Russia was to develop it as a theory of knowledge and a foundation of moral being. The founders of Marxism had failed to develop a theory of knowledge. Marx might have countered that he didn't need one to fight for workers' rights, but clearly Lenin did. As philosophical interest expanded in Russia in the 1900s, Marxists in Russia, that exaggeratedly theoretical place, were left particularly vulnerable to attacks from two varieties of idealist: neo-Kantians and 'Machists'. So Lenin studied the history of epistemology and wrote a riposte which put Marxism in Russia on firmer philosophical ground – firmer in the sense that a theory at least now existed which could become the quietly much derided but compulsory gospel of Soviet Russian philosophy.

Without training, with only the habits of a maniacal autodidact prepared to glut himself on world texts in the British Museum, Lenin resolved negatively to show why all idealist theories of perception, and all those under other names which resembled them, were untenable for a Russian Marxist. Idealism meant any description of individual minds as free to see the world in their own way. That was as unacceptable as the idea that men exercise free will in history. For, just as history develops according to the objective laws of dialectical materialism, so knowledge too works without any input from the subject. The facts are the facts. Our human job is to register them.

It took Lenin nine months, from genesis to publication, to see his extraordinary 350-page crusade against subjectivity into print. He should have been teased about the miraculous time-frame, for no ordinary person could have undertaken to see philosophy reborn as totalitarian politics in one semester and one long vacation. *Materialism and Empiriocriticism* remains a testament to Lenin's diligence and, despite the crudeness and haste, his political thoroughness. Meanwhile it had a texture like no other work in the history of philosophy. It was a delirium of quotations packed so densely on every page that the proliferation of speech marks seemed like a typographical illness. The tone was a mixture of rage, sarcasm and personal abuse, everything you might expect from an ignorant man with a grudge against 'philosophy' or a man trying to appeal to a mass audience.

Lenin attacked idealism in every form he came across. He tried to trump Bogdanov on every one of his historical sources from Berkeley on to sharpen the assault. If idealism was a tool used by the bourgeoisie to suppress the people, and if this was to be shown as an argument within philosophy by means of a cogent attack on the role of the subject in knowledge, then half of modern philosophy would have to be unpicked. In the event Lenin didn't so much unpick idealism as vilify and ridicule every theory which didn't appeal to him. Berkeley famously stated that *esse est percipi* – what is is what is perceived – a theory of knowledge which set the active and discriminating subject at the heart of reality. Lenin swung his hammer.

He didn't know it but in his philosophy-breaking he would use a form of materialism derived from Spinoza to see off Berkeley's 'subjectivism'. His conscious allies were, beside Spinoza, obscure and trivial men, but they served their purpose. One was Joseph Dietzgen, author of *Das Wesen der menschlichen Kopfarbeit* (1903). He was chosen because 'Joseph Dietzgen is a dialectical materialist'.[9] Half the Soviet future lay in that title alone, which Marxist historians wrongly translated as *The Nature of the Workings of the Human Mind* but which meant 'The Nature of Human Brainwork'. In a quarrel still central to Western philosophy today, a century later, Dietzgen opted for 'brain' over 'mind'. Where Hegel would have written *Geist* and meant an untranslatable composite of mind and spirit, Dietzgen chose the blunt and prosaic *Kopfarbeit* – 'work done in the head'. Thanks to the idea of head-work, Russian artists and intellectuals were about to take up their new roles as 'workers in ink' and 'engineers of the soul'.

Lenin explained his choice of Dietzgen:

Marx and Engels were partisans in philosophy from start to finish, they were able to detect the deviations from materialism ... And whatever particular mistakes he committed in his exposition of dialectical materialism, J. Dietzgen fully appreciated and took over this great and most precious tradition of his teachers . . . He firmly and categorically declared: I am a materialist; our philosophy is a materialist philosophy.[10]

More obviously to a reader today, Dietzgen offered a course in intellectual simplification coupled with a sharp tongue in the service of the cause. Lenin relished Dietzgenesque phrases like 'the scientific priestcraft' of idealist philosophy alongside 'the open priestcraft' of the church. Dietzgen's words appear in quotation marks here, supplemented by Lenin's bridging comments:

'In particular the sphere of epistemology, the misunderstanding of the human mind, is such a louse-hole' in which both kinds of priests 'lay their eggs'. 'Graduate flunkeys', who, with their talk of 'ideal blessings' stultify the people by their tortuous 'idealism' – that is J. Dietzgen's opinion of the professors of philosophy.[11]

Together, Lenin and Dietzgen declared epistemology to be a partisan science whose professors were, in Lenin's words, 'learned salesmen of the theologians'. The Russian master of Marxist polemic made clear that in both economics and philosophy the task of the home side was 'to lop off the reactionary tendency and pursue your own line and combat the whole line of the forces and classes hostile to us'. The switch in pronouns in mid-sentence suggests a desk-bound man suddenly carried away, imagining himself addressing the activist crowd.[12] *Materialism and Empiriocriticism* was a colourful sub-Hegelian work replete with pictures, personalities, colours and metaphors. Over its course idealism acquired striking synonyms: 'this naked "I" engaged in empty philosophical fancies. A stupid and fruitless occupation.' 'Empty scholasticism serving as a loophole for fideism.' 'This brainless philosophy', 'naked . . . solipsism . . . high-sounding trifling', 'an old, old sophism'.[13] Interesting then to remember that its 350 pages were dictated by a single phenomenon in

Russian intellectual history, which had brought home to Lenin the threat from Marxist 'revisionists' – neo-Kantians in the main, but in effect anyone who had a different idea and above all Bogdanov.

In *Empiriomonism* (1904–6) Bogdanov had the idea that not so much Russia but the proletariat had been short-changed by philosophy. The class which Marxism existed to defend, exalt and propel to the forefront of European culture needed an appropriate philosophy of its own.[14] The project ought to have appealed. But evidently if anyone was going to speak as a Russian Marxist for the proletariat Lenin was. So he took Bogdanov's project, saw its political weaknesses, ridiculed them, and replaced them. There would be a moral philosophy of being for that class, but it would not be empiriomonism.

What was the weakness in Bogdanov? Or, more realistically, who was the political enemy? It was Bogdanov's foreign sources of inspiration, the Austrian Richard Avenarius and the Swiss Auguste Mach. For ease of aim Lenin branded them all 'Machists' and dealt with them all together. Mach had called his philosophy empiriocriticism. That fool Bogdanov couldn't see that it left the door open for idealism. Bogdanov, that dolt, that liability to Bolshevism, was blind to 'the class utilization of empiriocriticism by bourgeois reactionaries'.[15] Bogdanov was one of those Russian Marxists like Lunarcharsky who had 'mutinied on his knees' against the epistemological inadequacy of Marxism.[16] The revision, or revisionism (for Lenin turned everything into a factional -ism), pioneered by Bogdanov and other 'blockheads' of his ilk, was completely wrong.[17] You *couldn't* be a Marxist and hold Machist views.

Bogdanov, who qualified as a doctor and returned to the laboratory after Lenin dismissed him from the Party (after the Revolution he was put in charge of an 'Institute for the Struggle for Vital Capacity'), lived his life as a passionate Marxist and Bolshevik. The experiment on his blood which killed him seems to have been in pursuit of a scientific key to Bergsonian vitalism – a typically bizarre Russian project.[18] He is worth studying in relation to Lenin because his genuine aim was not to write a philosophy of social control but one appropriate to the ways of the working man. The result was not one that the working man could read – there was still far too much epistemology and other -ologies in it for that – but one he might be persuaded to believe represented his interests more than Kantian or Hegelian idealism. Bogdanov's empiriomonism was a theory of perception opposed to any metaphysical explanation. It championed Feuerbach's natural man.

Bogdanov was such an ardent positivist that his tendency would have to be called 'scientism' today. In the 1920s he urged the abolition of philosophy altogether in the light of the primacy of the natural sciences.[19] It was his espousal of natural science that made his philosophy sound like the answer to Russia's philosophical dreams. As a 'monism' it sounded like a single vision of the truth, which would hold the country together. At the same time its truths were empirical – the result of experience, not speculation. Empiriomonism *sounded* as if it would provide a scientific basis for social unity, and it *sounded* as if that unity would be natural and uncoerced. As a side benefit of the wave of enthusiasm for positivism in Europe, Bogdanov's invention sounded like a way of discovering Hume for Russia. Its humanity was coarser than anything Hume imagined, but at least it was a stab at a grass-roots culture naturally binding people together. Tacked on to the Marxism that would put paid to tsarism, it was a bid at a good-enough theory to underpin a better practical future for the common man in Russia.

But the problem for which Lenin would never let Bogdanov and the Machists off the hook was that empiriomonism left individuals free to see the world in different ways. In the end, with a theory of perception based on the sensations the world excites *in us*, rather than on our direct apprehension of the world itself, empiriomonism had no need to prove or care whether an objective world existed. According to Lenin, the Machists didn't realize that in that respect what they purveyed was *extreme* idealism.

They thought they were common-or-garden realists, but in fact they were Berkelians, who said things in the world only existed when they were perceived. Or, more modestly described, on one of Lenin's gentler days, they were like Hume, who said that knowledge comes to us through sense impressions, each of us being a bundle of such impressions. Either way, to attribute to the common man a Berkelian freedom to inhabit his own head, or a Humean freedom to live in his own sense-world, was politically unacceptable. As Lenin put it, the Machists thought they represented 'the ordinary, non-philosophical naive view which is entertained by all people who do not trouble themselves as to whether they themselves exist and whether the environment, the external world, exists'. But the Machists were wrong. Their deviation was, as a modern politician still Leninistically moulded might put it, obscene, and they could not be left to exercise influence.[20]

In one of the key sections of *Materialism and Empiriocriticism*, worth reading for its historical import and battering turn of phrase, Lenin battled with Avenarius and Mach over who owned the title to the territory called 'naive realism'. The Machists of course had no claim. Their case was 'sophistry of the cheapest kind'.

> The 'naive realism' of any healthy person who has not been an inmate of a lunatic asylum or a pupil of the idealist philosophers consists in the view that things, the environment, the world, exist *independently* of our sensation, of our consciousness, of our *self* and of man in general.[21]

The emphases in the passage were Lenin's own. Russia's first Marxist-Leninist underscored his simple, single philosophical target. It was to stress that idealist claims to man's mental independence from the world around him were nonsense. What naive realism really meant was that there are men and there is the world, and nothing comes between them and nothing seems strange about our knowledge of how things are because that *is* how things are, and if you can't see that there must be something wrong with you.

> Our sensation, our consciousness is only an *image* of the external world, and it is obvious that an image cannot exist without the thing imaged, and that the latter exists independently of that which images it.[22]

This was Lenin's so-called 'copy theory' of knowledge. It has never been attacked enough.

It meant handing over the human subject, the space we tend to think of as inside us and containing our freedom, to an imagined impersonal process, constructed out of politics, economics and a theory of history. It meant making scepticism a thing of the past. It also meant, and means, denying ethical individualism, because this would need to be based on a perception of moral facts and moral facts can't be in the head of a man who only has a copy-image of 'what is there'. Moral facts don't after all look like anything. In effect Lenin's theory meant denying philosophy. It meant drawing a line under the subject, throwing the classics of sceptical inquiry into some muddy foundation pit on which, eventually, some vast, cheap concrete structure of no architectural or social merit would be erected to house the cheapened pleasures of a mass humanity unworthy of the name. It was a terrible betrayal of mankind, common or otherwise.

Lenin wanted the criterion of truth not to be 'how it strikes me', but 'the view from no one'. He wanted a theory of perception in which the 'I' of the individual mind was completely passive vis-à-vis the world out there, like a camera lens. He wanted a downgraded 'I' and an upgraded objective world, a balance which would afford something like the certainty and containedness of the medieval world. Accidentally, for Lenin was not so learned, his theory was the ultimate rebuttal of Descartes. It aimed to destroy the *cogito* which launched the modern Western world.

The copy theory of knowledge in Lenin's hands was nevertheless, by some mystery we will never be able to fathom, a deeply Russian response to the problems raised by Western modernity and Western philosophy, and Lenin was a Russian thinker, able to tap a rich emotional seam. His copy theory of knowledge ran parallel to the commonest and simplest Russian religious and spiritual response to the alien, questioning, individualistic, disruptive West. Philosophically, Lenin's theory of knowledge wasn't worthy of the name. At best it looked like a crude, scaled-down version of Spinozan rationalism, deprived of Spinoza's refinement and grace. But it was politically useful and it was appropriate, and it spoke for something in the Russian people.

A crucial sentence followed on directly from the definition of the copy theory of knowledge. Lenin penned it with a special emphasis:

Materialism *deliberately* makes the 'naive' belief of mankind the foundation of its theory of knowledge.[23]

Lenin didn't hide anything. He was deliberately simplifying Russia.

The political deliberateness of Lenin's choice should be underlined, along with his sincerity. He had just begun his research for *Materialism and Empiriocriticism* when, on 7 February 1908, he wrote with candour to the writer Maxim Gorky. Gorky was Lenin's sometime partner in philosophical discussion, and had even lured Lenin to the island of Capri, although in the last respect unsuccessfully, to share his cogitations with Russian exiles:

I am not a philosopher. I am badly prepared in this domain. I know that my formulations and definitions are vague, unpolished; I know that philosophers are going to accuse my materialism of being 'metaphysical'. But that is not the question. Not only do I not philosophize with their philosophy. I do not 'philosophize' like them at all. Their way of 'philosophizing' is to expend fortunes of intelligence and subtlety for no other purpose than to *ruminate in* philosophy. Whereas I treat philosophy differently, I *practise* it, as Marx intended, in obedience to what is. That is why I believe I am a 'dialectical materialist'.[24]

Lenin's tone here makes it just about possible to see why so many sensitive and intelligent and literate men and women over the twentieth century might have thought he was right and why they would push aside the suspicion that dialectical materialism was indeed a new form of idealism.

Lenin's friend Lyubov Akselrod explained the empiriomonist controversy by saying that subjective idealism would lead to social conservatism.[25] She made clear that the reason why mental autonomy was politically undesirable for Marxist-Leninism was that it could lead to psychological inwardness and escapism. Lenin found a way of forcing men and women to be what Chernyshevsky and Pisarev (and Hegel before all of them) only hoped they would be, that is active and practical and socially purposeful, not depressive, dissenting, irrational and bored. Psychologically speaking, Marxist-Leninism was a no-nonsense prescription against *anomie.*

The copy theory of knowledge justified treating those who could not see 'reality' as sick. If a person saw things not 'how they are' it could only mean his or her brain was out of order, because that *is* how things are. Hence the terrible justification, in Marxist-Leninist practice, for the Soviet *psikushki,* the psychiatric hospitals where dissidents like Vladimir Bukovsky and Leonid Plyushch were confined and medically tortured.[26] The copy theory of knowledge allowed Lenin to rage against all views of the world that diverged from one fixed picture, and punish all alternative thinkers. It had evil consequences. If you were a post-theodical thinker you might believe it was the work of the *malin génie.* That 'materialism [which] deliberately makes the "naive" belief of mankind the foundation of its theory of knowledge' sealed the intellectual fate of Russia for the next seventy years. Yet it was also terribly understandable. Thought officially became very simple in Soviet Russia because traditional life was chaotic. Philosophy, or a debasement of it, was needed to hold society together, because the real thing was too unreliable.

PART IV

The Long Tradition

11

How the Long Tradition Survived

Lenin turned philosophy into a totalitarian tool by combining an anti-personal realism – the copy theory of knowledge – with materialism and historical subjectivism. These were the main features of the only admissible Bolshevik view of life.[1] The shape of the copy theory of knowledge has already been drawn. Materialism shored it up as a Marxist theory. It meant that all thinking was generated by the material conditions of the thinker. Historical subjectivism described the belief that thought changed as material history changed. When the Bolsheviks became the sole ruling party in 1917, Russia's philosophical fate was frozen in these grooves for the next seventy years. The official philosophy wasn't watertight; a few independent minds managed to express themselves. But politically the idea of an official philosophy was hugely effective. In 1931 the Communist Party of the Soviet Union was declared the final arbiter of philosophical truth. Henceforth philosophers were required to be *parteiny* – party-minded.[2] For the next twenty-two years the Party was Stalin and the compulsory text in philosophy was *A History of the Communist Party of the Soviet Union: Short Course.* Forty pages headed 'Dialectical and Historical Materialism' presented 'the world outlook of the Marxist-Leninist Party'.[3]

In the rigorous 1950s, when Lenin's style of Communism achieved maximum expansion, every student in a Soviet empire of 200 million people, and every student in the newly acquired Soviet satellite countries – Poland, Czechoslovakia, East Germany, Hungary, Romania and Bulgaria – with a combined population of around 110 million, was required to master *diamat*. Students amounted to around 10 per cent of their generation, thus approximately thirty million people; in addition many more needed a smattering of *diamat* to allow them to get by in the workplace. Under mass conditions, official Marxist-Leninist philosophy became ever simpler and ever more ridiculous, though no one at the time dared say so. 'Stalin had dialectical materialism reduced to [a] bare skeleton.'[4] He made philosophy a catechism for students to learn by heart and turned its teachers into ideological placemen. 'The timidity of Soviet philosophers kept them for years monotonously and verbosely repeating those few statements, declining even to add flesh to the bones.'[5] Students of the *Short Course* learned that:

1) the world is by its nature material;
2) matter is primary, an objective reality existing outside and independent of our minds, while mind is secondary, being a reflection of matter;
3) the world and its laws are fully knowable, authentic knowledge being tested by experience and practice.[6]

Only the third of these propositions, concerning the dialectic, was of any philosophical interest. It belonged to Marx rather than Lenin, contained an element of freedom and came close to telling the discerning world that *diamat* was a kind of metaphysics in disguise. After Stalin died, *Fundamentals of Marxist Philosophy* (1958), reworked into a second edition, took over from *A Short Course* to provide a methodological foundation for all enquiry within a Marxist-Leninist society.

The method of dialectical materialism, applicable equally to nature and thought, functioned like the basic truth table used by logicians to determine all possible forms of sound arguments.[7] Values could be read off from it as if from a logarithmic grid. The method entailed the principles of historicism, evolutionism and sociologism – here was a world that, following Lenin's example, loved -isms. Historicism meant that the history of any natural or social thing or event was the condition of its being truly known. Evolutionism, the 'scientific' basis for Soviet optimism, said each thing evolved according to objective laws or principles, from lower to higher, from less perfect to more perfect forms. Sociologism configured history as the interaction ('struggle') of groups ('classes') rather than of individuals.[8]

Stalin modified historical materialism because he needed official Marxist-Leninist theory to correspond with his own practice as General Secretary of the Party. Not only material conditions but also and perhaps predominantly ideas, theories and political institutions were now said to shape Soviet society. *A Short Course* found a way of arguing this as a perfectly legitimate development of Soviet Marxism without denying the material origins of ideas.[9] But the effect was to make theory less of the creative interaction with experience imagined by the young Marx and more rigidly *dirigiste*.

Other areas of Soviet life lacked the privilege to alter *diamat* theory to meet their needs. In particular, the hard sciences struggled against ideological containment. 'In the West the physical sciences are usually considered immune from ideological encroachment. In the Soviet Union dialectical materialism provides a methodological foundation for the sciences. It also makes quasi-scientific assertions (e.g. that the universe is infinite) which must be accepted. Any theory which goes counter to these assertions is rejected not on the basis of experimental data but on the basis that it contradicts diamat, the truth of which is guaranteed by the Party.'[10] The considerable success of Soviet science and technology reflected the fact that in practice they ignored *diamat* wherever they could and that the likes of mathematics could hardly be tampered with.[11]

But collisions between science and ideology were bound to happen and several became notorious. In 1948 the fact that party-mindedness made Einstein's Theory of Relativity unacceptable – Lenin's *Materialism and Empiriocriticism* had denounced it directly – infuriated nuclear physicists instructed to develop atomic energy. Pyotr Kapitsa, internationally renowned and pre-eminent in his field, appealed to Stalin to remove his henchman Lavrenty Beria from chairmanship of the top scientific committee in the land, because Beria knew nothing about science. Relativity had to be an admissible theory if Russia was to build the atom bomb.[12] The ban on Einstein was pragmatically lifted. The same year another eminent nuclear scientist, Andrei Sakharov, who went on to become the most famous dissident of the Soviet century, publicly denounced the bogus agrobiology of Anatoly Lysenko. The theory that genes didn't matter and acquired characteristics could be inherited – laying the foundations for a drive towards supercrops and perhaps even supermen – owed more to Marxist-Leninist evolutionism than to empirical results. Sakharov reminded the Academy of Sciences that 'science remains a keystone of civilization and unwarranted encroachment on its domain is impermissible'.[13]

The Scottish philosopher and sometime Marxist Alasdair MacIntyre wrote in 1968 that Soviet Communism needed Lysenko to encourage belief in better and better Soviet agriculture, just as medieval Catholicism needed miracles. For a fine philosopher it was a regrettable remark to have committed to print, begging the question of Soviet cultural dishonesty.[14] As Chaadaev said in 1831 and endless Soviet examples later showed, the Russian temptation was perennially to handle truth cheaply. For the émigré philosopher Alexandre Koyré in 1922, it was precisely because a critical Cartesian philosophy had never taken root in Russia that such abuse of the truth was possible.[15] Western scholars in the 1960s soberly observed that dialectic materialism was a non-Cartesian methodology.[16]

Nevertheless there was something to understand behind what was not only a Soviet tactic but a longstanding Russian practice of adapting truth to hope, for had not Kireevsky in 1845 and Mikhailovsky in 1869 seen that Russia somehow needed two truths, one logical or technical and one 'integral' for its moral soul? The split truth which Soviet philosophy perpetuated was, at the point of invention, beneficially intended for Russian community. For this reason Soviet pronouncements, which in the West were simply dismissed as lies, were not quite lies for anyone prepared to admit the existence of 'moral' or 'emotional' truth linked to a better world. They were factual lies but they played on a human need – by no means restricted to Russia – for the truth to be emotionally satisfying. Many Western waverers were persuaded against the evidence that Soviet Russia was a decent place because of the heartfelt appeal of its communal social aims and declarations in favour of world peace.

The Russian truth-split not only illuminated the plight of fellow-travellers, it even had valid characteristics. Take a remark of Plekhanov's that might have been uttered by any Marxist or Marxist-Leninist propagandist over the next century: 'bourgeois scientists make sure that their theories are not dangerous to God or to capital'.[17] Plekhanov was pointing out that what we know is often what we choose to know for the sake of our moral or material well-being. In other words, to pay attention is not just a cognitive act. Pioneers of the atom bomb who later renounced their research in the interests of humanity – Robert Oppenheimer in the United States and Sakharov in Soviet Russia – acted on a belief that the fact/value connection could present the scientist with the worst possible dilemma, obliging him to turn his back on his discoveries for the sake of the quality of human life. A radical thinker like Solzhenitsyn would say today that Soviet political power, as it malignly tried to expand its global hold, exploited a traditional tendency in Russian ethics to link facts and values, but that that link was in its own way good.[18] His goal for Russia for many years was ethical socialism. That the potential link between facts and values was politically exploited by Marxism and Leninism does not mean that there is no link. It is a vexed issue which has subtly divided Western philosophers since Hume.[19]

Nevertheless the unscrutinized fact/value conflation was one of the weaknesses which made genuine philosophy in Russia impossible. It followed from the rejection of Descartes and the acceptance of values as facts because those facts were desirable. Sovietism was a form of extreme national subjectivism. What was a grand social vision worth if members of that society had never been schooled in impartial judgement and the integrity of facts? What was a modern society worth if its members could only be followers and loyalists? If Soviet philosophical culture incorporated many traditional Russian moral traits which retrospectively explain how the ideal held together and even had some appeal in the free world, it also showed up how weak that truth-seeking culture was because it didn't produce discriminating cognitive subjects. An interesting comparison could be made with Western Marxist experience, which also did not recognize impartial facts according to its ideology, but whose adherents followed normal humanist schooling, actually lived in free societies and therefore could protest when Party truths proved impossible to accept.

The idea of an absolute Party truth set up a potential conflict with the truths of natural science, but mainly it was felt as a strain on ethics. Communist parties everywhere through the twentieth century were traumatized by occasions when the call for Party loyalty and solidarity to predominate forced them to espouse a particular moral falsehood. Stalin's signing of his wartime pact with Hitler was a case in point, though to my knowledge the Russian experience is not well documented and has to be inferred. Two Western accounts of such a dilemma, one by a philosopher, one by a novelist, throw light on the general problem.

Alasdair MacIntyre, for instance, examined his own ethical dilemma as a Communist Party member, first in 1940, later in 1956 when the Soviet Union invaded Hungary. He judged that where his Communist ethic inclined him willingly to tune into and act upon the needs of the working class, in practice the moral imperative he signed up to was to further the interests of the Party at all costs.[20] He was a kind of Kantian volunteer for the good who had been subtly coerced into a nasty sub-Utilitarianism. He was a seeker (albeit misguided), ready to subordinate himself to the objective laws of history, who in reality was required to be a dumb political servant. The Hungarian-born writer and sometime member of the Moscow-centred international Communist movement, the Comintern, Arthur Koestler, captured the dilemma in his novel *Darkness at Noon* (1940). A 'militant philosopher' who had always believed he understood what the people needed, because he 'worked in the amorphous raw material of history itself'; who accepted that 'subjective guilt or innocence makes no difference', 'the individual is nothing, the Party is all' and that 'the Party can never be mistaken'; found, as he prepared for his own execution, that it was simply not true that 'I', the view from a discriminating someone, was only a 'humanitarian weakness'.[21] The repentant militant philosopher Rubashov acknowledged the harm which he – an active moral agent – had caused to an infinite number of unprotected human souls. Koestler's tone suggested a biblical Day of Judgement taking place in Rubashov's mind.

> Our will was hard and pure, we should have been loved by the people. But they hate us. Why are we so odious and detested? We brought you the truth and in our mouth it sounded a lie. We brought you freedom, and it looks in our hands like a whip. We brought you the living life, and where our voice is heard the trees wither and there is a rustling of dry leaves. We brought you the promise of the future, but our tongue stammered and barked.[22]

The revolutionary mentality, the attempt to justify Party terrorism as the pursuit of truth on behalf of the people, and for their own good, was the end of the road for one strand of Russian philosophy: the strand which linked the building project of reason to the inevitability of history and the willingness of Lavrovian disciples to act for the cause. It was the philosophy of revolutionary action interlaced with traditional anti-individualist communal mysticism and its outcome was two short centuries of intellectual and moral defeat for Russia.

Yet there are aspects of Russia's philosophical heritage which have to be appreciated independently of that defeat. They matter because they gave the grounds for the optimism and self-belief of at least half a century of ethically committed Communists – men and women whose personal ethics were hardly inferior to those of people living in the West, and often superior. They were persuaded by a socialist morality which was a secular version of Christian goodneighbourliness and, at a deeper, not always conscious level, by an argument as to why the world might every day approximate more closely to the utopian goal, if only people were willing.

Before the war, perhaps the majority of Soviet citizens were more or less Communist believers, the dissident Andrei Sinyavsky suggested.[23] The seductive idea, with a solid philosophical history, was that Communist truth might be created. What sounds today like a peculiarly British kind of political joke – being 'creative with the truth', an analogy with 'creative accounting' – was nothing of the kind in Communist-Marxist theory, which could trace its imaginative streak back to Aristotle.

The definition of dialectics said that both the laws of thought and those same laws as they governed objective reality could be analysed into contradictory elements which did not mutually exclude each other, but which made up the true nature of the analysed thing or process.[24] An ideology which encouraged acceptance of contradictions became the butt of more Western jokes, which were entirely justified by common sense but utterly failed to illuminate the Russian mystery for the general Western gaze. Why was a world power ready to deceive itself as to its own reality? The answer lay in a philosophical attitude – in its Soviet incarnation, historical materialism and evolutionism – which made it legitimate to believe in the reality of what was not yet present. This belief was much more complex than a simple commitment to the existence of the supernatural. In fact, it was its opposite. Several specialist Western observers of the Russian philosophical scene in the 1960s commented that they knew no other country in the world so permeated by Hegelianism as the Soviet Union.[25] Exactly Hegel made it possible to believe in the not-yet-real. The Russian Sophia – Wisdom as the Eternal Feminine, as Solvyov imagined her – never loved Hegel in the nineteenth century, but in the twentieth she became his arranged bride. Hegelian dialectic in its original form held out to Russia the romance of change. It offered a glowing vision of what the future could be by capturing thoughts in progress, from the simplest to the most complex. It argued, look, people mature in understanding and become fully fledged adults and this is how societies change too. They get cleverer, take in a wider range of experience, and finally add their wisdom to society which as a result becomes more progressive. Hegel is only difficult to read because of his extreme concentration on the thought process. The distilled result of his philosophy – a kind of happy outcome he forced on himself – is, unfortunately, much simpler.

The dialectical thought process started with a first idea encountering its antithesis, and showed how, out of that creative opposition, a richer third thought emerged. According to Hegel the best elements of contradictory ideas were always carried forward while inferior aspects were cancelled out; nothing good was lost as progress followed its course. The worst aspects of the past were thrown out, the best gained life in a new and higher form. Such was the process of *Aufhebung* – a term no single translation into English can account for. Somehow the very abstractness sticks in the English craw. Carlyle might have made a joke out of it in *Sartor Resartus*.[26] But because of the need for social construction the idea of a single principle of progress was hugely attractive in Russia. If Hegel said it was a rational principle so much the better. He had a twentieth-century audience captive.

What needed to be grasped about the philosophy of change, however much rationality Hegel and Marx attributed to it, was of course that it wasn't rational at all. Its origins were as mystical as any vision of the good life Russia could derive from its own Christian tradition – one reason why Hegelian hopes fitted so well with the Russian psyche. Hegel translated Christian hope for man's reconciliation with God into a miraculous mechanism for human progress. The Christian idea was that God had given the world his Son, Jesus Christ, so that men could understand the nature of God. The separateness of the ideal and the real was transcended in the Resurrection, when the real man in Christ was raised to the level of the ideal Son of God. The Christian story was the ultimate story of change: change as transfiguration, and as a miracle. How else could earth become heaven but by some process akin to the transubstantiation of bread and wine? A rationalist would call it a belief in magic; a Christian, supported by the vast and persuasive body of Western art, and two thousand years of moral aspiration, would refer to the power of faith.

Hölderlin, creator of poetry of unparalleled beauty in that longest of Western traditions, knew where his fellow seminarist and young philosopher Hegel was aiming. The Hegelian dialectic incorporated the Christian answer to the possibility of an upraised and transformed human life. That Christ had existed as at once the Son of God and the Son of Man made Hegel's idea of progress possible. The origins of ideas do not determine their nature, but in the Russian case they point to their double, their emotional shadow, the continuing religious hope affecting their aura. They show how dialectical materialism was essentially a philosophy of hope with religious ingredients which could readily build on the emotional-communal tradition.

The immediate consequence of the dialectic's underlying spiritual nature was that the concept – the tool of rational human understanding – was deemed only to represent a passing, incomplete stage of truth. The presently valid concept was only one aspect of reality in the making. To a Hegelian, therefore, reality was always poised to become something other than it seemed, although how it seemed was part of the truth.

Hegelian philosophy was about concepts on the move. It tried to catch the moment between their first speculative formulation and their pending redundancy. What is the value of a concept when reality has already moved on? The only ultimate truth is the process of change. A Western historian of philosophy who immersed himself in Soviet ways in the mid-1960s finally threw up his hands and cried: 'I defy the Soviets to show me a fluid concept!'[27] But that was exactly what Hegel and Soviet philosophy thought they could do. In a dialectical materialist world no concept was supposed to be fixed: theory was constantly modified by new practice and further thought. The result ought not to have been totalitarian at all because knowledge was continually in the process of being tested by experience. Marxist-Leninism was infinitely experimental. Communism necessarily resisted definition because it was a future condition.[28] A Derridean post-structuralist – essentially a post-Marxist – would say that the definition of truth was indefinitely deferred.[29]

German Romantic religious philosophy, in the way that it was based on open-ended human creativity – and even, one might say, an open-armed response to God – was a kind of dream that humanity might never make a conceptual mistake it could not undo. The dream was misplaced because the consequences of concepts applied to real life and real people could not be readily undone. As the tragic twentieth century showed, they had horrific consequences.[30] But something like the opposite was intended in this, one of the key sources of totalitarianism. This source was not authoritarian. It rather entailed subordinating reason to the needs of the heart – the kind of needs, Kant would say in his *Critique of Aesthetic Judgement*, which meant that the human mind searches for unity and harmony in everything it touches upon, and often misguidedly imagines that what exists in art also exists in nature and society.

The strain of philosophy which German Romanticism and later Russian *diamat* drew on, in this aspect much older than Hegel, was of a special creative tension between matter and ideas. Hylomorphism was a theory, argued by Aristotle and Spinoza, detested by Kant, revived by

Goethe and Schelling, that matter had the same innate properties as mind. Hylomorphism – from the Greek *hule*, meaning matter and *morphe*, form – said mind and matter were of the same substance, with a constant active interplay between them. A lump of clay was predisposed to become the sculpture into which the artist moulded it. The clay had a kind of formal yearning within it to take a superior shape. Its material truth was the story of the potential for form it contained. Soviet philosophy was still alive when it was arguing about the relevance of Spinoza to dialectical materialism, roughly during the years 1925–32.[31] Russian interest in Spinoza stretched from the *lyubomudry* to Frank, who published his critical views on Spinoza just before the Revolution.[32] Plekhanov named Spinoza as his favourite philosopher.[33] Lunacharsky wrote a book called *From Spinoza to Marx* just after the Revolution, when philosophy made a fresh start. The year of publication was 1926. About the same time Abram Deborin (1881–1963) reaffirmed Spinoza's relevance for the new materialist century by calling him 'Marx without a beard'.[34] Spinoza, as no other philosopher, understood the potential of matter and its relation to perfection.

A powerful and controversial figure, Deborin immediately split Soviet Russia's neo-Spinozans into, in effect, open-ended Romantics set against precise rationalists.[35] The Deborinites insisted on man's freedom to make his world and his values out of given material conditions. The mechanicists – the philosophers Alexander Bogdanov and Lyubov Akselrod and the Bolshevik author of *The ABC of Communism* Nikolai Bukharin – preferred the supremacy of the natural sciences. Soviet history presented the issue in a typical Leninist way, as if it were a clash of political factions. Today it seems to have been a battle for a degree of intellectual freedom – though taking the mechanicist side one might feel that common sense in Russia would have been a more promising value than the intellectual freedom to go terribly wrong.[36]

The battle took place in 1929 when Soviet philosophy revisited the development of Idealist philosophy after Feuerbach succeeded Hegel.

The Deborinites argued rightly that philosophy was a superior instrument in Hegel's hands and should remain the science of the sciences. But by 1931 they had lost their authority, having been branded 'too abstract'. *Diamat* was set to become more 'scientific-mechanicist' and less 'creative-Deborinite'. But that was just the problem. It wasn't genuine science that the mechanicists were in a position to defend for the Russian future. It was the Romantic kind, which only meant something if it was kept open and creative. In effect, both imagination and science lost the battle, and totalitarianism stepped in, making use of these ingredients where it was so inclined. The battle was lost as Stalin met no resistance when he insisted ideas rather than immediate material conditions shaped Soviet reality. These combined moves ensured that any remaining openness to experience disappeared from the Soviet philosophical scene. Science became a form of philosophical bluffing – the greatest hoax of the twentieth century. A 'command metaphysics' took the place of a metaphysics of creativity. Command metaphysics – my term – meant that reality could be summoned into being. If ever fluid concepts were operational – and perhaps they did reside at least in the minds of designers of society who saw themselves as, in Goethe's sense, 'active sceptics' – this was the moment when fluidity became petrified and the sceptics were annihilated. All through the Russian nineteenth century, the impulses to creative anarchy on the one hand and social construction on the other had fought for the higher ground. Now the romantic-anarchists were utterly vanquished.

Not that it would take a Stalin to crush the delicate and tentative hope enshrined in 'the fluid concept' or its reincarnation in Derrida's 1970s notion of *différance*.[37] Tentativeness is surely an improbable way to build a society and maintain a state. But more than that the comings and goings of human intellect in search of pollination are mostly crude. All intellectual and artistic finesse – and it can't be over-emphasized how much the dialectic was originally a poetic imagining – gets simplified as it passes through successive minds.[38] Normative tendencies are universally at work in human understanding. Only Romantics like Marx and Abram Deborin and Derrida believe they can master a process out of human control.

Russia as a whole in fact did retain its fundamental interest in the Romantic philosophy of creativity because the religious idealism of Berdyaev and Frank and others perpetuated it almost in its original spiritual form. The yearning for an interactive spiritual reality linking man and God, the real and the ideal, was anathema to Lenin and seemed naive to rationalist outside observers like Isaiah Berlin, but it was the other side of the Russian twentieth-century phenomenon – its complement – worth taking seriously for that reason alone. The religious philosophers were the Romantics and the anarchists who had to be banished for their fondness for 'openness'. They too represented no way to build a modern state. But intellectually their function in Russia was vital. In partnership with the constructionists, the anarchists gave Russia its one native form, in the culture and thus in the politics, of checks and balances.

During the long philosophical ice age a few Soviet historians of ideas were in fact aware of the greater philosophical tradition in Russia. They knew it had split into conflicting extreme dialectical materialist and religious doctrines and that the religious-anarchic-creative form had been pushed beneath the surface of permissible Russian life. Discreetly they tried to keep something closer to the creative-spiritual version alive or not entirely lost from distant sight.

The following story is my own observation of a concealed commentary on the German Idealist origins of official Soviet philosophy – a commentary which dared to express itself in the 1960s. The springboard period 1961–4 was a time of relative political relaxation in the Soviet Union, which made the idea of criticizing 'the system' possible after a long period of terrified silence. The incumbent Communist Party General Secretary Nikita Khrushchov, trying to rid the country of the legacy of Stalin, seemed almost to encourage freer speech. The third thaw, as Russians came to know it, was signalled to the world by the publication, in 1962, of Solzhenitsyn's *One Day in the Life of Ivan Denisovich*. That novel, set in a prison camp, appeared in *Novy Mir*, the most prestigious literary journal, which gave it an implicit seal of Party approval (although this would be disputed by functionaries later held to blame). *Ivan Denisovich* made 'the point not only that the inmates of Soviet prison camps were for the most part innocent of any crime, but also that official Soviet policies contradicted the innate moral sense of an honest Russian man or woman.'[39] Solzhenitsyn's novel spoke up for Soviet reality against theory, and common sense against ideological norms.

Imagine then that a similar window of opportunity presented itself, all too briefly, in philosophy. A subject rich in possibility for coded critical comment on the Soviet status quo was 'philosophical aesthetics', first named as a legitimate Soviet area of inquiry in 1962 by Valentin Asmus (1894–1975). Asmus called himself a 'professor and a philosophical writer'. He taught at the Moscow State University and was much loved for the courses he gave to students out at his Moscow countryside home in the writers' colony of Peredelkino. 'One of the last carriers in Russia of the native philosophical tradition, he relied in his pedagogical activity on the experience gathered when he was a student.'[40] His early enthusiasms included Spinoza, Schopenhauer, the neo-Kantian Wilhelm Windelband and, surprisingly but instructively, Descartes and the Cartesians. In Peredelkino, where his students in the 1960s and 1970s could fix their eyes on reminders of Pasternak on the walls, the course Asmus delivered was on Kant. Kant was the subject of his last book before his death, published in 1973.

The symbolism of those Peredelkino occasions embraced what Asmus stood for in philosophy and no doubt as a man. The writer and poet Boris Pasternak, born in 1890, had died in 1960. He and Asmus were of the same philosophical generation, they were neighbours and they shared many interests. Pasternak had studied neo-Kantianism in Marburg and was also deeply immersed in the Symbolist poetry and the philosophies of culture of the Russian Silver Age which grew out of the ideas of

Solovyov.[41] *Doctor Zhivago*, written in the 1930s and published abroad in 1957, was nominally a novel about how a Russian beautiful soul endured the Revolution, the civil war and the Sovietization of his beloved country. In truth it was a kind of poetic-philosophical odyssey, a spiritual *Bildungsroman*, about how Yury Zhivago became the man he was through the inspiration of his uncle, Nikolai Vedenyapin, a fictional historian-philosopher of Solovyov's generation. Zhivago believed in the integrity of truth preserved in the symbolic realm of culture.[42] He was formed by the same turn-of-the-century German ideas which would give rise to the career of Ernst Cassirer and *The Philosophy of Symbolic Forms* (1923–31). Cassirer grounded his thought in a study of *Kant's Life and Thought* (1918). Pasternak thus created two generations of fictional thinkers who were educated along the same neo-Kantian German lines as Asmus and himself.

For Pasternak-Zhivago, however, the greatest cultural symbolism and the source of any genuine Russian philosophy was the story of Christ. Like Alexander Blok in his famous revolutionary poem 'The Twelve', through Yury Zhivago Pasternak measured 1917 in apocalyptic-religious terms. The resulting vision soared above the tawdry reality of Bolshevism and remained there as an eternal poetic moment. When *Doctor Zhivago* was finally published – and became the inspiration for Pasternak's 1958 Nobel Prize – Pasternak was ostracized by the Soviet establishment. His spirit was alien and, worse, he had published in the West and made his easily offended country lose face. His life was made deeply unpleasant for these reasons and he died not long after. His Peredelkino funeral was famous for the betrayal of his memory by yet another German-educated, Russian writer, Konstantin Fedin (1892–1971), who, unlike Pasternak, succumbed to official pressure and mislaid his early talent. At Pasternak's grave Asmus on the other hand not only paid him open tribute but daringly included in his speech mention of 'the great' Solovyov. In words not quite spoken, but which would be understood by a few minds still carrying the torch, Pasternak perpetuated the Romantic-ethical tradition of Solovyov.[43]

In contrast to official philosophy, which in the words of a contemporary Russian commentator was 'more like a lobal attack than serious and deep analysis', Asmus spoke at Pasternak's graveside of Solovyov's 'exclusively moral purity and his moral charm'.[44] Such words in the Russian tradition could only mean that Solovyov was a beautiful soul with a ready place for him – and anyone like him – reserved in the Russian heart. Pasternak and Asmus and a handful of others continued to keep alive and to defend the Romantic idealist tradition in its personal aspect where they could.

That Asmus had studied with its last representatives on Russian soil shaped his life. He heard lectures by Vasily Zenkovsky (1881–1962), who left Soviet Russia to become a leading religious figure and historian of Russian philosophy in emigration.[45] The young Asmus also read the work of Father Pavel Florensky, who published his most influential work, *The Pillar and the Ground of Truth*, in 1914. In touch with the best of the Silver Age, Asmus also eagerly devoured the output of the idealist publishing house *Put'*, which in the short time fate allotted to its existence between revolution and extinction published Berdyaev, Bulgakov, Kireevsky, Chaadaev and others.

Asmus's first published work, in 1924, was a contribution to the still live debate on dialectical method. Perhaps the bravest thing he did was to write a whole book on Solovyov, in 1940, three years after Florensky and Shpet were shot by the NKVD, Stalin's political police. During the war, and with the destruction of spiritual Russia around him, with the horror of Stalin and the camps, a Russian humanist scholar consoled himself by studying Russia's greatest beautiful soul, even though his book could never be published. It appeared for the first time in print in 1994, when the Soviet era was over.

One of Asmus's students, Yury Mann, took up the Romantic idealist torch in the 1960s by continuing a less overtly subversive line of thought, but one which was bound to enrich specialist Soviet readers who still possessed a grain of independence. Without fanfare, *Russian Philosophical*

Aesthetics, published in Moscow in 1969, reopened the story of dialectical materialism by going back to its German and Russian Romantic origins. The subject legitimated talking of Schelling and Schellingists and of Russian beautiful souls like Venevitinov and the great Hegelian Stankevich, and the *lyubomudrets* Odoevsky and others. Mann rendered his due to Caesar by acknowledging that the methods and values he was discussing were *not* those of the Soviet world, indeed quite the reverse, for Soviet philosophy was materialist, was it not, and as Engels put it, 'German Idealism was materialism stood on its head'.[46] The habit was called quotationism by those who despaired of it but had no choice but to toe the line.[47] Mann paid the obligatory tribute incumbent on all writers in the Communist world by citing one or all of Marx, Engels and Lenin, whatever their subject.[48] Meanwhile intelligent Soviet readers could not fail to ask themselves: what exactly did it mean to stand Idealism on its head? As Mann evoked a philosophy linking the ideal and the real, and talked of the wholeness of 'the system' and its ability to deliver a complete account of life and the universe, was he not bound to set off a certain train of thought? Readers would think: surely this is the philosophy by which we still live? Or some corrupted version of it? In which case the outcome ought to have been different.

Mann surveyed how the German Romantics had passed on their key idea to the founding fathers of Russian philosophy. He named and investigated Chaadaev's editor Nadezhdin, Venevitinov, Kireevsky, Odoevsky, Stankevich and the critic Shevyryov, all of whom suddenly entered a picture normally reserved for revolutionary history. Shevyryov's Romantic aesthetics, which influenced Belinsky, gave Mann a special chance to highlight the origins of dialectical method in a poetic vision of truth. Shevyryov stressed that practice should precede theory, that action should precede knowledge. Having taken this idea over from the Germans, Shevyryov wanted to develop it into a theory appropriate for Russia.[49]

As of 1969 what exactly did Mann want to say about this German heritage in present-day Russia? Quietly, that it had provoked not one but two core responses in Russian culture. There had been two strains of Russian response: the first creative and open-ended, the second, 'alas', a hunger for utopia. In suitably convoluted terms that would keep unwanted critics off his trail, the true disciple of Asmus, a second scholar-philosopher in hiding, described

> a tendency in which social criticism mostly took the form of 'antisystematism' (both scientific and social) while an irrepressible fullness and vitality of elements, whether they were facts in a scientific theory or people in the community, was advanced in the guise of an unknown quantity or, alas, a utopian ideal.[50]

Mann's unmitigated criticism of what Soviet official philosophy had made of the ideas it inherited from German Idealism hung on that tiny word 'alas'. Soviet Russia had failed to keep the dialectic open. It had banished the 'irrepressible' anarchic elements so deeply embedded in Russian thought, and rejected the testimony of everyday experience, in order to adhere to a utopian ideal. It was in its way a true u-topia, a non-place.

In the early 1960s the Ukrainian-born future dissident Leonid Plyushch was also reading, teaching and discussing philosophy in Moscow, Kiev and Kharkiv. His way back to the days before Russian philosophy had solidified came, as it also did in the contemporary West of the 'New Left', with a passion for reading the newly discovered 'young' Marx of the 1843–4 Paris Manuscripts.[51] Marx's still vital response to Hegel contained crucial remarks on alienation. Alienation suggested factors of mental origin making the world an unhappy place to live in – a poor home for the spirit. The idea had a peculiarly powerful effect in the repressed and alienated post-Stalinist east. Unlike Asmus, Plyushch was not a Romantic idealist. He regarded himself as an unconstrained materialist. But what he learned from the young, still Romantic Marx put him in touch with a deep-rooted Russian anarchistic rebellion against the inert rational concept. In turn he realized what Soviet life had become and wanted to evoke a kind of common sense to defend it against the horrific effects of whoever and whatever had put ideas in charge. 'I learned that everything created by man has a tendency to escape his control and to become alien and hostile to him ... ideas, labour, products of labour, as well as organization and the state.'[52] Teaching in Moscow in 1966 Plyushch noticed: 'In philosophy, treatises on alienation were sprouting like mushrooms after rain. At first the philosophers argued that they were studying the young Marx before he became a Marxist ...'[53] Three years later Plyushch and friends were still discussing the young Marx and 'ethical problems and the meaning of life'.[54] Briefly the philosophical critics of Sovietism had found a pretext to express themselves.

But time was running out for these not quite – or not yet fully declared – Soviet heretics. Yury Mann published his book just in time in 1969, which was the same year Solzhenitsyn was expelled from the Writers' Union. Khrushchov had been ousted in 1964. A year before Mann's book, in 1968, one of the crucial years for the Communist world, a philosopher of ethics had published a paper suggesting, as Plekhanov and Bernstein had done sixty years earlier, that Marxist morality was an insufficient guide to the good life, and needed to be supplemented by the ethics of Kant. The venture was a quiet invitation to Russians, or a plea to their rulers, that they be allowed to think for themselves; and also that their politics should not be aggressive. The timing of the article coincided with the Prague Spring of reform Communism in Czechoslovakia, one of the more intellectually agile Soviet satellite cultures. But a higher Kantian law applicable at all times to all men and which would draw attention to the quality of moral motives rather than useful results was more than Soviet officialdom could tolerate. A special Union-wide congress of philosophers was hastily called in Moscow in February 1968 and the Kantian argument of Iakor Abramovich Mil'ner Irinen was forcibly committed to the dustbin of history.[55] (A Kantian moral outlook would of course have challenged the 'utility' of a Soviet invasion of Czechoslovakia which took place in August that year.)

By 1970 Soviet life under Leonid Brezhnev was poised to enter a new period of conservative and punitive stagnation. Plyushch's friend Oleg Bakhtiarov was tried in February 1970 for possessing copies of unacceptable works like Berdyaev's *The Origins of Russian Communism* and sent to prison for three years.[56] Plyushch himself would be arrested in 1972 and horribly mistreated in a mental hospital – a *psikushka* – for more than three years before mounting Western pressure helped to get him and his family released abroad. The sentence on him was absolutely consistent with Lenin's copy theory of knowledge: what is true is true and if you can't see it there must be something wrong with you. Quietly, meanwhile, the study of how German Romantic philosophy impacted on nineteenth-century Russia was restored to the ideological straight and narrow in two crushingly conformist volumes of *Russian Aesthetic Treatises of the First Third of the Nineteenth Century*, published in 1974 by Z. A. Kamensky. Dialectical materialism was fully recovered as a command metaphysic and the Party was in charge of ethics. Potentially life-giving thoughts were re-frozen in dead forms.

Just one more way in which the older German-Russian Idealist tradition lived on into Soviet times, but was swiftly deprived of any meaning, needs to be mentioned: it lay in the idea of work. In a country which still idealized its peasant communities on the threshold of the twentieth century, both the idea and the reality of work brimmed with nostalgia and hope – and tentatively coalesced with what Marx had to say on labour and the working class.

The idea of work, at once a fact and a value, had a double power in philosophy. It was moral-communal in social practice while in theory it proposed an ingenious modern solution to the old philosophical problem of how mind relates to world, spirit to matter. Hegel – in the end the man without whom Russian philosophy would not exist – had set the precedent by showing how work-in-the-world acted as a bridge between the ideals in men's heads and real social life. In work men were both fully themselves and fully part of universal being.

> Whatever it is that the individual does, and whatever happens to him, that he has done himself, and he *is* that himself. The individual therefore, knowing that in his actual world he can find nothing else but its unity with himself, or only the certainty of himself in the truth of that world, can experience only joy in himself.
>
> In his work he has placed himself altogether in the element of universality, in the quality-less void of being.[57]

Hegel brought to the problem of how the mind can have true knowledge of the world the psychological solution of the satisfaction of work. We know what we work on, because in working on something we make it our own; we make it useful to us. But also work gives us a social identity. In both these functions work counters alienation and recreates nature as a suitable human home. Hegel thus showed how work provided a spiritual home for the individual as well as social glue for society. As men make their material homes in the real present so the ideal truth of a perfect future society becomes possible.

In Russia Pisarev was one of the first philosophers to talk about work. It had an ethical application, because it modified the Romantic ideal of introspection. It was not through private moral self-knowledge but through work that men would realize their full organic potential. In fact, work made people good. Pisarev developed an idea of work as the basis for unselfish moral community. A man who had found his rightful work in the world could not be selfish, Pisarev said, because he did that work out of love and so loved the world.

Relying on the work they love, which is advantageous to them and useful to others, the new men arrange their lives so that their personal interests in no way contradict the real interests of society.[58]

The metaphysical and the empirical qualities of work as a solution to nineteenth-century problems gave it huge appeal to social thinkers, and not only in Russia. The way Pisarev cherished the moral outcome of satisfied labour recalled Ruskin and William Morris in Victorian England and also chimed with Herzen's enthusiasm for the communal peasant workshop or *artel'*. Craftsmanship and vocation supplied a new idea of wholeness. The craftsman and the man doing a job he loved were the latest beautiful souls. Meaningful, unalienated work was the new good in itself. Herzen and Pisarev and, a generation later, Kropotkin, all saw work in the community as the way to prevent the social atomization of modern life.

The beautiful worker rose from the ashes of the beautiful soul and took over his metaphysical task: to bridge the gap between reason and imagination, between fact and value. The beautiful worker stood in worldly terms for a progressive goal, but in his philosophical genesis he was almost a religious figure. Because of the strength of the Russian tradition, and the enthusiasm with which the work ideal was taken over, early Soviet enthusiasm for work and workers, especially as expressed in poetry and the graphic arts, had a visionary quality, and all through the Soviet period the idea, at least, of the sanctity of work, of work as a moral tool, refused to leave the air. Corrupt, bored and inefficient Soviet reality was absurd, but the idea of work was beautiful.

Work was beautiful because it answered that fundamental problem, shared by philosophy and society, of where unity was going to come from to give men ethical standards. How were men with minds going to feel at home in the world of nature and with each other? How could they share values and meanings? In the period when Marxism grew in popularity across Europe, and labour reform was on every radical political agenda, work seemed to be the philosophical panacea. The classical good man was a reflective soul; the new good man was a worker. To be in charge of one's own resources, to apply one's labour to the world and benefit from the result, was true human being which brought with it a hint of the transcendent. Faith in humanity as an ideal entity was possible because work was ultimately meaningful. The impact of practical labour idealism on social history was enormous in terms of campaigns for workers' rights, labour unions and so on, and seemed terribly new. But behind it philosophy was toying with an old, old problem.

The two streams of thought which came together in Russia on the cusp of the twentieth century, one concerned with the actual conditions of the working life, the other with providing a quasi-metaphysical justification of why work was the great solution, were rich and needed no Western supplement. Both affected Tolstoy, who now talked about work in a philosophical context and now personally adopted the way of life of a labourer in the fields. How the peasants on his estate lived at ease with nature impressed him because of his hatred of the self-consciousness and intellectual isolation in his own soul. For an antidote to his feeling of critical divorce from life he looked to monotonous days of faith and toil when he would be one with the suffering mass.

The ethical power of work to discipline a man's soul, to keep his intellect from individualistic Western arrogance, is well known as a strong nineteenth-century Russian motif. For Dostoevsky's characters who longed for delivery from the strain of Western independent-mindedness work was also a solution. For Tolstoy and Dostoevsky faith and work were a double harness into which the potentially errant modern soul should strap itself for the sake of its redemption. As Shatov advised the demonic Stavrogin in *The Devils*:

You are godless because you are the son of the idle rich, the last of the idle rich. You've lost the ability to distinguish between good and evil because you've lost touch with the people of your own country . . . Listen, Stavrogin, find God through labour. That is the essence of everything. Find God or you'll vanish without a trace like a rotten fungus. Find God through labour.

What sort of labour? [asks Stavrogin]

The work of a labourer, a peasant [replies Shatov].[59]

For the great nineteenth-century Russian writers, to work was to be restored to God, or to be able to be good.

The idea of work as the perfect ethical life and the perfection of human knowledge was finally expressed for Russian philosophy by Nikolai Fyodorov that ascetic philosopher who was so admired by Tolstoy and others. His most famous book *The Common Task* was finished in 1902 and published posthumously. It contained a defence of the life of labour that began with an attack on Kant's idea of what linked men universally. Kant's notion of universal humanity was an abstract idea held in the minds of reflective individuals. It did not emanate from the real fraternity of suffering, working people. Indeed, it was not an expression of common human interests at all.

> *The Critique of Practical Reason* knows nothing of a united mankind; it gives no rules for the common action of the whole human race ... It does not know the experience which is had *by all people everywhere and always* ...
>
> The whole negative doubt of the *Critique of Pure Reason* is based upon the presumed inevitability of division among men and the impossibility of their unification in a common task ...
>
> *The Critique of Practical Reason* is also based on the unconscious acknowledgement of the inevitability of division, the vice of division ... Kant ... has transferred the principles of enlightened absolutism to the moral world; it is as if he were making God say: 'Everything for people and nothing through people.'[60]

Fyodorov struck a chord for the working man as philosophy's new source of definition – or perhaps made a definitive mark with his pickaxe would be a more accurate expression – when he insisted that not reason but real people realizing actual projects generated the good. Kant's universal moral law was only a dream. To bring good into the world takes action, and, specifically, it takes physical work to bring all men together. An ethical world must be built with love and sweat, hammer and sickle, not just abstract thought.

In *The Philosophy of Economy* (1912) Sergei Bulgakov, knowingly having studied Marx, tried to infuse the lives of Russian peasants with Solovyovian creativity. Their task, as it was once similarly expressed by John Locke, was to breathe life into the physical world by their creative and transformative labour. On the eve of the Revolution the idea of the good, unalienated society united in manual work was above all a Christian and an ethical vision in Russia. Chekhov's middle-class young women who cried wistfully 'We must work!' showed how far the idea permeated in a general moral form through the levels of society.

Fyodorov was the mystical extremist to Chekhov's sensible doctor. He embodied that anti-intellectual and quasi-anarchic Russian philosophy which was ready to sacrifice all products of mind for the sake of social harmony. Like Lavrov he blamed educated men for Russia's misguided progress, or lack of it. But unlike Lavrov he was ready to wrench control of the common task from those educated softies' bungling hands. Since all through the nineteenth century educated men had failed in the common task, 'the unlearned ... who put work above thought' would now take up the burden. Russians in the tradition of Tolstoy and Dostoevsky and Fyodorov were more in touch with the real labouring life than Marx but at the same time they were mystical in a way Marx would have found utterly alien. For its part the essentially populist Russian tradition differed radically from Marx's incitement of the workers of the Western world to class vengeance and the imposition on them of Party political discipline. But clearly the idea that the working man could rescue the stricken Russian *intelligent* and give him the community he craved would be no hindrance to the growth of Marxist labour ideology in Soviet Russia. The Russian *intelligent* had no reason to be interested in the cohesion of the international proletariat, but Marxism gave him something he could use within Russia to good communal effect.

'A great deal of Marxist-Leninism's appeal is moral . . . this was often lost or submerged in the writings of Lenin and Stalin.'[61] Certainly it was. The moral appeal – and even the Christian nature – of the Soviet Union was usually felt by Western visitors in inverse proportion to their dislike of official ideology and their subliminal sense of what lay beneath it. Some of this moral value lay in the natural sense of egalitarianism and community which was visible at its best. As I have tried to suggest, it was partly that the undying Romantic idealism of the country's philosophical history did somehow shine through the deadened forms of official materialism. But also the strict Russian moral code tacked on to the Marxist-Leninist theory of knowledge created an authoritarian world with an edge of moral quality. The official texts of the late 1950s and early 1960s drew on classic Russian anti-individualism and selflessness to define the Communist ethic. 'Bourgeois morality is characterized by the principle of individualism and egoism; proletarian or Communist morality by devotion to communism, collectivism and mutual help.'[62] Good Communists were exhorted to purge society and their own lives of 'the remnants of capitalism: lust, covetousness, greed, envy, anger, sloth and the desire for possessions or honours'.[63] *Bourgeois Morality – A Tool of Imperialist Reaction* (1951), *Questions of Marxist-Leninist Ethics* (1960) and *Fundamentals of Marxist Ethics* (1961) – all by the Party philosopher Alexander Fyodorovich Shishkin – enshrined the Russian sense of moral superiority over a morally debilitated West. The positive desire for Russia to be a non-Western 'otherland' was most acutely felt in the moral sphere both by its own people and by discerning visitors.

The Communist ethic combined socialist cooperation with Marxist class solidarity, and ancient Russian fondness for community with the newer Russian dislike of Western Utilitarianism. The Kantian Kingdom of Ends, which stated that no man should treat another as a means, found a natural home. Marx hijacked a true ethical ideal to justify the utterly false one underlying his invention of the class war. It was the most absurd claim of Marxism that the working class was by definition the class which did not exploit any other and therefore proletarian morality was the best in the world. Many Soviet Russians would have admired the principle of non-exploitation if only because it expressed an idea of goodness. They were happiest with their Kantianism neat. No other modern civilization seems to have produced so many volunteers for the moral life, though the forms that voluntarism took under pressure could become perverse.[64]

The strength of the shared moral life compensated to a degree impossible to measure for the factual falsehoods embedded in Soviet ideology. It created a world which it was possible to understand and be proud of as a true ethical alternative to the Utilitarian West. The moral culture also compensated for the depleted material culture. Old Orthodox habits perhaps, but generally a sense of non-materialistic moral priority encouraged acceptance of physical hardship. The Soviet Union was a congregation of millions singing the self-confirming *doleo, ergo sumus* – 'I suffer, therefore we are'. Of course, not all sang the same tune and not all non-materialists with high ethical priorities were slaves to collective masochism. Meanwhile, as the century progressed consumerist habits grew. Embourgeoisement was only retarded in ethical Russia; it wasn't prevented. But these are ideal tendencies, which help to understand the Soviet phenomenon and the ideas behind it.[65]

Berdyaev characterized the Communist world as 'asceticism without grace'.[66] It harnessed the ethical resources of a population of Christians, Kantians and simple peasant communities for a worldly political end. Because of Communist self-belief it was all the more horrific to hear that the West was a threat to world peace and, for those without the information to counter the official line, one more reason why Russia should be the good society.

Soviet practice institutionalized and not quite destroyed the old Russian habits of voluntarism and Populism. It introduced the 'voluntary' extra day of labour, the *subbotnik*. It called on the people's unfettered and selfless desire to build socialism and made it ideologically compulsory. Meanwhile the Populist teachers of the nineteenth century became the political commissars of the twentieth – the *politruki* in the armed forces and the Party advisers in every workplace. Their job was to help the mass of people understand the Soviet Communist way.[67] Teachers were assimilated to the Populist tradition with a special authoritarian twist. Following on from the admirable habits of nineteenth-century students to go out to remote villages and even to give up their own education, the Party learned to send any independent-minded graduates with potentially disruptive political ideas to as faraway communities as possible, where their ambitions could come to nought. Another form of institutionaliza-tion of nineteenth-century habits of course happened in literature and to a less obvious extent in all the arts. The Russian tendency, first set out as principles for literature by Belinsky, was to conceive of art as socially useful. With Chernyshevsky's simple aesthetics to build on, and some reduced Hegelian theory about the tension between the ideal and the real through Plekhanov, the Soviet doctrine of socialist realism was made. Agitprop was a short-lived avant-garde phenomenon which combined the Populist desire to teach with an almost dionysian desire to celebrate shared truth in the streets. The element of genuine novelty – and stronger connections to Nietzsche and Wagner than to Chernyshevsky and Plekhanov – ensured it couldn't survive as a Soviet cultural practice.[68]

For most of its duration the Soviet Union was regarded as an experiment projected at a possible human future. But it was a drastic attempt to retard moral modernity. The difficulty most modern minds would have in accepting it was that Communist ethical code, whatever its intrinsic appeal, was devalued because it was simultaneously used as the means of primitive political-ideological control. Arguably it had to be, because Russia needed to be 'constructed'. It needed to be made coherent. Ethics had to stand in for tradition and create a powerful moral law requiring people to supervise each other. But the degree of coercion was unacceptable.

The extent to which the authoritarian world was anti-modern can be seen by comparing it with what the autocracy wanted to retain for Russia despite the French Revolution. One has the sense of a Russian twentieth century institutionalizing the ideals of Lammenais-Odoevsky: strict moral faith, rejection of the free market and rejection of selfish individual freedom. As an ideal place Soviet Russia was as Hegel imagined the world to have been before criticism began, which for him meant before the French Revolution took place. Hegel saw that a certain idyll – which he set back in Homeric Greece! – was bound to collapse in the free modern world, unless it was unnaturally defended. What he saw has been neatly paraphrased by one of his best political interpreters:

> [Hegel's] people of the Heroic Age have the spontaneous inner integrity of a whole people. Collectively these citizens are an individual people, and a whole which acts freely. The situation cannot endure. The inner harmony of such a people is unreflective and that is its great defect.[69]

But that also was the Soviet foible – it dared not reflect on the nature of its harmony. When Khomiakov and Kireevsky read Hegel they decided to resist, to hold on to the idyll, to buy 'naivety' for their country at the price of modernity, and Sovietism took that habit of naive community over as a totalitarian institution. All cultural input was scrutinized for the potential harm it might do to social harmony. The result was, at last, the emergence in Russia of a single educated and egalitarian society, uniting both workers and *intelligenty*. A likemindedness was achieved – and happiness for many, it must be said, and social order – but at what price?

The cost of its social unity and order is something Russians still have to come to terms with, in their past and in the present day.

A Russian psychological-philosophical habit which would need to be studied by those who lived it, but probably never will be in that country, was the way in which Communism was unreflectively believed in – almost with deliberately closed eyes, not because it was economically successful, not because it was just, not because it never told lies nor imprisoned, murdered and otherwise wasted human beings, since the opposite of all those things was true, but because it provided the long sought-after Russian foundation of moral being. Odoevsky's *Russian Nights* of 1844 contained the proposition that 'whether one begins from a true or stupid position, a stupid one can steer a beautiful and correct path'.[70] The habit predated Sovietism and as late as 1990 an American sociologist found Russians who accepted their lives had been based, à la Pascal, on 'a beautiful error'.[71] When he was a student the future dissident Andrei Sinyavsky approached a much older friend, a Party member, with his worry that the authorities were torturing political prisoners in order to extract confessions of guilt. 'Fortunately he wasn't an informer. But his utterly sincere response, not prompted by fear, was this: "Don't talk to me about any torture. Even if this is true I don't want to know about it. Because I want to believe, I have to have faith." '[72] In 1991, more than forty years later, the last Soviet leader Mikhail Gorbachov told an interviewer that 'I do not merely believe in socialism. It is my knowledge, it is my thinking.'[73]

Gorbachov's words were particularly interesting because they made clear that the idea of 'belief' alone was not enough to convey what Soviet Communism embraced. There had to be a sense in which belief was not optional even though it was personal. Gorbachov repeated three times that the truth was 'his'. What he conveyed was a world-view which combined voluntary commitment with factual certainty. He felt his commitment to what was true and at the same time he knew without doubt how the world was. This was exactly how Soviet truth was taught as philosophy: Communism was the inevitable outcome of history and at the same time only what any good person would freely choose.[74] In two short sentences Gorbachov told the outside world – an uncomprehending world, it must be assumed – what it was like to have a mind and a heart shaped by the dialectic. The collapse of that Soviet way of life at the end of 1991 was as deeply shocking to the Russians who had lived it as the French Revolution was in Paris in 1789. Not only did they lose all their certainties but at last the real modern revolution was allowed to happen. Russia was exposed to the unlimited pursuit of individual freedom and the free market of Adam Smith and a different kind of logic.

Soviet Marxism, Gorbachov's type of belief, was never a form of rationalism. It was an existentialism in disguise. It required the kind of Pascalian leap of faith which Kierkegaard and Heidegger and Sartre had also demanded in philosophy, if the modern world was to have moral meaning. The Soviet world gave existentialism a totalitarian framework. Because this was Russia, a spiritual place with a long Pascalian tradition, a place with Pascal as its only real philosopher, it was almost as if the Russians were primed psychologically to take a chance on Communism. It was, if you like, an institutionalized form of existentialism on behalf of an existent country desperately seeking to create its collective essence. Jean-Paul Sartre told a discussant after the first delivery of his lecture 'Existentialism and Humanism' in 1946: 'For us the real problem is to define conditions in which there can be universality.'[75] Seven years earlier, at the start of the war which created his moral outlook, he told Simone de Beauvoir that to be 'authentic' was to live with a conscious, active attitude towards one's historical situation. 'I considered it as my fate, understood that in choosing to be of this era I was choosing myself for this war.'[76] He put the existentialist dilemma in terms any traditional Russian *intelligent* could sympathize with when he claimed that shared objective knowledge – the truths of science and everyday facts – was not the problem. What men needed was a shared feeling for truth. Sartre claimed that existentialists created their values freely – because they were free individuals – but that their choices were not arbitrary because their thought proceeded from their being and their being was from the outset social. 'Man finds himself in an organized situation in which he is himself involved; his choice involves mankind in its entirety, and he cannot avoid choosing.'[77]

The existentialist attitude, proceeding from the primacy of social reality, was evidently in conflict with Sartre's election of Descartes as the guardian of the primary personal freedom of each of us to live in our own heads. Since Sartre worked in a free country his critics pointed this out. Nevertheless, once the emergency of the war was over, existentialism was the philosophy he wanted to espouse. Embedded in the eighteenth-century Counter-Enlightenment, it had been refreshed in the nineteenth century when Kierkegaard and Nietzsche – and also Feuerbach – thundered against the tyranny of the Hegelian concept and insisted on the subject's responsibility to create meaning.[78] In the twentieth century this counter-rational tradition split into two branches, though few of us were aware of it at the time. While the West talked passionately about existentialism – roughly from 1945 to 1965 – Russia put existentialism into totalitarian practice in the East.

In the Counter-Enlightenment the gist of existentialism was contained in Vico's idea of the *verum factum* – that man can know completely and with certainty only what he has fashioned himself. Goethe eloquently upheld existentialist practice when he explained that 'theory and experience/the phenomenon stand opposite each other in constant conflict, all unity in reflection is an illusion [and] they can only be united in an active dealing with the world'.[79] The Soviet secular form of existentialism coexisted with the suppressed religious form of Berdyaev's.[80] But what if, despite Vico and Goethe, Berdyaev and Sartre, Russia was the most unsuitable culture in the world for existentialism to become the official philosophy in disguise? What if, despite the good will of subjects ready to take the leap and convert existence to essence, there was no social world for the individual to join with? What if the existential 'I' – looking for conditions in which there might be universality, interested in leading the authentic life – was actually in a position where he had no chance of succeeding? Dostoevsky had seen the nightmare possibility already in his own pre-Soviet day, and in the worst Soviet times it is surely true to say that genuine society almost vanished. The weight of a punitively enforced official truth almost crushed subjectivity and the possibility of value at all out of existence. These questions and this experience produced a single truly alternative philosophy in twentieth-century Russia, at once a comment on what had happened and a rediscovery of Russian anarchism as the way out.

Mikhail Bakhtin (1895–1975) took up the challenge to show what became of the creative subject under totalitarian political pressure. Along with an inevitable and invaluable portrait of the meaning of life under Stalin, he developed a theory of residual individuality in the kind of eclipsed humanitarian world Sartre could not begin to imagine. Bakhtin theorized a unique ethical experience of repression which he also lived through himself.

A man who shared the same neo-Kantian background as Pasternak and Asmus, but who only ever studied in Russia, Bakhtin published his first book, *Problems of Dostoevsky's Art*, in 1929. He learned his neo-Kantianism from his friends who had studied in Germany, while Lossky and Lossky's colleague, the university Kantian Vvedensky, versed Bakhtin in the native Russian tradition.[81] The Dostoevsky book, and perhaps also the fact that his brother Nikolai had fought on the White side in the civil war and emigrated to England, got Bakhtin into immediate political difficulties when Stalin took Russia in his grip. Already in 1929 he was sentenced to five years in a labour camp in Mordovia.[82] But due to ill-health he only served out that period in exile in Kazakhstan and thereafter was only allowed to work at the Pedagogical Institute, later University, in the Mordovian town of Saransk. He remained at the university as a literary theorist and historian until 1961 – when again ill-health caused him to resign – and stayed in Saransk for almost the rest of his life. One way or another he made a good job of his survival and gradually became known abroad. In his last illness the Kremlin looked after him in a special hospital – a suggestion of how aware the authorities were of this semi-banished scholar's Western following.

> We have seen how cosmic fear, and the images of world catastrophe, and eschatological theories bound up with it, cultivated in the systems of the official world-view, found a laughing equivalent in the images of carnival catastrophes, parodic prophecies and the like, which freed people from fear, brought the world closer to the person, lightened the burden of time and its path and transformed it into the festive path of the joyful time of changes and renewals.[83]

The writing from Bakhtin's 1946 work on Rabelais was opaque because its author had disguised his function. Bakhtin as a philosopher wrote in a kind of code. As he talked about the literature of seventeenth-century France, however, it was clear to those who cared to reflect that he was also and perhaps mainly talking about Stalin's Russia. Thus in the paragraph above the values that mattered fell either side of a clear equation. On the one side 'official world-view', on the other 'laughter', 'carnival', 'parody'. The latter three joined forces with 'freedom' and 'light' to bring 'the world closer to the person' and ease the burden of temporal circumstances. The message was clearly anti-utopian for those who could read it. Soviet reality was an 'eschatological theory' and an 'official world-view' which inspired fear and took the world away from the person. The system justified itself as staving off world catastrophe, in reply to which claims the people laughed, got drunk, fornicated and swore. 'The joyful time of changes and renewals' was reminiscent of a religious hope for transformation often detectable in Bakhtin. But what he mainly seemed to be writing with his theory of 'carnival' was an ethic of survival.

He set out the terms of that ethic by celebrating what the novel could do on behalf of Life. His 'literary theory' in fact re-energized the anarchism which was a traditional pillar of Russian philosophy. Here was the time-honoured Russian way to undermine any inflicted order that threatened the truth of life-as-it-was-lived. The novel was associated with anarchic 'holiday forms, familiar speech, profanation'.[84] With the power to satirize and parody, its task was to

> liberate the object from the power of language in which it had become entangled as if in a net; destroy the homogenizing power of myth over language; free consciousness from the power of the direct word, destroy the thick walls that imprison consciousness within its own discourse, within its own language.[85]

Its agenda was to undo false connections.

> Amid the good things of this here-and-now world are also to be found false connections that distort the authentic nature of things, false associations established and reinforced by tradition and sanctioned by religious and official ideology ... by scholastic thought and theological and legalistic casuistry ... It is necessary to destroy and rebuild the entire false picture of the world ... It is necessary to liberate all these objects and permit them to enter into the free unions that are organic to them.[86]

Like Asmus and Mann in the innovative domain of philosophical aesthetics, through his own invention of a literary theory Bakhtin found a disguised way of highlighting how official philosophy had made a deadly shackle of a living idea. Even more boldly he created a heroic alternative to the imprisoning dialectic, a counter-theory provocatively called dialogism but mostly expressed in other words. What the theory worked on – the 'speaking with many tongues' of the Greek word *heteroglossia* – was also a clue to its own polyvalent nature. The good dialectic would be 'a system ... [in which points of view] mutually and ideologically interanimate each other', 'a living mix of varied and opposing voices [*raznorechivost'*]'.[87] Simply put, a true philosophy would not impose a single construction upon the nature of reality. When extracted for concentrated scrutiny like this, however, Bakhtin's philosophical criticisms sound bolder than they were when buried in literary commentary. In the original text they described the variety of language in Pushkin's *Eugene Onegin*. On the other hand it was useful, to say the least, that literary texts could also be described in structuralist terms as systems – and a sufficient reason for inventing structuralist methodology in a totalitarian country. Henceforth dialogism would pick holes in Communist authoritarianism while the living reality of literature would reflect how it was possible for flesh-and-blood people to escape some of the constraints.

The official Soviet world-view forbade speaking in many tongues. It suppressed all individuality. At the same time it almost destroyed social truth by killing off language. Official language, instead of picking out the diversity of life-as-it-was-lived, petrified everything it touched. Reality was completely obscured by ideological fabrications. Bakhtin countered by trying to measure the truth of natural contact between persons through speech and gesture. The truth, he suggested, lay in the scope for an open-ended and unpredictable outcome when any two living beings encountered one another. The theory would apply to connections between people and also connections between individual consciousness and the world beyond. His neo-Kantian reading of phenomenology gave him this primary interest in how consciousness exists in tandem with what is to be understood. For a phenomenologist consciousness opens up the possibility of many aspects of understanding what is given. Thus dialogism became a method to undo the workings of a dictatorial one-way reality.

'[Dialogism] is an idea drawn initially from phenomenology, from a philosophical analysis of the "thing" called meaning. [It] is indeed about the two-sided aspects of meanings, but not in any sense necessarily about two people. Rather it refers to what other writers would call the intersubjective quality of all meaning: the fact that it is always found in the space between expression and understanding, and that this space – the "inter" separating subjects – is not a limitation but the very condition of meaningful utterance.'[88] But dialogism also rediscovered what first made 'dialectic' appeal to the Romantic imagination. As for Goethe, it was a search for truth through 'active scepticism' and 'participatory observation'. Dialogism was fashionably and elusively expressed as a linguistic theory, and was received that way in the West, in the 1970s, on a wave of enthusiasm for Bakhtin's 'structuralism'. But in the Russian context Bakhtin always saw himself a philosopher who turned to theory of language because he had no other politically permissible way to express himself.[89] His philosophical task was through non-verbal communication and street language to establish a moral value for personality in its minimal form.

How Bakhtin disguised his philosophical activity may be seen from the following passage in which he discusses the role of the novelist in understanding life. Was it a simple code he used to express his true ideas? Even if it seems so now, surely the censor would not easily have alighted on the clue.

The novelist stands in need of some essential formal and generic mask that could serve to define the position from which he views life, as well as the position from which he makes that life public.

Precisely here … the masks of the clown and the fool (transformed in various ways) come to the aid of the novelist. These masks are not invented; they are rooted deep in the folk. They are linked with the folk through the fool's time-honoured privilege not to participate in life, and by the time-honoured bluntness of the fool's language; they are linked too with the chronotope of the public square and with the trappings of the theatre. All of this is of the highest importance for the novel. At last a form was found to portray the mode of existence of a man who is in life but not of it, life's perpetual spy and reflector; at last specific forms had been found to reflect private life and make it public.[90]

The novelist sees how people liberate themselves against the confining inhumanity of official truths. They hang on to their humanity by evasion and dissembling. And so now must the Russian philosopher. Substituting 'philosopher' for 'novelist', and retranslating the folk of Rabelais' seventeenth century into 'the people' of Russia's twentieth, and 'theatre' into 'media', the paragraph reads like this.

The *philosopher* stands in need of some essential formal and generic mask that could serve to define the position from which he views life, as well as the position from which he makes that life *knowable.*

Precisely here ... the masks of the clown and the fool (transformed in various ways) come to the aid of the *philosopher.* These masks are not invented; they are rooted deep in the *people.* They are linked with the *people* through the *philosopher's* time-honoured privilege not to participate in life, and by the time-honoured bluntness of the fool's language; they are linked too with the chronotope of the public square and with the trappings of the *media.* All of this is of the highest importance for *philosophy.* At last a form was found to portray the mode of existence of a *philosophical subject* who is in life but not of it, life's perpetual spy and reflector; at last specific forms had been found to reflect *the life of the subject* and make it *knowable.*

241

A traumatic experience for philosophy was reflected in this paragraph and for the humanity of the philosopher who had to be ever on guard even as he dissembled, mingled with ordinary people, skimmed the lies of the newspapers, tried to find ways of turning the official life inside out and therefore to show what was 'true' about it. Life itself could survive perhaps, but could the philosopher make meaningful statements about it? His first task in circumstances of oppression is to say that life is incommensurate with any statement made about it. Still philosophy should try to capture the life of the subject as it is lived – perhaps in the end by joining forces with literature. A philosophy true to life should somehow be able to capture that sense that every single human consciousness has of being in life but not of it, not wholly determined by it. Probably not by coincidence the phrase about being in life but not of it was a direct quote from Schiller, the greatest German philosopher of freedom through inwardness.[91] Bakhtin could turn the tables on the culture of quotationism too. He made the ultimate comment on his own work, which was theory of the novel, when he described Socrates as the first novelist. Clearly their task was the same.[92]

The task was to unpick nonsense. In the Soviet context it was to try to lift the stranglehold official discourse had laid on life and let people live in an unalienated society again. But in Bakhtin's move to bring philosophy and literature closer, in the interests of the living truth, there was an element of thought which can also be found in almost contemporary Western philosophizing: the idea, expressed for instance by Martha Nussbaum, that general terms are so poor with respect to real human lives that they have to be offset with personal stories, told orally, one by one, because all of us, when we say 'I', are both in life and not of it. In our apartness we retain a grain of inalienable integrity.[93]

Yet still in another sense again Bakhtin was only coming back to that old Russian feeling for the truth of 'being' – that foundational link between living and knowing which was always a guide to authenticity, albeit in extremis. It was a way of finding truth in the very condition of remaining oppressed and unfree. When Sinyavsky wanted to round off his *Soviet Civilization* he quoted a poem by Olga Berggolts, written about the siege of Leningrad during the Second World War.[94]

> In those days, daily life
> Disappeared, reappeared.
> And bravely, being
> Came back into its own.

The contrast in these lines was between daily life, *byt*, and *bytie*. Belief in *bytie* made it possible to squeeze a spiritual value even out of terrible suffering. It gave at once a sense of communal endurance and of individual escape into mystical contemplation. *Bytie* could even suggest a non-banal order of things which might be the foundation of the good life still possible to realize. *Bytie* might promise the 'joyful sense of renewals and changes' of the first Bakhtin passage quoted above.

Admirable as the typical Russian philosophy of being seems, in truth it is surely not a viable universal moral theory. It is more like a kind of perennial Russian hallucination brought on by a constant series of emergencies such as war, hunger and political repression. Such disasters give an illusion of a pared-down authentic existence waiting around the corner for our grasp, if only we would give up our cowardly obsessions with immediate order and happiness. Only because the sense of higher reality so quickly recedes does it seem so meaningful. But normally it is the trivial world which has meaning. Bakhtin, against, say, an extreme mystic like Shestov, was able to say this. He was not, in the end, a mystic, but a lover of a rumbunctious Russian community of individuals: something actually closer to *byt*.

The achievements of Soviet life, and of philosophy to the small degree that it could reflect that real life, concerned the ethics of the people, the cleverness of dissent and a subtle sense of connection with the banished broader tradition. The difficulty for the historian is the degree to which alternative lives were led but not expressed in a way that would enable posterity to hold on to them. Bakhtin is an exception to be treasured as much for what he reveals as what he argues. Otherwise we have only the testimony of a few lucid witnesses like Andrei Sakharov's widow Elena Bonner, who wrote a few years ago that 'those who sensed the falseness of Soviet society intuitively fled the lies of the humanities and took up concrete professions'. This was why

> with the fall of the totalitarian regime – with Stalin's death, Khrushchev's speech, the Thaw, and the emergence of the liberals of the 1960s, came the era of the dissidents. Among them were disproportionately large numbers of physicists, mathematicians, engineers and biologists, and almost no historians or philosophers. The dissidents were only a handful . . . It is hard to say whether they had a distinctive philosophical view, but the clarity of their vision differed from that of millions of other people. This gave them the strength to reject lies and preserved their self-respect, without which there is not respect for others and for life in general, and which in the final analysis brings a sense of happiness.[95]

The humanities in Soviet Russian society were corrupted by that same lack of respect for truth which philosophers had noticed when they detected the lack of a rational tradition around the beginning of the twentieth century. The arts as they were affected by Chernyshevskian optimism were insultingly childish. Bonner spoke of the difficulty that, when 'brought up on lies, a society cannot mature or take on responsibility'. Her judgement was of a society cut off from the Western classical tradition and with no adequate morality of knowledge to fill the gap. Just as in the nineteenth century, when it came to terms with the immovability of the autocracy, so the later twentieth-century Russian intelligentsia saw that it had no alternative but to give up its natural calling to work in the humanities and take to political protest. The revolutionary political tradition had to be reopened.

As for Soviet official life, any history has to take note of the small provision it did make for exceptions. A handful of brilliant individuals were allowed to flourish under near-perfect conditions for the development of their science or art. This was the message behind Solzhenitsyn's portrait of the scientists at Mavrino. Exactly because so many political and cultural controls were in place it was possible for these beautiful Platonic souls to devote themselves to the ideal reflective life. By the same token the Soviet Union was able to support a restricted culture of high artistic excellence. A century of authoritarian cultural protectionism also meant that the high standards of the traditional intelligentsia, in the form of a broad education and a requirement that every educated person should actively cultivate art (not that bourgeois hybrid 'the arts'), also lived on in Soviet life. That superb artistic-intellectual culture which Soviet Russia nourished – the last surviving example of a world respectful of beautiful souls – was revealed to, and alas forced to sell itself to an astonished West, in the 1990s. Paradoxically, all through the Soviet period Russian culture continued to believe in itself as its own realm of truth. Where it could survive the boorish and punitive pressures, the neo-Kantian Russia of Pasternak lived on.

A tiny time-capsule of Russian greatness was somehow preserved in the artistic culture at the same time as philosophy disintegrated. Here I want to use the word to mean no more than the average man's grip on the truth. The only justification for calling it philosophy is a sense that that grip does depend on what is emanating from the sources of cultural authority or whatever has stepped in during their absence. In the 1960s Plyushch portrayed an intellectual life secretly full of self-proclaimed Sartreans, neo-Kantians, logical positivists and followers of Wittgenstein, but in which in practice everyone conformed. Thus to hold a belief had no meaning.[96] As a young man Plyushch's task was to teach *diamat*. When he recorded that some of his university colleagues simply did not turn up for these tedious sessions and the rest spent their time discussing Tolstoy and the meaning of life, it seems clear that he was showing us how Russian intellectual life preserved some sense of its own value in abeyance, as it were by abstention. But when we read in the same breath that they turned from the meaning of life to experiments with hypnosis we get a sense of that life going astray which is amply confirmed by other sources. Meaningless Soviet ideology bred disoriented generations to come.[97] A short century of intellectual self-defeat entailed the bizarre removal of far too many *intelligenty* from the mainstream rational world.

In his 1970 novel *Moskva-Petushki*, translated as 'Moscow Stations', Venedikt Yerofeyev tried to capture the sense of his country dying. A drunk driven to desperation by the Soviet system reaches the last stop and the existential end of the line, just as Russia does too. In the world around him a travestied version of philosophy has been used to construct the Russian moral cause. But the cause is rubbish and has infected all the men and women who live by it with the desire to obliterate themselves.

> I remember distinctly, it was Hegel. Yes, he used to say: 'There's no difference, apart from difference of degree, between degrees of difference and the absence of any difference.' Meaning, translated into good Russian, 'Who doesn't drink these days?'[98]

A few years later Alexander Zinoviev's novel *The Yawning Heights* (1979) featured a country called Ibansk in which by definition – *yebat'* is to fuck – everyone was fucked by the nonsensical system.

For the contemporary novelist Viktor Pelevin a short century of nonsense has produced one of the most bizarre and endangered societies in the world, unable to escape its own fantasies. The brilliant *Yellow Train/Omon Ra* (1993) and the chaotic *Clay Machine-Gun* (1997) describe a form of dementia and randomness that might have been dreamed up by

Descartes' *malin génie* determined to spoil human belief in a coherent world. Pelevin told a Western interviewer that his stories of bizarre, off-the-rails, mentally aberrant Russian life were what he encountered, not what he invented.[99]

The origins of *diamat* suggested on the one hand a Marxist-Leninist obsession with technological advance, on another a Spinozan-Schellingian query as to when God and Man would become one substance again. Something of that mixture of science and mysticism came to express itself in a people scientifically educated but invaded by New Age wackiness. In *Dead Again. The Russian Intelligentsia After Communism* (1997), Masha Gessen, whose grandfather was a leading publicist in the Silver Age and later in emigration, found in a survey in the early 1990s that one after another *intelligenty* of every generation seemed to be living in private universes shaped by vast nationalistic or religious or paranormal theories, many of them 'ugly, frightening . . . and hopeless'. None of her interviewees ever thought of putting their theories to the test of truth; enough believed that their theory was about to explain the universe.[100]

Russian philosophy in the twentieth century became an almost unfathomable marriage of hope and necessity, values and facts and malign experience. It was a hybrid of Marxist theory and Russian social need constantly tugged in a third direction by residual mysticism. As for Soviet life, Sinyavsky said it destroyed the intelligentsia, although Solzhenitsyn, now in his eighties, insists it should remain in being to continue to play a moral role.[101]

12

On the Edge of Reason

It seems possible that the long tradition in Russia ended in 1991. This is not intended to mean that Russia has given up its characteristic ways in philosophy, torn between constructionism and anarchism, but that it can as a culture no longer pretend that the French Revolution didn't happen. What its thinkers have feared since 1789 – the negative effects of individualism, selfishness, atheism, competition, prosperity – have burst in through the door and changed the frontiers of the philosophical domain. Why did Russia hold out so long as an Otherland, to be created by philosophy as a non-Western place? It may not have escaped the reader that Odoevsky's description in 1843 of that terrible Western place, Newbenthamtown, in which every last citizen grabbed what he could get and bled society dry without care for his neighbour nor the state of nature, more closely resembles Russia today than it ever did the actual West. Russian disdain for the West, its sense of being morally superior, always contained the shadow of a fear that Russia was the inferior place. In his uncertainty the good man in Russia wanted the very ground of his being to be moral, to support him. To be a good man in Russia – to be better than a typical Western man – he needed to be surrounded by encouragements to be moral. He was ethically realistic about his limitations. Subliminally he has known for two hundred years that whereas the degree of available individual freedom in Russia has generally risen in moments in its history when it has been prepared to tolerate chaos (like the present), the quality of intellectual, literary and moral life has generally soared with the effort to find cohesion. The sense of an end comes with a new sense of uncertainty where Russian culture belongs. Russia has suddenly been precipitated into a world too modern – too uncontained – for its comfort.

The philosopher Alasdair MacIntyre, once a Marxist, now a Catholic, argued a quarter of a century ago that the moral West had arrived at a condition he called 'After Virtue'. The predominant I-centred morality seems to be 'the obscure manifestation of massive dislocations in society'. Only a chaotic world eschews those 'social ties and modes of life which alone can give meaning and dignity to human activity'.[1] There cannot be a coherent morality without a closed set of values to which that morality can refer – values of reason, or the Church, or the community. In which case the only way for a meaningful ethics is backwards. In some sense that Russians have already recognized MacIntyre expresses typically Russian feelings. Russians proud of their communal ethics have spent the last two centuries trying not to move forward. Neither MacIntyre nor the kind of traditional moral Russia Communism encouraged – and Solzhenitsyn still stands for – is liberally inclined.[2]

MacIntyre has always been aware of the pathos of what holds societies together as ethical wholes. In an early essay on Hume he imagined Hume meeting Marx. Hume opened the conversation by asserting that it was common interests which made morality possible. In eighteenth-century England, a nation which had those interests, he could speak with confidence. But for Marx, despite what Hegel had said about nations, common interests in the modern world were more likely to be at once inter-national and class-defined.[3] The problem that MacIntyre faced personally more than a quarter of a century ago was that suddenly Marxism was revealed to have solved the coherence problem artificially and temporarily. In *Marxism and Christianity* (1968) he said of 'the Marxist project' that it 'remains the only one we have for re-establishing hope as a social virtue'.[4] But only a few years later he had to admit that it had failed. Living 'after the hope for virtue' is now Russia's experience. Will a philosopher emerge to urge like MacIntyre that the only way to ethical meaning is backwards, towards a new or renewed form of moral protectionism? It seems likely.[5] But how can it be done? MacIntyre needs to advocate what Leontiev chose to do in the mid-nineteenth century: retreat to a monastery. Contemporary Russian thinkers, respectively drawn to and repelled by moral protectionism, are evidently keeping alive the tension between Slavophiles and Westernizers with which this history opened.[6]

At the time of writing, Russian philosophers seem caught between the seductions of postmodernism and the renewed discovery of their own religious philosophers.[7] One way to see the situation of Russian philosophy in a wider context, however, as this history has repeatedly tried to do, is to see Russian thought passing through a crisis which hit the Continental West about thirty years ago. Russian philosophers without Communism – their particular Russian form of 'the Enlightenment project' – are facing the same cataclysm as befell French philosophy about the year 1970:

> Beyond reason, implacable ruses muzzled the hopes of creating a better world ... It was no longer possible to naively exalt the continuous progress of freedom and human lucidity, nor to sustain the humanist vision according to which man is the perfectible master of his destiny, marching towards perfection.[8]

On the edge of postmodernism or post-structuralism French philosophers saw that 'it was no longer possible to naively exalt the continuous progress of freedom and human lucidity'. Marxism was revealed as a form of naivety. It had been a deliberate step backwards to preserve community and an idea of humanity against the forces of individualistic disintegration – only those who espoused it had not understood the difference between a benevolent fiction and the objective truth. The Slavophile Russians were never so naive. They had known from the moment the Enlightenment project was held out to them that 'reason' was 'an implacable ruse'. On the other hand, without the Westerners' willingness to believe in reason, not a form of naivety but a genuine desire to encourage the best in human nature, a modern Russian culture might never have come into being, bringing with it a desperately overdue respect for individuals. Nor out of the conflict between reason and obscurantism would the philosophical anarchists have established their bridgehead, attacking reason-as-social-glue and defending the integrity of souls. Reading the Russian spiritual tradition from the beginning of the nineteenth century, it seems clear that Russian philosophy has always been about the issues which made the West self-destructively postmodern in the last third of the twentieth century, with continuing effect today. Bakhtin on any reckoning ought to be considered the first postmodernist or deconstructionist in Russia.[9] On the other hand, the 'reason' it was his task to undermine was evil. The effect of Enlightenment reason in the West certainly was not.

Postmodernism since Foucault and Derrida has flirted with Western fringe experience. But Russia *is* the philosophical fringe of the West, and for as long as it has realized its role it has courted chaos and included elements of mischief in its anti-Enlightenment role. One of the saddest products of Russian philosophy in the twentieth century was Alexandre Kojève (1902–68) who left Russia after the Revolution, studied philosophy with Karl Jaspers and then moved to Paris, where he lectured a generation in how to understand Marx through Hegel. In between driving home a view of Hegel as the last philosopher who predicted the end of history, and working for the French government on the European project, Kojève spread his vision of extreme contempt for both East and West by imagining a single form of uncritical mass material contentment achieved sometimes through totalitarian politics and at other times through the totality of consumer satisfaction. He has been seen as the pioneer of postmodern politics.[10]

Kojève's Russian background has never been satisfactorily untangled. A philosopher and namesake of his father's generation was a disciple of Solovyov and friend of Fyodorov, the philosopher of 'the common task'. It seems possible that Kojève, whose father died when he was two, who lost his stepfather in violent circumstances in 1917, and who was traumatized by a spell in a Bolshevik prison at the age of fifteen, may have invented a patrimony to take with him to the West. One of the few certain biographical details is that he was the nephew of the painter Vassily Kandinsky and came from a wealthy family steeped in the culture of the Silver Age. Kojève studied the beautiful soul of Solovyov and Solovyov's longing to join the Churches of East and West, and read his way through Dostoevsky. He noted Solovyov's late fear of 'false wholenesses' and the coming of Antichrist and then in his own work put these horrors forward as the future of the world. Kojève envisaged a sated East–West dystopia in which an undifferentiated mass of materially contented people had settled for a life of less than freedom. His life's work could be read as an act of vengeance for Russia's suffering, for its violation by Communism, and its position on the Western fringe. Steeped in Europe-hating Dostoevsky, Kojève revelled in exploiting and mocking Western naivety.[11]

Critics of postmodernism as a superficial cultural phenomenon in the West seem not to realize that its fissiparous ways lie in the desperately serious problem of coming to terms with loss of hope, as successive positions from Hegel to Marx have had to be abandoned. The idea that the heritage of the Enlightenment – a belief in the human capacity to reach perfection through reason – ended in the double horror of Nazism and Stalinism, of the Holocaust and the Gulag, that the Enlightenment culminated in the consummate modern experience of evil, has led to the demise of its cultural influence. The argument seems both wrong and ill-advised. To go wholeheartedly down the postmodern path, whatever the apparent justification, is to risk giving in to Kojèvian mischief. It means giving in to a value-free world where freedom and dignity no longer matter. Better to accept, as the more sedate post-metaphysical German philosopher Jürgen Habermas has argued, that we are all post-Hegelians now.[12]

However, Habermas might have said: now we are all companions of Belinsky. For as Belinsky argued in 1841, no higher ideas are acceptable if they justify the loss of a single innocent life. I make these remarks not because there will be any drawing together of Russian and Western philosophy in the foreseeable future – the traditions remain deeply divided and differently dedicated – but because over the last thirty to forty years, during the time of the collapse of humanist certainties in the West, more common experience has been revealed between Europe and Russia than I can be comfortable with as a Cartesian rationalist. I find myself defining as Russia's richest heritage ideas which, to my classical Western cast of mind, informed by postmodernism but formed by humanism, seem uncommonly dangerous.

Nevertheless the truth of the Russian position is on the edge of reason. Even its humanism is extreme. The non-Cartesian Russian tradition also defines the end of the West: the far limit. On the other hand, this does not mean that non-Cartesian or counter-Cartesian thought does not have a positive value nor that it cannot revitalize the more rigid aspects of classical Western philosophy. Three strains of Russian thought, a mixture of politics, morality and poetry, seem to me particularly poised to clarify and enrich philosophy's understanding of the human condition.

In an obscure corner of *The Republic*, Plato wondered through Socrates how the good man ought to live in an unfriendly world. How should Socrates, a good man, appear in society, if he wanted people to *know* he was good and learn from him?[13] The trouble with seeming good is that mostly bad men do it. Socrates would have to try to appear bad, otherwise people would take him for a bad man pretending to be good. To resemble a bad man he would put himself outside society, cherish no friends, give up love, growl at strangers, let his appearance grow shabby. The general public would soon be convinced and never suspect that for good reason he was not what he seemed. When Plato considered whether Socrates should dissimulate, he touched on the first philosophy of 'living in truth'.

Those born into despotic and totalitarian societies recognize this moral problem but have rarely recorded it. Fifteen years ago the British novelist Anthony Burgess offered an interesting reading of Griboyedov's classic 1831 play, *Woe from Wit*. In that play the main character has to disguise his intelligence and potential goodness in order to survive. Burgess subtitled his English translation of the play 'The Importance of Being Stupid'. Bakhtin made disguise the central topic of his philosophy. He questioned whether the moral life was possible under conditions of extreme repression. Griboyedov's original title was *Gore ot uma* – 'How One Comes to Grief from Having a Mind'.

The good man in Russia, with a history of living under political repression, has often not had the freedom to be his moral self. In difficult times his moral choice has been narrow and extreme: to conform or not. If he decided not to conform, would he do so passively or actively? Passive non-conformity would consist in a dialogue with himself in which he would remember values outside his present situation. Yet to be sure of his moral authenticity he would have to act on his beliefs – take an existential leap or a leap in protest. A second question would then arise: would his gesture – living-in-truth – have moral value, except to himself?

Protest has value because it is courageous and because it acts as a reminder of non-standard values in a standardized society. On the other hand, the self-destruction of moral men is surely a waste, because a morally exiguous society needs all the examples it can get. Emergency situations, times of repression, of the kind with which Russia is long familiar, create a tension in ethics between being and showing. Is it better to be a good man in one's own eyes or to show oneself to be a good man in the eyes of others? In the case of the good man who decides not to protest openly and destroy himself by that means, but to hold on to life so that now and again he might provide an example while still saving his skin, the question arises: how small can he make himself and still retain self-respect? Should the moral man pass himself off as something he is not in order that one day he will reveal the values he really believes in? Should he in fact learn to speak the language of the enemy because that is the only way potential dissent can be effective? These questions have been lived through by generations of Russians and also more recently in Central and Eastern Europe. The Czech playwright and dissident under Communism, Václav Havel, has written and acted on stage and acted out in life the dilemmas of the life-in-truth.[14] That active protest could make the openly declared life-in-truth a moral fact was surely sufficient to make that the crucial argument in a totalitarian society, because it showed the totality did not quite hold; that conscience as the ultimate ethical value came from somewhere else.

But it is not only in totalitarian societies that the desire to show values drawn from outside feels like a valuable ethical impulse. The protester in a Utilitarian society also has a problem of being noticed. If the good society is one where the pursuit of self-interest swells the common interest, how can my single act of defiance register its value? I am not asking to be seen as a heroine, only for the value of my position to be accepted as such, and not as part of an overall computation. A moral society has to pay active attention to, and not just tolerate, individual protest. When contemporary Utilitarians insist there is a place for everyone in an inclusive society they forget the need certain individuals have to set up their moral camp outside anything that present – or possible – society provides. A person wishing to show that he holds values different from the prevailing society may feel he must jump from a tall building or set fire to himself, or, to take an example from American newspaper headlines in 2001, fly a microlight plane into a tall building to show that he too disapproves of the conventional values with which he has been brought up. Being a protesting individual does not guarantee that one's actions and values are good. The man who sets fire to himself or the boy who crashes the plane may have no greater good cause than self-expression. But because it is difficult to be an individual everywhere, and under every modern political system, and because individual discretion seems to be the right foundation for the moral life, these gestures show the need for moral territory to be mapped. The overt experience of repressive societies like the Soviet Union ought to make Western weaknesses apparent. Kojève saw them immediately. Because the West is 'free' it thinks it is better than it is.

The place of rebellion has to be understood. There is an urge in certain moral individuals not to be included in assessments of what is good for society because they can't find their reflection there. They can't find their morality in Hegel or Marx but also not in Utilitarianism. They want to be good in themselves and seek the test. Protest is not an a priori moral activity. Protesters are not good people because their cause is good. Berdyaev would argue that protest loses its moral value the moment it is 'objectified' or 'socialized', because in that moment it loses its guarantee of personal authenticity. The more moral values are socialized in the form of organized causes the more the genuine moral man comes under pressure to demonstrate that his commitment is personal and genuine.[15] And perhaps that self-individualizing moment is just what moral philosophers should seize on: the moral potential in wanting to be an individual. Berdyaev would say that what men and women are really like in conversation with themselves is what matters. Who Koestler's Rubashov actually *is* when he talks to the 'silent partner' of his conscience is the ethical core of *Darkness at Noon*. The important thing for ethics, more than ever in the wake of the Eastern intelligentsia's experience of political repression, is to put that desire to be a moral individual centre-stage and to respect it.

Russian philosophy alone can never deliver a value for protest. Since the early Russian martyrs – Radishchev and Chaadaev – protest as a moral value in Russia has mostly arisen out of contact with Western reason and thus out of the negative difference between Russia and the West. In fact Russian philosophy may turn out to have made its greatest contributions to almost a non-subject, but one which again should no longer be ignored – let's say the philosophy of happiness. When Khomiakov elevated *sobornost'*, the traditional form of God-fearing Russian communal life, to be his first principle of being *and* knowing, the result was clear: to be happy in Russia the peasant had to sacrifice his individuality and freedom. But only a critical (Western) outsider would see that epistemic gesture as sacrifice. 'The blind student of optics' was a man able to trust the community to give him knowledge he could not obtain first-hand. The community formed him as one whose pleasure in belonging to the group outweighed his personal interest in truth. He was, because of his willingness to accept epistemic limitations, able to be happy.

The knowledge and happiness displayed in Khomiakov's examples are of the simplest kind. The peasant who responds to his community and enjoys knowing his place in the world is like the dog who responds to her master's call. She comes running not because she fears him and submits to his orders but because she enjoys their contact. Belonging to her master defines the scope of her being and precisely her joy introduces a degree of freedom into the relationship. Khomiakov saw this primitive, poorly individualized world as Russia's greatest moral asset. The joyful confirmation of social identity at the expense of individual freedom remains characteristic of the most intelligent animals, however, not of Socrates. Thus what a dominant strain of Russian philosophy makes available for our scrutiny are, even when they are positive, ideas of extreme moral and epistemic simplicity.

In simple peasant Russia the way 'blind students of optics' learned to orientate themselves was not so much through their own discriminations as through personalities fit to convey what was good. The peasant looked to community leaders and great men as special men in touch with wisdom. Tolstoy – with more than a touch of irony, says Isaiah Berlin – included in *War and Peace* the peasant Platon ('Plato') Karatayev as a model of knowing-in-being. On a different level, not ironic at all, however, was the related character of General Kutuzov. The victorious Russian leader against Napoleon existed as a foil to Napoleon's individualistic Western rationalism. Kutuzov was a good man and took the right decisions because his soul was mysteriously embedded in the flow of Russian being. His ultimate wisdom came from passively committing his country to God's way, not from wasting himself in self-assertive action. He was what Russian culture wanted him to be, an epistemic hero – a man who showed how to know.

Communist political leaders, and the Party itself, were invested with the same infallible wisdom in the twentieth century as these folk heroes were in the nineteenth. The elevation of the personality expressing it over the actual testibility of the truth-claim established itself as a feature of Russian life which has remained to this day. A leading Western authority on Bakhtin was astonished to find his Russian counterpart in the mid-1990s praising Bakhtin's work as true because Bakhtin was a great personality. Vadim Kozhinov was writing in 1995:

I think that Bakhtin is a very great figure. Above all because this person was a representative of that essentially heroic type in Russian culture, to which there is none comparable in the world, especially in the twentieth century . . . And it seems to be that this heroism enters into the concept of culture as a constituent part of it, that is, raises it still higher, because culture, if you like, is intrinsically valuable . . . In what sense? It is intrinsically valuable within humanity and in the end it is a kind of exit in a higher sense out of the narrow limits of the temporal, the spatial, the everyday, even the historical boundedness of the individual.[16]

The American scholar Ken Hirschkop rightly observes that this attitude elevates personality over science. When Kozhinov credits Bakhtin with higher insight into truth because of his character he seems to operate in a primitive pre- or post-literate world in which all teaching is done by example rather than argument. His 'critical' assessment of Bakhtin's personality is wildly out of touch with Western academic standards. One thinks rather warily of the timeless big 'progressive' personality also common on the Russian scene, whose democratic politics are ambiguous, but whose capacity to lead and inspire is unquestionable. The idea is of the folk hero, and it is in the folk tradition that personality matters as a gauge of the good man. The old Soviet habit of the 'cult of personality', from time to time opportunistically denounced as a crime, was the political extension of a folk habit.

What follows from personality being taken as an indicator of true knowledge is the elevation of personal qualities to the level of 'epistemic virtues'. The exemplary personality on the primitive Russian pattern has special personal virtues which give him access to truth. He may be strong, or pious, or physically handsome or able to hold his liquor or a great womanizer: his virtues need not bear directly on knowledge-seeking. In fact, to be consistent or diligent or patient would surely spoil his aura. The primitive theory of epistemic virtue singles out as exemplars of knowledge those who seem somehow to have been 'blessed by the gods'. The practice is not confined to Russia of past centuries. Populist Western societies like Britain in 2004 practise it every day without recognizing its primitivism.[17]

Classical philosophy however is extremely uncomfortable – and rightly so – with such theories of 'epistemic virtue'. They are unscientific. They defy the fundamental endeavour of the *cogito* to remove all personal variables and uncertainties from the truth picture. Knowledge is 'an equal matter for discernment by competent persons' but that competence has nothing to do with personal virtues like patience or diligence or doggedness or a capacity to hold one's drink or exude sexual attractiveness. Some of those qualities may make inquiry easier – all but the last would certainly result in longer hours at one's desk – but none of them can *cause* knowledge to be true, which is what exponents of epistemic virtue would have to argue. In the matter of scientific truth the facts speak for themselves. Their value is sovereign.[18]

Nevertheless peasants prefer epistemic virtues to scientific procedure and so do Romantics. For a Romantic the presence of a divine spark in her being will lead her where reason alone cannot reach. Or maybe certain substances in her bloodstream will open the gates of perception or with or without them she will get to heaven in her dreams. The German Romantics believed in glamorous epistemic virtues like divine blessing and poetic intoxication and, steeped in their ideas, Dostoevsky carried their habit of mind forward. Prince Myshkin in *The Idiot*, the man who believed beauty would change the world, was the bearer of such epistemic privileges, which is why others were almost prepared to love him, despite his clumsiness, despite his otherworldliness, because something about his epilepsy hinted that he had special insight and would be worth following. Dostoevsky's attempt to make illness an epistemic virtue – he did it again with Kirilov's revelatory epilepsy in *The Devils* – was philosophically primitive, richly poetic, nothing unusual for a novelist.[19] But where did it leave Russian culture if truth had no firmer foundation than the enchanted empyrean? When Kirilov asked his mentor Stavrogin whether, if it were mathematically proven to him that the truth lay with science, he would remain with the truth-in-Christ, Stavrogin, Russian man-of-the-cross, seemed to say yes.[20] Stavrogin believed in a theory which would justify his own position in the novel as an epistemic hero and an exemplary personality. But since he was also a murderer clearly even Dostoevsky had his doubts about the proposition.

Descartes laid down classic conditions for testing scientific truth. They included the need to doubt the evidence of our senses, to exclude any distorting influence which might be caused by sickness and fever and dreaming. Anyone persuaded of the basic wisdom of Descartes must conclude that Russian philosophy can't begin until it leaves behind the superstitious, pre-scientific world of the nineteenth-century peasant community and the Romanticism which replaced it in educated minds. It has to separate values from facts, personalities from truth if it wants to be considered as more than poetry.

Yet the poetic element is so important in Russian thought that in a sophisticated form it will insist that the Russian contribution to the Western mind must reflect an alternative epistemic world. Knowledge is incomplete if it resides in a detached Cartesian 'I'. Epistemic sophistication destroys the natural bond between man and world on which happiness depends. Let science be respected in its own instrumental sphere. Something remains to be known in a different way.

Khomiakov spoke of 'God's world' as the world before the human mind impinged on it. For Kant such a world was unknowable. Yet what satisfaction is there in a philosophy which can tell me precisely about the contents of my own mind and nothing about my place in the world? Three successive moments in European thought raised that objection to Cartesian rationalism and to Kant's critical rationalism. It came from the men of the Counter-Enlightenment, the German Romantics and the Russian religious philosophers, who each in their turn insisted that reality was absolutely knowable, but through intuition, which mattered more than reason. Russian idealist philosophy defined itself by putting intuition at the centre of its epistemic stage. It gave intuition this epistemic value, and also an additional moral value because of its capacity to restore man's bond with the world. That we *have* poetic vision within us, says Odoevsky, that we have epistemic imagination, means that we can avoid the chaos of the world of objects falling apart and the feeling that we exist in no necessary connection to nature.[21] A certain instinct to preserve things whole also preserves our humanity from rational excess. Instrumental reason asset-strips what it touches. Knowledge as belonging leaves the world intact.

Russian idealism, of which Berdyaev nominated Khomiakov as the founder, consistently made two points clear. One was a desire to defend the integrity of the world against the interference of the human mind. The other was a Pascalian defence of the supreme integrity of the heart. Both followed from a circumspect view of the *cogito*. For a Russian idealist critical thought has to be secondary to that first moment of being when we affirm our essential position in the world. Not 'I think, I am' can be the beginning of philosophy but 'I am, I think'. Cogitation is an aberration if it does not respect the prior integrity of the world, of which the thinker is an ineradicable part.[22]

Russian peasant wisdom could immediately supply a simple model for this kind of integral knowledge. Think of the farmer who 'knows' what the weather will be like tomorrow. He reads the clouds, sniffs the air, holds up a finger. His predictions stand a good chance of being right because of his long grass-roots experience. Even if he turns out not to be right, his way of living and knowing seems impressive, as if nature were rewarding him for abiding with her. He is the late European equivalent of the Greek hero chosen by the gods, one of Hegel's Heroic people. The wind and the sky and the earth have chosen to confide in him. His visible reward is epistemic grace. He knows the world the way animals know it and animals are always epistemically impressive. My husband's dog knows it's raining without looking; she doesn't need external evidence, whereas he and I have to feel the rain for ourselves, or see it, or hear it. We are dignified by our truth-seeking, at the same time as nature seems to mark us down as epistemically cumbersome creatures. We have to work so hard to be sure what is there. By contrast the farmer and the dog have an epistemic aura. But the belief that animals and 'naturally chosen' people have a special gift of knowledge may be misleading because the essence of the belief is poetic and sentimental. Tolstoy's admiration for the simple peasant life was of that kind. He wanted simple knowledge because it seemed to reinforce the existence of a natural order of things in which man had a coherent and valuable place.

Simple knowledge often entails passivity. The simple mind is more of a receptacle or a pregnable surface than a sharp tool – more feminine than masculine as it used to be said, before those cultural stereotypes were abolished; and the Russians always saw their nineteenth-century Oblomovian, anti-Hegelian tradition as 'meek'.[23] These are interesting and genuine precedents for the peace cult which Soviet politics exploited as part of the Russian Communist image. Once again a grain of truth was at the core of a political lie. Tolstoy's Kutuzov did nothing against Napoleon in order to steer the right course for Russia. By his passivity he invited in God's wisdom. The peace-loving Oblomov did the same.

God's world, integral knowledge, blessed passivity. By these routes Russian philosophy finally arrives at a serious question, namely: how can we offer epistemic hospitality to the world rather than confrontation? The Russian question might be: how in our knowledge-seeking can we be more like singers than warriors? It is almost what Goncharov asked in *Oblomov*. (I take the singer to exemplify passive knowledge and the warrior to represent the active kind.) Can there be a kind of knowledge without individualism and pride? On the model of the singer the answer is yes. For the singer when she sings is not really present in the music as her 'self'. The technique which makes her a great singer lets the breath flow freely through her. Air makes use of her to produce sound, in which moments her body does not belong to her but to nature and to the truth of music. Not to interfere with these objective processes is the singer's training and her art and the more she manages not to interfere the truer will be that art. Russian idealism implies this 'passive' attitude to knowledge as an art which consists in less than self-assertion.

'Implies' is to say that no Russian philosopher to my knowledge has explored passivity as a conscious model. It was first identified as a moral philosophy of being, in a way which would be immensely useful to twentieth-century Western thought, however, by the Prague-born German poet Rilke. Rilke came to Russia in 1899, and again in 1900, the year Solovyov died. Over the next five years he immersed himself in the literature and thought, and in the reality of peasant life.[24] He travelled widely in the Russian countryside in the company of the brilliant Lou Salomé, met folk poets, great writers and ordinary people; and he read. He wrote about Russia, and came to feel that he could be that country's voice. As he put it more than a decade later:

All the home of my instinct, all my inward origin is there.[25]

Rilke's mentality harmonized with an outlook he found prevalent in Russia. He loathed the approach to the world of scientific positivism. Everything he stood for, and was, was opposed to the overreach of instrumental reason. By contrast he wished to embody a pure openness to the world. Knowledge should alight like a blessing on consciousness. It should happen as a response to cognitive patience, like a prayer being heard. The poet hoped to be in the world as 'a fleeting moment in which the morning comes to consciousness'.[26]

It was a Russian monk who spoke through the first two books of Rilke's early masterpiece *The Book of Hours* (1899–1903). A worshipful man out of the same stable as Dostoevsky's Zosima, this monk told how the proud (*hofartig*) Renaissance spirit was dead and a new humility had come to replace it. He expressed a vision to which Khomiakov – and perhaps even Aristotle – could have owned. The truth was embedded in a divine darkness to which animals and things have more ready access than men.

There is rarely sun in the Russian cathedral.

And

The darkness holds everything to itself
Forms and flames, animals and me.[27]

Spiritual power consists in accepting darkness as the basis of our companionship with the world. 'Seeing always away from oneself' is the route to understanding.[28]

> Knowledge is only in time.
> You are the dark Unconscious
> From eternity to eternity.[29]

> But the living all
> make the mistake that they differentiate too much.
> Angels (they say) often don't know
> whether they are among the living or the dead.
> The eternal current drags every age through both realms
> and drowns them out in both.[30]

Rilke's position was one of extreme cognitive passivity.

> Why say what *is*? Why afflict things with their meaning? I can imagine only a longing that with continual wandering traverses the world. All things are so ready to host for a short time our many and often confused thoughts and desires.[31]

Against the Western cognitive tradition he suggested a metaphysic based on an *absence* of self-assertion.

Semyon Frank cited the most directly revealing words Rilke ever wrote about Russia and his view of what the Russian tradition could mean.

> Russia became for me . . . the deep, daily insight that reality is something strange, something which comes infinitely slowly to those who have patience. Russia is the country where the people are lonely people, each man with a world inside him, each man

full of darkness, like a mountain; each deep in his humility, not fearing to lower himself, and pious therefore. People full of warmth, uncertainty and hopes: people who are in the process of becoming.[32]

Rilke, a German poet, created a Russian metaphysics of *sobornost'* that would because of his name become better known than any other in the world. *Sobor* was the Russian word for that cathedral into which sun rarely penetrated, and he used the Russian word in his German line: *Selten ist die Sonne im Sobor*. His sympathy for spiritual Russia led him to hymn that integral knowledge admired by Khomiakov and Kireevsky as the right way to live.

> Every single thing is watched over
> by a goodness ready to fly
> every stone and every blossom
> and every small child at night.
> Only we in our arrogance push
> because of a few connections
> into a room empty of freedom
> instead of trusting to clever powers
> and raising ourselves up like a tree.[33]

Freedom consists in opening ourselves to truth. Predatory concepts obscure our freedom to know the world as it is – which without cognitive fuss includes us.

There are obvious limits to the use philosophy can make of this model of embedded, passive knowledge. Animals can't do science, nor can stones or blossoms know anything as we would recognize it, nor can small children know much, however readily they 'raise themselves up like a tree'. Farmers and singers would have to learn a different technique to acquire some scientific knowledge. But the Russian theory of naive knowledge was really meant as a moral philosophy of being in just the way Rilke understood it. It was, historically, an ethics of knowledge and as such a way of living with the modern individualistic and critical spirit.

Rilke was born in 1875 and died in 1926. In their own right Russian idealists of the same era reached for models obviously comparable with his vision of cognitive gentleness. One was Sergei Bulgakov's idea that nature could be treated fairly and made sacred through labour. As Hegel first understood, labour was a tool, just as thought was a tool. The use of these tools defined our relation to nature. Marx followed in the Enlightenment-Hegelian tradition of seeing thought and labour as active instruments by which man builds himself a home out of the raw material nature offers. Nature exists to be exploited and reworked for man's use. But against this technical use of thought, and this purely technical interpretation of labour, the early twentieth century began to rebel. In contrast to the harsh Marxian view of man as technical master and exploiter of nature, Bulgakov's 'sophic economy' was a romance of the soil which transformed the idea of labour from active exploitation to tender cooperation. The sophic economy – expressed in *The Philosophy of Economy* (1912) – took the cognitive aggression out of work and recast it as sympathy with nature. Work should not be an attack on nature, like conceptual thought on reality, but empathize with the material it works upon. Bulgakov, having passed through a period of Marxism, accepted that philosophy was no longer a matter of how we perceive the world but how we act upon it.

The leap from cogitation into practicality forged a powerful link between instrumental reason and the carelessness of industrialization, as two related undesirables. Philosophers felt it as well as poets. As a recent commentator put it, the Russian Silver Age hated 'improvements in living'.[34] Bulgakov wrote into Russian philosophy that as the ultimate object of knowledge the physical world must have its integrity respected. It should not be abused by intrusive and destructive abstractions. The soil

of every place has its specific integrity. Treat your part of the world with
integrity and you have a basis for communal living. With this kind of
argument Bulgakov added a poetic epistemology to the longstanding
Russian communal ideal. With work as non-aggressive knowledge – the
basis of the sophic economy – he revamped Tolstoy's praise for peasant
life into a sophisticated moral option which more than peasants might
choose as the right way to live.

Bulgakov's contemporary, Semyon Frank, was also concerned to
formulate on the right level for philosophy an ideal non-aggressive
knowledge to respect the integrity of the world. He defined philosophy
as a rational approach to the limits of reason. *Nepostizhimoe* (Paris 1939)
was a translation of Goethe's *Das Unerforschliche*, and meant 'what is
beyond the mind of man'. Frank spoke of a 'transrationalism' which did
not reject rational perception but replaced it at the summit of
understanding with pure receptivity.[35]

Frank saw an alternative German poetic discourse – one from the end
of the eighteenth century – as providing a conceptual apparatus through
which the Russian vision could be expressed. Goethe's pursuit of the
'pure phenomenon' at last opened up an acceptable epistemic world at a
high intellectual level. Goethe the poet-scientist, who had made it his
philosophical task to 'take things to be what they are', whose method was
'participatory observation' and 'intellectual-spiritual participation' and
who believed that 'through intuition of a constantly creative nature'
he could make himself worthy of 'intellectual-spiritual participation in
nature's products', maintained that his reward as a scientist was to be
able to see that the natural world contained symbols of its own self-
transcendence.[36] The basis of Frank's philosophy was to make Goethe's
intuition of pure symbolic phenomena a philosophy of knowledge
crowned by religious intuition. The transrational method – Frank's term
for the search for the pure phenomenon – confirmed that God's world
existed. Frank spoke of the mind's *metalogical* unity enabling it to reach
out to the unattainable and of 'a better way of knowing'.[37]

Frank raised up the simple Russian idea of protecting 'God's world' and made it a moral-ontological imperative: the good man must accept that the meaning of life lies beyond him and is greater than anything he can invent. He must not only accept it but actively respect it. As Goethe puts it in a favourite quotation of Frank's: 'Existence is duty, and it would be even if it only lasted a moment' (*Pflicht ist Dasein, und wär's nur ein Augenblick*). Duty is not just a matter of right conduct, but of right living from moment to moment. We carry out our wider duty as human beings by caring for the ungraspable total reality of which we are part.

On a historical note, Russian cognitive idealism in defence of the integrity of the world developed in two main waves. The first wave came in the 'remarkable' decade with the reaction against German Idealist abstraction; the second was part of the reaction against positivism and Marxism. Solovyov pioneered an anti-positivist religious idealism which provided a way for thinkers of the next generation like Berdyaev, Bulgakov and Frank to attack Marx. First against Fichte and Hegel, then against Marx, Russia's redoubled response within fifty years to the problems posed by modern rationalism strengthened the sense of a native tradition at last. Its position was disarmingly simple. It was what Belinsky suddenly woke up to one day when he decided he would read no more Fichte:

> Being will always be for me more than I know . . . logically it is
> so, but in practice it is different, will always be for me the words
> of a wise man.[38]

To argue against Fichte ('The German Descartes') and Hegel, Russian philosophy had to put a premium on the non-individual and the non-rational in its scale of values. The result was a meek, passive, 'feminine' philosophy to refute the combativeness of concepts. Through the nineteenth century the *raison d'être* of such an alternative philosophy grew ever more apparent. Rapid European modernization threatened Russian simplicity. The perceived enemies were individualism and technology. Russian philosophizing about moral being contains an implicit search for ways *not* to industrialize. The overarching anxiety as to whether concepts – rational thought as such – were likely to misjudge life and damage its substance was most plausible at a poetic and personal level. In the Silver Age of Russian culture, a term Berdyaev coined to describe the richness of poetic discourse from about 1890 to the Revolution, the strongest common feature between poetry and philosophy was an attachment to symbolic objects which confirmed the existence of transcendent values. Here was a realm for living and a method for thinking which was fundamentally non-rational and sensitive to the eternally inviting otherness of the world.

In a passage that might have excited any of the Silver Age poets and philosophers, Goethe defined as symbolic objects those 'which, in a certain characteristic multiplicity, stand there as the representatives of many others; they contain a certain totality within themselves and invite a certain order. They awaken in my mind similarities and differences and so from both without and within they lay claim to a certain unity and universality. They are therefore, what a good choice of subject is for a writer, fortunate objects for humanity.'[39] On the other hand, Russia had been living more or less happily with this poetic-moral outlook for many decades when suddenly in the period 1890–1920 the West identified it as Russian. Suddenly the West, which came to terms with technology and Marxism rather later than Russia, could see that Russia's choice was not only poetic and personal but possibly, to echo Goethe's words, something fortunate for humanity, a true alternative. Suddenly – on the threshold of the twentieth century – it was to poetic Russia's great advantage not yet to have abandoned primitive knowledge when the advanced world was on the edge of catastrophe. Rilke was a product of the Western rebellion against technological culture which turned to Russia for consolation, just as was his fellow German writer, Thomas Mann. In

Mann's earlier work Russian characters acted as foils of naturalness to self-destructive Western complexity.[40] This was also the sense in which in *The Decline of the West* Oswald Spengler looked to Russia as a new start for European civilization.

As Berdyaev who, in his vast unsystematic body of thought actually excelled at expressing the Russian spiritual project, put it:

> Adaptation to the meaningless, given world can only hinder us from comprehending meaning; but the partisans of scientific philosophy demand this adaptation, that is they deny the creative nature of philosophy. It is true that they are striving to lift the rank of science, to recognize it as a creative act and to see a higher meaning, the Logos, in the logical categories with which science operates. But this raising of the rank of science and its extension into higher spheres can be achieved only by bringing philosophy down into science, consciously or unconsciously.[41]

In the early twentieth century, the Germans and the French and the British realized that Russia, through its literature, its ideas, its experience, its art, was different. What began then, with a less fortunate outcome for Russia than might have been, because it was not honoured for its contribution by name, was a seeping out of Russian ideas into new Western ways of thinking: a poetic revolution which still marks Continental philosophy a century on. Naive poetic Russia was truly the antidote to Hegel and Marx, and to the legacy of the *cogito*. Rilke idealized Russia, no doubt. But the result of his reading and his travels and his absorption of Solovyov was a small miracle in the history of European thought, because it created a conduit for Russian ideas to flow West. As a result, the force of Russian spirituality, all that its philosophers had worked out through their reading of the German Idealists and the great mystics before them, and what they had married to Russian ideals of ethical community and non-individualized, non-assertive knowledge,

271

would help to found the most influential philosophy of being in twentieth-century philosophy, that of Martin Heidegger. What Heidegger grasped, in the spirit of Solovyov and Dostoevsky, and against Marx, was that the world might be re-enchanted.

Like the mystically minded Russians who responded to the French Revolution, and a century later to the Bolshevik Revolution, Heidegger entered the story of modern philosophy out of a world which seemed to have broken apart. All around him, either side of 1914–18, German culture and philosophy were obsessed with the spiritual loss accompanying the arrival of a modern industrial consumerist society. For Heidegger the tradition of Western 'instrumental reason' was to blame. The impulse to dominate the earth through scientific classification and technological use was destructive. With it Western metaphysics had entered a dead end. The only way for man – humanity – to recover was to give up his cherished 'privileged subject' point of view – the Cartesian *cogito* of modern science – and begin to rethink 'the sense of being'.

In his lecture 'What is Metaphysics?' (1939) Heidegger described three adjustments towards the world that would revivify philosophy:

Philosophy – what we call philosophy – is metaphysics' getting underway, in which philosophy comes to itself and its explicit tasks. Philosophy gets underway only by a peculiar insertion of our own existence into the fundamental possibilities of being [*Dasein*] as a whole. For this insertion it is of decisive importance, first, that we allow space for beings as a whole; second that we release ourselves into the nothing, which is to say, that we liberate ourselves from those idols everyone has and to which they are wont to go on cringing; and finally that we let the sweep of our suspense take its full course, so that it swings back into the basic question of metaphysics, which the nothing itself compels: why are there beings at all, and why not rather nothing?[42]

Heidegger's position is post-scientific and anti-technical, in the sense that he sees his approach to being coming into operation after science has done its instrumental work. He is not interested in 'putting things to use'. His way is explicitly anti-Cartesian, opposed to the idea of a pure, cognizing subjectivity. Indeed, Heidegger is drunk on the contrary desire to bring epistemic 'moods' into the act of knowledge: joy, boredom, excitement and, crucially, anxiety, express being-in-the-world. In George Steiner's words, Heidegger rejects 'the seductions of "technicity" . . . the egocentric humanism of liberal enlightenment and, finally, logic itself'. A better kind of thinking would be pre-subjective and pre-logical and would let being be.[43]

The Russian comparison provides a rather sobering context in which the rejection of humanism and logic might be measured. Pre-subjective, pre-logical thinking is hard to imagine beyond the examples of the cognizant farmer and the responsive dog, unless all men are to have the genius of Rilke. But Heidegger's evident point is that thought need not be a confrontation between subject and object. In *What is Metaphysics?* he speaks, even in scientific procedure, of an attitude which brings about a disclosure. When science 'breaks in to being' the result brings 'a fire of simplicity and sharpness of being-there into scientific existence' and 'in the sciences there occurs, according to the idea, a coming close to the true nature of all things'. Yet science ignores the Nothing, which is the source of the openness of Being and of the brilliance which surrounds whatever comes to light, and science's superiority is absurd if it does not hold itself out in mystical expectation, ecstatically or ek-statically, as Heideggerians write, into the Nothing.

> Only when science ex-ists out of metaphysics, can it constantly conquer afresh its essential task, which does not consist in amassing and ordering knowledge, but in performing the always freshly required task of opening up the whole realm of truth about nature and history.[44]

The 'What is Metaphysics?' lecture was printed with an introduction and afterword in 1943 and again in 1949. Another 1949 work of Heidegger's, *The Letter on Humanism*, took up the idea that *Dasein* or *Ek-sistenz* was beyond the reach of Cartesian subjectivism. The spelling *Ek-sistenz* emphasized man's 'standing out' into 'the truth of being'. Parallel to the way man brought luminosity to scientific existence he brought *Lichtung*, 'clearing', to being. That was what his *Ek-sistenz* was for. The 'Letter' argued that humanism underestimated man's active role, his 'out-standing stance' in this *Lichtung*. But Heidegger did not mean illumination, direct light, for that would point to what the Enlightenment achieved in the scientific spirit he wanted to get away from. Instead, in *Being and Time* he had spoken of the 'pre-predicative simple seeing of the invisible world' which *Lichtung* made possible. *Dasein* was immediate radiant understanding of being's fundamental but hidden qualities. The mystical word 'radiant', the spontaneous, self-combusting light emanating from Christ and from saints, neologism of the once passionately Catholic Heidegger, must surely play a part in any translation into English of *Lichtung*. He trails with him a religious heritage as rich as that which equipped Hegel and Schelling and Khomiakov's paradoxically 'blind' students of optics.

Heidegger's values arced back to those which Russians of the previous century associated with the good man and the ethics of being. The beautiful soul, with his superb openness to beauty, and his mystical sense of the oneness of being, and his steady cultivation of his personal life through art and personality, was needed by Solovyov, by Berdyaev, by Frank, just as by Heidegger, to say how a non-Cartesian set of truths could be perceived. In the Russian religious idealists and Heidegger alike philosophy had as its goal re-enchantment or spiritual happiness, and if what they wrote tended away from philosophy into literature that was because happiness was not a matter for mentality alone but involved all the senses, and the response to art. Heidegger rejected philosophy as a professional, specialized, occasional pursuit. Rather it was the condition of any authentic personal life and its most intimate event. Moments spent reading a poem or contemplating a landscape or a painting were the most truly philosophical.

Both Frank and Berdyaev would have recognized Heidegger's central idea of *Lichtung*, rather unhappily translated as 'the clearing of being', as a fair description of their own work. Whatever the exact wording, what was meant was the desire to get away from an artificial social truth and back to an unmistakable ontological truth. Russian philosophers had been crusading against instrumental reason since the 1820s. The strongest original position in Russian philosophy was that fully *to be* matters more than to acquire knowledge. In fact one has to *be* one's way to knowledge by allowing being to live through one's existence. Ordinary language makes it difficult to say this. The intransitive verb 'to be' has to be rethought as an openness to being. By chance the Russian language is actually better able to make these points than either German or English. In Russian the present tense of the verb 'to be' only exists in the infinitive form. Usually no verb is written but occasionally the infinitive form is used. I to be, you to be, and so on. The personalized and inflected power of *est'* is thus invisible, even if it is possible. At the same time it corresponds to a noun for truth, *istina*, whose essential distinction from *pravda* is that it is not man-made. *Istina* refers rather to the truth of the universe. The twentieth-century thinker Father Pavel Florensky, murdered by Stalin's NKVD, was so fascinated by the Russian case that he compared the etymology of the word for 'truth' in various languages. The Greek word *alethiea* drew attention to that aspect of the unforgettable or indelible nature of truth. Latin *veritas* had the same root as the Russian verb *verit'*, to believe, and laid the emphasis on belief. The ancient Hebrew word *emet* emphasized the aspect of trustworthiness or security. But the Russian word *istina* emphasized being, 'that which is'. It seems like a story tailor-made for Heidegger, who was often moved to see obscured spiritual truth in forgotten etymologies.[45]

Heidegger shared with the Russians his sources from Plato and

Aristotle, through Eckhardt and Boehme, to Schelling, on the need for art to bring about a clearing of being. Like Solovyov, Berdyaev and Frank, and like their shared mentor Goethe, Heidegger was interested in symbols, 'pure phenomena', as Goethe said, which were 'fortunate for mankind'. Among those symbols were painting and literature and music, for they showed something beyond themselves.[46]

All philosophies seem to need enemies, ways of defining what they are not, and clearly what Heidegger and the Russians most had in common was distaste for the modern West. The attitude remained relevant for over a century, from the 1830s when the Russians first gave voice to it, to the 1930s when Heidegger, despite becoming embroiled in Nazism, was thinking some of his best anti-modern thoughts. The Russians from Khomiakov to Solovyov and beyond had wanted to defend nature, something like the cause of Heidegger's *Erde*, on both poetic and ecological grounds. They too disliked the man-made world, Heidegger's *Welt*. Their enemy was typically that model of bourgeois, capitalist, industrial society, Odoevsky's 'Town without a Name'. Tolstoy set Russian nature against Western progress, as did the *pochvenniki*, the adherents of *pochva*, the soil, who included Dostoevsky.[47]

As Odoevsky had seen it as far back as 1844, already then the typical Western man could no longer hear his own inner voice, while the good Russian had never lost his attunement to spiritual goods. And so Odoevsky objected to capitalism, and to the industrial technology which supported it. But importantly, against the future Marxist template imposed upon Russian thought, he did so on spiritual, not class-based grounds. The same could be said for Heidegger's actual opposition to Marxism, and the campaign Berdyaev and Frank would maintain against Soviet Communism from their exile abroad. Their mutual complaint was against a false metaphysics. Frank for one knew the affinity to Heidegger was there, though he was understandably reluctant to recognize the link to an atheism and a philosophy which quickly overshadowed his own.

To my knowledge Heidegger never acknowledged and maybe never knew of the coincidence of his thought with Russian traditions. He learned so much about being from Rilke, but seemed unaware of the degree of Rilke's debt to Russia. Unknowingly therefore, he brought two great Russian ideas to fruition. He overturned traditional metaphysics rooted in the encounter between a coercive subject and dead object, and he insisted on the truth of man's bond to the earth rather than the man-made world.

Both in Russia and in Germany a raft of alternative poetical-philosophical thinking would move forward in the twentieth century: anti-technological, anti-materialist and what the Russians would call personalist – a last bid to hold on to spiritual enchantment. Berdyaev and Frank read Goethe and the German mystics. Heidegger read Hölderlin – the poet of 'Bread and Wine' – and Rilke. If Life itself, what Kant called 'things for us' as opposed to things-in-themselves, and what Nietzsche called 'things to hand', was rich in meaning before any man started to analyse it, precious too were the persons of men and God and their unique intimacy.

In Russian religious philosophy from Solovyov onward, persons were moral personalities who accepted responsibility towards a world greater than themselves. The thesis of Berdyaev, Frank and others was that a good Russia needed moral persons but expressly not Western-style competitive individualists. Russia could build a good world so long as it had morally creative individuals. Personalism also continued to insist that if we want to *know* truth then there is a right way to *be* in the world. Personalism asked for respect for reality as if it were another person. This reality could be described as God, or as the continuity of being.

Marxism was deficient in persons and all the values dear to personalism. It is important to note that from a Russian spiritual point of view, the kind that informed the judgements of a whole century of men from Odoevsky to Berdyaev to Solzhenitsyn, Marxism was essentially 'Western' and 'individualistic' and even 'bourgeois'. Berdyaev expressed his hostility in strong terms, in prose which four generations of Soviet

Russians never knew existed but which they have passionately welcomed in the post-Soviet era:

> Marxism is in essence an atomistic world-view. Marxism asserts the social consciousness of hostile, disjunct and separating atoms. In the Marxist consciousness there is nothing organic, no recognition of the reality of the general and suprapersonal. In it there is not even the recognition of the reality of the personal. Marxist social consciousness is something which arises only after the sin of individualistic disunion.[48]

In Russia, Lenin and the rise of Marxism and then the Revolution distilled the views of the spiritual opposition, just as the Great War and the rapid spread of modern technology had their effect on Heidegger. The Russian emphasis, however, remained emphatically on persons and also, as had been the case since Belinsky, on less articulate, defenceless simple souls who might be crushed in the modern stampede. Every man is valuable, say the Russian and German ethical neo-Kantians, trying to put the Hegelian idea of competition against the other, of self-definition *against* the other, finally to rest. Ethical Kantians believe in non-exploitation of the other. The work of Frank and Berdyaev found its European counterpart not least in the poetic mysticism of the Jewish philosopher Martin Buber, who argued in *I and Thou* (1923) that we should know the world on I–Thou terms rather than I–It: if we relate to an It we only dominate, we don't really *know*. True knowledge is a coming together, a middle. The other becomes an 'it' as soon as it becomes an extension of the subject. The subject must allow the other to be a Thou. Buber suggested that it was possible to be consciously in the world and among other men without dividing off that world and one's fellow human beings as separate and 'other' objects. Frank had expressed this view in many earlier works, as had Berdyaev. Berdyaev had specifically decried objectification, by which he meant turning the world into a cold detached object out there rather than a warm one still part of us.

> Objective processes *abstract* and disrupt existence. They substitute society for community, general principles for communion ... the result of objectification in knowledge ... is not only to isolate man but also to confine his activities to an essentially alien world ... Reality is originally part of the inner existence, of the inner spiritual communion and community, but it becomes degraded in the process of objectivication and of having to submit to social necessities.[49]

The 'I and Thou' theme lay at the heart of the Russians' Christian socialism. It could be traced back to Feuerbach, for whom it was a utopian criticism of Hegel.[50] But its development in Marxism was disappointing and degrading. Thus the early twentieth-century thinkers went back to the final expression of German Idealism to see what went wrong, and begin again. In Buber and in Solovyov, and in Berdyaev and in Frank, was over and over again a critique of Hegel as a theologian who went wrong. Hegel allowed the attraction of reason to carry him away from the reality of individual men and women and situations. Hegel, like all his subsequent Christian critics, understood that central to an ethical philosophy of being, in which the good man could find a home, was the idea of the Incarnation, a paradigm of non-separateness made possible through the continuous presence of divine love. But he sacrificed his insights. He gave them away in favour of a systematic account of social and political change in a world completely conquered by reason. His finished system of thought drained his insights of their real human content and downgraded real individuals to the status of endless active egos in competition with each other.

There is a sense in which every modern thinker must come to terms with Hegel, that no progress can be made without returning to where he left Western thought. Marxism, last child of Hegelian dialectic, failed humanity precisely because it did not come to terms with Hegel. And now that Marxism has failed Russia, a new generation of thinkers is looking back to the generation which tried to resist Marx before the cataclysm. Because Marxism has let the world down, philosophy has a task in a post-socialist world to come back to where Hegel left off and start again. 'I suspect that our point of departure is not essentially different from that of the first generation of the pupils of Hegel.' 'There is nothing for it. We are philosophically still contemporaries of the young Hegelians.'[51]

The anti-Marxist, personalist argument was taken up in European thought by Buber's disciple Emmanuel Levinas (1906–95). There is something wrong when being is appropriated by knowledge and the two become identical. The source of the aggression against being is traced back first to Descartes and then implicitly to Hegel.

The wisdom of first philosophy is reduced [by Descartes' *cogito*] to self-consciousness. Identical and non-identical are identified. The labour of thought wins out over the otherness of things and men.[52]

For Levinas, true knowledge 'will . . . come to constitute the mystery of being qua being'. He goes on to argue, famously, that not the Cartesian theory of knowledge, but ethics, should be 'first philosophy'. That 'the labour of thought should not win out over the otherness of things and men' is a sentiment which expresses the strength and the best aspiration of the Russian tradition. No Russian has perhaps ever said it so well, but the tradition exists, of a culture which above all things wishes to be moral by preserving the integrity of the world and the integrity of others – not their right to be fully fledged individuals so much as their right to be private souls. By happy chance there is a cognate bond between the Russian word for 'friend' and for 'the other', *drug* and *drugoi*. The two belong together as the fundaments of any viable modern philosophy. They wait for a Russian philosopher to become their author.

Evidently Russian philosophy is not quite its own subject. It is a branch of German philosophy, perhaps even of German poetry, and has always needed outside thinkers to make clear what it holds as its own. Its originality has lain in what it has made of Western thought in a unique Russian situation, and, as I hope these last two chapters have shown, what subtly it has been able to give back to the West as something forgotten there or new; something valuable as a marker because it is extreme.

My final Russian philosopher is Isaiah Berlin, and in a way his life and work in Britain should be seen as a small ironic postscript to the history of Russian philosophy told in the course of this book. He was, in my view, a man with an aversion to religious thought, but a Russian philosophical anarchist and a defender of souls. For his thought to have gone by those names in the repressed culture England was in the 1950s would have been far too emotive, a decision he surely reached for himself. So instead of talking about anarchism in his political philosophy he talked about positive and negative liberty. The classical essay was 'Two Concepts of Liberty' (1958). Negative liberty was the right of individuals not to be interfered with by the state or by other men. It sounded like a reprise of J. S. Mill. In its postwar way it was perhaps a subliminal defence of quiet English privacy against aggressive German lunacy.[53] But at the same time its roots were in European Counter-Rationalism and, finally, in Russia.

One way to trace that link is to observe what Berlin had to say about the counter-rationalist Herder:

For Herder men are men, and have common traits at all times; but it is their differences that matter most, for it is the differences that make them what they are, make them themselves, it is in these that the individual genius of men and cultures is expressed. The denial, at any rate in Herder's earlier writing, of absolute and universal values carries the implication, which with time has grown increasingly disturbing, that the goals and values pursued by various human cultures may not only differ, but may, in addition, not all be compatible with one another; that variety, and perhaps conflict, are not accidental, still less eliminable, attributes of the human condition.[54]

Of those who believed that 'differences... matter most', 'perhaps his [Herder's] most characteristic descendants were to be found in Russia' and it was 'the pre-Marxist Russian intelligentsia who took over Herder's passion for the whole man'.[55]

The Russian anarchists – Russian Herderians, extreme liberals – insisted concepts could not be used as social glue without harming souls. From Khomiakov to Belinsky to Shestov souls had to be protected from the reach of ideas. Souls were not Western-style individuals whose rights to become their best selves required positive respect and encouragement. They were rather an infinite unknowable number of others who needed to be protected against the intrusions of external authority, whether that reason emanated from concepts or from political power or, as the personalists began to understand, from technology. This Russian anarchist attitude, based on a rejection of the triumphant Hegelian concept, was surely the foundation also of Berlin's idea of 'negative liberty'.

Negative liberty was a rejection of Hegelian perfectionism and tellingly of what Marx went on to call 'positive criticism'.[56] Negative liberty told the old Russian story of the need to resist philosophy as social glue. Berlin would implicitly agree with Belinsky in 1841 that 'All Hegel's talk about morality is utter nonsense, since in the objective realm of thought there is no morality.'[57] By contrast, 'political liberty in this [negative] sense is simply the area within which a man can act unobstructed by others'.[58] This vision brought Berlin close to both the Russian personalists and to his fellow Balt Levinas. Positive liberty, about which he had almost nothing positive to say, was a neutralized – not to say neutered – way of referring to the Hegelian tradition of self-realization. In it lay the roots of Western liberal individualism and Marxist dialectic, two traditions tainted by their common assumption of a right to dominate based on a sense of an objectively certifiable hierarchy of values. The problem for Berlin amongst his British and American contemporaries was how to secure his pluralism against the charge of relativism. 'It may be that the ideal of freedom to choose ends without claiming eternal validity for them, and the pluralism of values connected with this, is only the late fruit of our declining capitalist civilization' sounded almost as chaotic as his core proposition, though perfectly fitting for a Russian anarchist in mild Oxford disguise.[59]

What Berlin would have needed to argue, but in England more like confess, would have been the continuing presence of Hegel in the argument. For what pluralism amounted to was keeping open the dialectic; accepting that for every thesis or belief an open, eternally unfinished society would generate more than one antithesis, and the antitheses would keep on coming; that this was unquestionably better than living under the domination of one idea; indeed, it was the only acceptable, if decadent, modern way to live. Modern life was defined by some doubt and social confusion, but it was as far as possible unfettered. As crucially Berdyaev once wrote:

Hegel's monistic philosophy is redeemed by his vision of a dialectic and a struggle of opposites at the heart of existence.[60]

Positive and negative liberty – essentially two visions of the good life – were the two dominant forces in Russian philosophy before totalitarianism took hold. Their interplay was the first and last hope of balance in the Russian tradition. As the most humane Russian thinkers debated what to do with potential social chaos in a world which lacked grass-roots social traditions and a corresponding empirical tradition in philosophy, they oriented themselves towards the defence of souls. They wanted to know how to be realistic and tolerant in a world without Hume; how to make life bearable in a world prey to being organized from above, by rulers and by ideas which cruelly overlooked what Berlin called 'differences' and Levinas 'the otherness of things and men'. Shestov's anarchism was one way of compensating for the absence of Hume in Russia.[61] Berlin did something similar, forging a marriage of Russian anarchism and English common sense. Common ground between the two cultures lay in their utter distrust of the application of abstract universals to real, warm, living life. Against German and French rationalist tendencies the Russians and the English believed reason had no claim on ways of personal and national and cultural growth.

Berlin was in one way a man who lived and worked in the nineteenth century. He could never have appreciated that his insistence on the dialectic remaining unresolved, his idea that there should be no conclusion to the syllogism, would lodge itself also at the heart of post-modern opposition to closure. But in another he was a man who foresaw the near-chaos lying ahead of a Western world that dared to remain libertarian under pressure to privilege certain cultural values over others; and he knew that potential future Western chaos because he knew the Russian past – what Russia would be without an ideological harness.

In my life Berlin became part of the mystery of where Russia fitted in the greater world. In conclusion it seems possible to say that the last two hundred years in Russia have been an intellectual disaster but not an imaginative or a moral failure. Russia is its own place, by turns primitive, non-rational, powerful, careless with human lives and deeply humane. It exists on the edge of a Western culture where we too no longer live in the centre.

A Comparative Chronology of Russian and Western Philosophers

		René Descartes	*1596–1650*
		Blaise Pascal	*1623–62*
		Baruch Spinoza	*1632–97*
		Gottfried Leibniz	*1646–1716*
		Earl of Shaftesbury	*1671–1713*
		Bishop Berkeley	*1685–1753*
		Giovanni Batista Vico	*1688–1744*
		David Hume	*1711–76*
		Adam Smith	*1723–90*
		Immanuel Kant	*1724–1804*
		Johann Georg Hamann	*1730–88*
		Friedrich Jacobi	*1743–1819*
		Johann Gottfried von Herder	*1744–1803*
		Jeremy Bentham	*1748–1832*
Alexander Radishchev	*1749–1802*	Johann Wolfgang von Goethe	*1749–1832*
		Friedrich Schiller	*1759–1806*
		Claude Henri de Saint-Simon	*1760–1825*
		Johann Gottlieb Fichte	*1762–1814*

		G. W. F. Hegel	*1770–1831*
		François Fourier	*1772–1837*
		Friedrich Schelling	*1775–1854*
		Arthur Schopenhauer	*1788–1860*
Pyotr Chaadaev	*1794–1856*	Auguste Comte	*1789–1857*
Vladimir Odoevsky	*1804–69*		
Aleksei Khomiakov	*1804–60*	Ludwig Feuerbach	*1804–72*
Ivan Kireevsky	*1806–56*	John Stuart Mill	*1806–73*
		Joseph Proudhon	*1809–69*
Vissarion Belinsky	*1811–48*		
Alexander Herzen	*1812–70*		
Nikolai Stankevich	*1813–40*		
Mikhail Bakunin	*1814–76*	Karl Marx	*1818–83*
		Friedrich Engels	*1820–95*
Fyodor Dostoevsky	*1821–81*		
Apollon Grigoriev	*1822–64*		
Pyotr Lavrov	*1823–1900*		
Nikolai Chernyshevsky	*1828–89*		
Nikolai Fyodorov	*1828–1903*		
Lev Tolstoy	*1828–1910*		
Konstantin Leontiev	*1831–91*		
Dmitry Pisarev	*1840–68*		
Nikolai Mikhailovsky	*1842–1904*	Eduard von Hartmann	*1842–1906*
		Friedrich Nietzsche	*1844–1900*
Vladimir Solovyov	*1853–1900*		
Vasily Rozanov	*1856–1919*	Sigmund Freud	*1856–1939*
Georgy Plekhanov	*1856–1918*		
		Henri Bergson	*1859–1941*
Lev Shestov	*1866–1938*		
Vladimir Ilyich Lenin	*1870–1924*		
Nikolai Lossky	*1870–1965*		
Sergei Bulgakov	*1871–1944*		
Alexander Bogdanov	*1873–1928*		
Nikolai Berdyaev	*1874–1948*		

Semyon Frank	*1877–1950*	Martin Buber	*1878–1965*
Gustav Shpet	*1879–1937*		
Pavel Florensky	*1882–1943*		
		Martin Heidegger	*1884–1976*
Boris Pasternak	*1890–1940*		
Alexandre Koyransky (Koyré)	*1892–1964*		
Aleksei Losev	*1893–1988*		
Mikhail Bakhtin	*1895–1975*		
Alexandre Kojève	*1902–68*		
		Jean-Paul Sartre	*1905–80*
		Emmanuel Levinas	*1906–95*
Isaiah Berlin	*1909–97*		
Alexander Solzhenitsyn	*1918–*		
		Michel Foucault	*1926–84*
		Bernard Williams	*1929–2003*
		Jacques Derrida	*1930–*
		Alasdair MacIntyre	*1929–*

Notes

Preface

1. Frederick Copleston, *Philosophy in Russia*, Notre Dame, 1986, p. 4.
   Andrzej Walicki, *A History of Russian Thought from the Enlightenment to Marxism*, Oxford, 1980, p. xiv.
2. Isaiah Berlin, 'Thinkers or Philosophers?', *Times Literary Supplement*, 27 March 1953.
3. G. P. Fedotov, *The Russian Religious Mind*, Cambridge, Mass., 1966, II, p. 355.
4. Ibid., pp. 4, 344.

Chapter 1   *The Men of the 1820s*

1. Walicki, 1980, p. 59. For the Decembrists see Marc Raeff, *The Decembrist Movement*, Englewood Cliffs, NJ, 1966.
2. Walicki, 1980, pp. 57–8.
3. Cynthia H. Whittaker, *The Origins of Modern Russian Education*, Dekalb, 1984, p. 47.
4. Walicki, 1980, p. 57.
5. Ksenofont Alekseevich Polevoi, *Zapiski K. A. Polevogo*, St Petersburg, 1888, p. 86.
6. A. I. Gertsen, *Polnoe sobranie sochinenii* [PSS], Moscow, 1955, V, p. 13; IX, p. 17.
7. F. W. J. von Schelling, *Werke*, ed. Manfred Schröter, Munich, 1958, IV, pp. 385–6.
8. M. G. Pavlov, *Atenei*, 1828, No. 1, 'O Vzaimnom otnoshenii svedenii

umozritel'nykh i opytnykh' [On the Inter-relation of Speculative and Empirical Knowledge].

9. I. I. Ivanov, *Istoriya russkoi kritiki*, 2 vols, St Petersburg, 1898–1900, II, p. 282; *Brokgauz i Evron Entsiklopedichesky Slovar'; Russkie esteticheskie traktaty pervoi tret'i XIX veka*, ed. Z. A. Kamensky, Moscow, 1974.

10. Whittaker, 1984, pp. 78–83. See also C. H. Whittaker, 'From Promise to Purge: the First Years of St Petersburg University', *Paedegogica Historica*, 1978, XVIII, pp. 148–67; J. T. Flynn, 'Magnitsky's Purge of Kazan' University', *Journal of Modern History*, 43, no. 4, 1971, pp. 598–614. The most eloquent and moving account remains Alexandre Koyré, *La philosophie et le problème nationale au debut du XIX siècle*, Paris, 1923. pp. 99–112. Koyré, born Aleksandr Koyransky, emigrated from Russia in 1919 and pursued an academic career abroad.

11. A. V. Nikitenko, *A. I. Galich*, St Petersburg, 1869, p. 17.

12. Nikitenko, 1869, p. 20.

13. P. N. Sakulin, *Iz istorii russkogo idealizma Knyaz V. F. Odoevsky*, Moscow, 1913; I. I. Zamotin, *Idealizm v russkom obshchestve i literature*, St Petersburg, 1908; Neil Cornwell, *The Life, Times and Milieu of V. F. Odoevsky 1804–1869*, London, 1986.

14. For the doctrine of 'Official Nationality' devised by Count Uvarov, Nicholas I's Minister of Public Instruction in 1833, see Whittaker, 1984; Nicholas Riasanovsky, *Nicholas I and Official Nationality*, Berkeley, 1959, pp. 70–72 and *A Parting of Ways. Government and the Educated Public in Russia 1801–1855*, Oxford, 1976, p. 116.

15. *Mnemozina*, ed. V. F. Odoevsky and V. Kyukhel'beker, Moscow, 1824–5.

16. V. I. Sakharov, 'O zhizni i tvoreniyakh V. F. Odoevskogo' in V. F. Odoevsky, *Russkie nochi*, in V. I. Sakharov (ed.), *Sochineniya v dvukh tomakh* [Works], 2 vols, Moscow, 1981, I, p. 6.

17. R. T. McNally, *The Major Works of Peter Chaadaev*, London, 1969, pp. 30–31 (First Letter). This is my translation from the French.

18. McNally, 1969, p. 200.

19. M. Lemke, *Nikolaevskie zhandarmy i literatura 1826–1855*, St Petersburg, 1908.

Chapter 2 *The Beautiful Souls*

1. I. S. Turgenev, *Polnoe sobranie sochinenii v dvenadtsati tomakh* [PSS], Moscow, 1983, XI, 'Vospominanie o Belinskom', p. 27.

2. Isaiah Berlin, *Russian Thinkers*, London, 1978, p. 126.

3. Turgenev, PSS, 1983, XI, p. 27.

4. V. G. Belinsky, *Polnoe sobranie sochinenii* [PSS], Moscow, 1953–9, XII, pp. 656–7.

5. Belinsky, PSS, 1953–9, XI, p. 152–3 [to Ivanov 7 August 1837].

6. Belinsky, PSS, 1953–9, XI, pp. 307ff [to Bakunin 12–24 October 1838].

7. Belinsky, PSS, I, p. 465.

8. Belinsky, PSS, 1953–9, XII, p. 69.

9. Ibid.

10. Belinsky, PSS, 1953–9, XII [to Botkin 27/28 July 1841].

11. Gertsen, PSS, 1955, VI, p. 60.

12. Gertsen, PSS, 1955, VI, pp. 101–2.

13. Gertsen, PSS, 1955, VI, p. 67.

14. Gertsen, PSS, 1955, III, p. 56. Mill, Comte, Bakunin and many others disliked specialists. Walicki, 1980, p. 257; J. S. Mill, *On Liberty*, ed. John Gray, Oxford, 1991, p. 124fn.

15. Gertsen, PSS, 1955, VI, p. 129.

16. Gertsen, PSS, 1955, VI, p. 119.

17. Berlin, 1978, p. 117.

18. Berlin, 1978, p. 133.

19. Friedrich Schiller, 'Uber Anmut und Würde', 1793 [On Grace and Dignity] in *Dtv-Gesamtausgabe*, Munich, 1966, Band 18, (Theoretische Schriften), p. 36.

20. V. F. Odoevsky, *Russkie nochi*, in V. I. Sakharov (ed.), *Sochineniya v dvukh tomakh*, Moscow, 1981, I, p. 238.

21. Ivan Kireevsky, *Polnoe sobranie sochinenii*, Moscow, 1911, reprinted London, 1970, II, pp. 26–7. On the history of the beautiful soul, excluding Russia, see Robert E. Norton, *The Beautiful Soul*, London, 1995.

22. I. S. Turgenev, *Polnoe sobranie sochinenii*, Moscow/Leningrad, 1960–68, VI, pp. 394–5.

23. Martin Malia, 'Schiller and the Early Russian Left' in *Harvard Slavic Studies*, IV, 1957, p. 196. See also Martin Malia, *Alexander Herzen and the Birth of Russian Socialism*, Cambridge, Mass./Oxford, 1961.

24. Odoevsky, 1981, I, p. 116.

25. Nikitenko, 1869, pp. 89–90.

26. P. V. Annenkov, *Literaturnye vospominaniya* [Literary Reminiscences], St Petersburg, 1909, p. 79.

27. 'A. S. Khomiakov ego lichnost' i mirovozrenie' in *Izbraniye sochineniya*, pod. red. N. S. Arsenievom, New York, 1955, p. 13. James M. Edie, James P. Scanlan and Mary-Barbara Zeldin, *Russian Philosophy*, 3 vols, Chicago, 1965, I has an excellent introduction to Khomiakov's life and work in English.

28. A. S. Gertsen, *Byloe i dumy* [My Past and Thoughts], Part 4, Ch. XXX, p. ii.

29. Edie et al., 1965, I, p. 235.

30. 'The factory process...' quoted in N. Berdyaev, *Sub Specie aeternitatis Opyty filosofskie, sotsial'nye i literaturnye*, 1900–1906gg., Moscow, 2002, p. 220. See also A. S. Khomiakov, *Sochineniya*, Moscow, 1994, I, p. 302.

31. See Golo Mann, *The History of Germany Since 1789*, Harmondsworth, 1974, pp. 84–91, for a kindred interpretation of Hegel's place in history and his achievement. An excellent guide is also Judith N. Shklar, *Freedom and Independence. A Study of the Political Ideas of Hegel's 'Phenomenology of Mind'*, Cambridge, 1976.

32. Copleston, 1986, pp. 74–6. Walicki, 1980, pp. 102–3. See also Dmitry Chizhevsky *Gegel' v Rosii* [Hegel in Russia], Paris, 1938, p. 176. The Slavophile thinker Yury Samarin writes in a letter to Khomiakov that the Orthodox Church can be given a philosophical underpinning through a demonstration of its similarities with Hegel. Which culture should lead the world becomes the question of which church. Catholicism is the thesis, Protestantism is the antithesis, Russian Orthodoxy the synthesis for the new age. Khomiakov prefers to retain his simple vision.

33. For *Mitwissenschaft* see Andrew Bowie, *Schelling and Modern European Philosophy*, London, 1993, p. 113. Feuerbach called it *Mitgewissen*, see Eugene Kamenka, *The Philosophy of Ludwig Feuerbach*, London, 1970, pp. 135, 144.

34. Copleston, 1986, p. 64.

35. Copleston, 1986, p. 56.

36. I. V. Kireevsky, *Polnoe sobranie sochinenii*, ed. Mikhail Gershenzon, Moscow, 1911, reprinted London, 1970, I, 'Devyatnadtsaty Vek' esp. pp. 89–94. S. P. Shevyryov, *Teoriya poezii v istoricheskom razvitii u drevnykh i novykh narodov*, Moscow, 1836. *Russkie esteticheskie traktaty v pervoi tret'i XIX veka*, ed. Z. A. Kamensky, 2 vols, Moscow, 1974, II contains many typical passages.

37. See N. I. Nadezhdin's articles on Romantic poetry included in S. A. Vengerov (ed.), *V. G. Belinsky Polnoe sobranie sochinenii*, St Petersburg, 1900, I, p. 504.

38. Kireevsky, 'Obozrenie sovremennogo sostoyaniya literatury 1845g.' and 'O kharaketere prosveshcheniya Evropy i o ego otnoshenii k prosveshcheniyu Rossii' in Kireevsky, 1911, I, pp. 127–74 and 174–223. The second of these articles 'On the Nature of European Culture and its Relation to the Culture of Russia' appears in English in *Russian Intellectual History: An Anthology*, ed. Marc Raeff, New Jersey, 1978. Dostoevsky, *The Brothers Karamazov*, tr. David Magarshack, Harmondsworth, 1958, I, p. 69.

39. Copleston, 1986, p. 53.

40. Walicki, 1980, pp. 108–9.

Chapter 3 *The New Men*

1. Walicki, 1980, p. 202.
2. Kamenka, 1970, pp. 124ff.
3. Edie et al., 1965, II, p. 60.
4. Edie et al., 1965, II, p. 52.
5. Cf. Walicki, 1980, p. 160 and pp. 349–51.
6. Edie et al., 1965, II, p. 59.
7. *What is to be Done?* tr. Benjamin Tucker, revised and abridged by Ludmilla B. Turkevich, with an introduction by E. H. Carr, New York, 1961.
8. Edie et al., 1965, II, p. 28. See also Rufus W. Matthewson, *The Positive Hero in Russian Literature*, New York, 1958, for Chernyshevsky's rejection of tragedy.
9. Emma Rothschild, *Economic Sentiments. Adam Smith, Condorcet and the Enlightenment*, Cambridge, Mass., 2001, p. 116.
10. Edie et al., 1965, II, p. 59.
11. Edie et al., 1965, II.
12. Edie et al., 1965, II; Copleston, 1986, p. 116.
13. Edie et al., 1965, II, p. 102.
14. Edie et al., 1965, II, p. 66.
15. Edie et al., 1965, II, p. 75.
16. Edie et al., 1965, II, p. 272.
17. Marina Kostalevsky, *Dostoevsky and Soloviev. The Art of Integral Vision*, London, 1997, pp. 146–7.
18. Walicki, 1980, p. 374.
19. Edie et al., 1965, III, p. 99.
20. Semyon Frank, *The Listener*, 28 April 1949, p. 709.
21. John Mander, *Our German Cousins. Anglo-German Relations in the 19th and 20th Centuries*, London, 1974. Iris Murdoch was greatly interested in Dostoevsky and the spiritual Russians.
22. V. S. Solovyov, *The Crisis in Western Philosophy*, Chapter IV.

Chapter 4 *The Populists*

1. Walicki, 1980, pp. 222–3: 'Populism should be understood not as a specific trend in revolutionary thought but as a dynamic ideological structure within which many positions were possible. The significant feature of this ideology was that it combined bourgeois democratic radicalism with opposition to capitalism as a social system.'
2. See Peter Kropotkin, *Memoirs of a Revolutionist*, 2 vols, London, 1899, and for

studies of his life and work Martin A. Miller, *Kropotkin*, Chicago, 1976 and George Woodcock, *Anarchism. A History of Libertarian Ideas and Movements*, London, 1963 (note 86).

3. Aileen Kelly, *Mikhail Bakunin*, Oxford, 1982, pp. 24–8.

4. Kelly, 1982, p. 112.

5. Woodcock, 1963, p. 152.

6. *Karl Marx, Friedrich Engels, Collected Works*, London, 1975, III, 'Economic and Philosophic Manuscripts of 1844'. See also David McClellan, *Marx before Marxism*, Harmondsworth, 1972.

7. G. W. F. Hegel, *Phenomenology of Spirit*, tr. A. V. Miller, Oxford, 1977, p. 406 [para 668].

8. Walicki, 1980, p. 277.

9. Leszek Kolakowski, *Main Currents of Marxism*, 3 vols, Oxford, 1981, I, pp. 246–8.

10. Walicki, 1980, p. 273.

11. Walicki, 1980, p. 279; Kelly, 1982, p. 157.

12. Walicki, 1980, p. 279.

13. See Kelly, *passim*. Leonard Schapiro commented in the *Times Literary Supplement*, 13 May 1983, that her treatment of the Nechaev controversy 'is the most illuminating treatment of the question to date'. See also Walicki, 1980, pp. 244–5.

14. Samuel H. Baron, *Plekhanov. The Father of Russian Marxism*, London, 1963, p. 14.

15. Baron, 1963, pp. 14, 31.

16. Baron, 1963, p. 15.

17. Edie et al., 1965, II, p. 136. Also in *Lavrov. Historical Letters*, tr. and with an introduction and notes by James P. Scanlan, Berkeley, 1967, reprinted Knoxville, 1976, 1984.

18. Edie et al., 1965, II, p. 137.

19. Edie et al., 1965, II, p. 139.

20. Edie et al., 1965, II, pp. 143–4.

21. Copleston, 1986, p. 270.

22. Phillip Pomper, *Peter Lavrov and the Russian Revolutionary Movement*, London, 1972, p. 35. Edie et al., 1965, II, p. 120. Scanlan, *Lavrov. Historical Letters*, pp. 18–19. See also Kolakowski, 1981, II, p. 320.

23. Edie et al., 1965, II, p. 126 (Letter I).

24. Edie et al., 1965, II, p. 151 (Letter VI).

25. Edie et al., 1965, II, p. 153 (Letter VIII).

26. Pomper, 1972, p. 182.

27. Pomper, 1972, p. 9, pp. 75–6.
28. Proudhon believed that Communism would never be compatible with the dignity of the individual. See Kolakowski, 1981, I, p. 207.
29. Kolakowski, 1981, II, p. 320.
30. Walicki, 1980, p. 253; Edie et al., 1965, II, p. 179.
31. Edie et al., 1965, II, p. 179.
32. Alain Besançon, *The Intellectual Origins of Leninism*, Oxford, 1981, p. 148.
33. Walicki, 1980, p. 263.
34. Walicki, 1980, pp. 256–7. Kolakowski, 1981, II, p. 322.
35. Edie et al., 1965, II, p. 175.
36. N. A. Berdyaev, 'Filosofskaya istina i intelligentskaya pravda' in *Vekhi*, Moscow, 1909. Available in English as *Landmarks*, ed. Boris Shragin, Albert Todd, tr. Marian Schwarz, New York, 1977, and *Landmarks*, tr. and edited by Marshall S. Shatz and Judith E. Zimmerman, Armonk, New York, 1994.

Chapter 5   *The Impact of Marx*

1. Marx in fact was far less Marxist than the Russian Marxists about their country. See Kolakowski, 1981, pp. 323–4.
2. Baron, 1963, p. 60.
3. Baron, 1963, p. 143.
4. Walicki, 1980, p. 415.
5. Walicki, 1980, p. 409.
6. Cf. Baron, 1963, p. 116.
7. Baron, 1963, p. 163.
8. Kolakowski, 1981, II, p. 340.
9. Baron, 1963, p. 151.
10. Walicki, 1980, pp. 409ff; Kolakowski, 1981, II, p. 350.
11. Baron, 1963, p. 174.
12. Copleston, 1986, p. 266, 270–71. Baron, 1963, p. 179.
13. Kolakowski, 1981, II, p. 352; Walicki, 1980, p. 421.
14. Baron, 1963, p. 354; Walicki, 1980, p. 421.
15. V. I. Lenin, *Collected Works*, London, 1962, XIV, p. 20.

Chapter 6   *The Silver Age*

1. Roman Jakobson, *Language Poetry and Poetics. The Generation of the 1890s: Jakobson, Trubetskoy, Majakovskij*, ed. Katerina Pomorska et al., Amsterdam, 1987, p. 10.
2. Kolakowski, 1981, II, pp. 354, 362.

3. *Vekhi*, 1909 (Preface to the 1st edition). See above chapter 4 note 36.
4. Nicholas Berdyaev, *Dream and Reality*, London, 1950, p. 19.
5. Berdyaev, 1950, p. 27; Berdyaev, *The Meaning of the Creative Act*, London, 1955, p. 72.
6. Timothy Ware, *The Orthodox Church*, Harmondsworth, 1963, pp. 75, 254.
7. Berdyaev, 1950, p. 30.
8. Edie et al., 1965, III, p. 190 [*Solitude and Society*, London, 1939].
9. Fedotov, 1966, II, p. 355; Ware, 1963, p. 236.
10. Berdyaev, 1955, p. 72.
11. Berdyaev, 1955, p. 41.
12. Philip Boobbyer, *S. L. Frank. The Life and Work of a Russian Philosopher*, Ohio, 1995.
13. Catherine Evtuhov, *The Cross and the Sickle*, London, 1997, and see below.
14. Preface, note 2.
15. Berlin, 1978, p. 155.
16. Berdyaev, 1950, p. 87.
17. Robert Service, *Lenin. A Biography*, London, 2000, p. 59.

Chapter 7   *The Moral Map*

1. Odoevsky, 1981, I, pp. 49, 87, 146.
2. Odoevsky, 1981, I, pp. 87–8.
3. Aleksandr Solzhenitsyn, *The Russian Question at the End of the 20th Century*, London, 1995, pp. 116–17.
4. *John Stuart Mill, Jeremy Bentham, Utilitarianism and Other Essays*, ed. Alan Ryan, Harmondsworth, 1987, p. 31.
5. Rothschild, 2001, p. 74.
6. Rothschild, 2001, p. 38.
7. 'Pervaya vstrecha' in Gertsen, PSS, 1955, I, p. 119.
8. 'Zapiski odnogo cheloveka' in Gertsen, PSS, 1955, I, p. 278.
9. Edie et al., 1965, II, pp. 143–4.
10. Ibid.
11. Ibid.
12. Hegel (1807), 1977.
13. N. V. Stankevich, *Perepiska*, Moscow, 1914, p. 594.
14. Ivan Goncharov, *Oblomov*, tr. Natalie Duddington, London, 1932, p. 55.
15. Goncharov, 1932, p. 5. Sabine Melchior-Bonnet, *The Mirror. A History*, London, 2001, p. 189, notes that Thomas Aquinas denounced the *libido sciendi* as the first degree of pride.

16. Kelly, 1982, p. 32.

17. Kelly, 1982, p. 38.

18. Kelly, 1982, p. 39.

19. Georgy Florovsky quoted in Evgeny Lampert, *Studies in Rebellion*, London, 1957, p. 32. Sergei Bulgakov also speaks of 'the religious Russian soul lacking in cultural self-discipline'. N. O. Lossky, *A History of Russian Philosophy*, London, 1952, p. 97.

20. Edie et al., 1965, II, p. 238.

21. Fedotov, *The Russian Religious Mind*, Cambridge, Mass., 1946, I, pp. 123–30.

22. Daniel Rancour-Laferrière, *The Slave Soul of Russia*, New York, 1996, p. 244.

23. Lou Andreas Salomé, *En Russie avec Rilke 1900. Journal inédit*, texte établi par Stéphane Michaud et Dorothée Pfeiffer, Paris, 1992, pp. 133, 138–9. The translation is mine.

24. Thomas Garrigue Masaryk, *The Spirit of Russia*, 3 vols, London, 1955–67, I, p. 527 observed the Russian pursuit of 'a mystical form of aristocracy'. Berdyaev takes up aristocracy as a spiritual concept but transmutes it out of characteristically passive Russian communalism and defines it as personal and creative: 'Aristocratic morals (in the metaphysical rather than the social sense of the word) are morals of value, of quality, of individuality, of creativeness.' Berdyaev, 1955, p. 266.

25. Edie et al., 1965, II, p. 75.

26. Georg Lukács, *Goethe and His Age*, tr. R. Anchor, London, 1967, p. 127.

27. Alexander Solzhenitsyn, *The First Circle*, London, 1968, pp. 386–9.

28. Ibid.

29. Ibid. The character Shulubin makes the same spiritual journey in Solzhenitsyn's *Cancer Ward*, London, 1986.

30. Odoevsky, 1981, I, p. 307.

31. Edie et al., 1965, I, p. 251.

32. Solovyov, *Sobranie sochinenii*, ed. S. M. Solovyov and E. Radlov, St Petersburg, 1911–14, VII, pp. 64–81: 'I call a true or positive universality that in which the one exists not at the cost of all or to their detriment, but to the benefit of all. False, negative unity crushes or swallows the elements entering into it and seems itself empty; true unity preserves and strengthens its elements, realizing itself in them as the fullness of being.' ('The First Steps towards a Positive Aesthetic', 1894; my translation.) Berdyaev, *The Philosophy of the Creative Act*, 1955, repeats the point: 'The falsehood in Marxism is in that it presents itself as a metaphysic of being' (p. 140). 'Sociologism is a false sense of community, a community of individualistic disunion, a degraded

community of men estranged from each other' (p. 274) and 'In the highly developed capitalistic economy ... there is the black magic of false and fictive being' (p. 293).

33. Belinsky, PSS, XII [to Botkin, 1 March 1841].
34. Walicki, 1980, p. 329.
35. Berlin, 1978, pp. 73–4.
36. 'The one who builds and destroys worlds' (1909), quoted in Leon Chestov, *L'homme pris au piège*, Paris, 1966, p. 6.
37. Fyodor Dostoevsky, *The Devils*, tr. David Magarshack, Harmondsworth, 1953, p. 255.
38. Evtuhov, 1997, p. 63.
39. Evtuhov, 1997, p. 49.
40. Edie et al., 1965, II, p. 240.
41. Edie et al., 1965, II, p. 272.
42. Edie et al., 1965, II, p. 231.
43. Edie et al., 1965, II, p. 223.
44. Edie et al., 1965, II, p. 242.
45. Edie et al., 1965, II, p. 273.
46. *The First Circle*, 1968, pp. 357–8.

Chapter 8   *Rejecting the View from Descartes*

1. *Cancer Ward*, 1968.
2. *Cambridge Companion to Descartes*, ed. John Cottingham, Cambridge, 1992, p. 417. See also 'Sayings Attributed to Pascal', IX, in Pascal, *Pensées*, tr. A. J. Krailsheimer, Harmondsworth, 1966, p. 356.
3. Copleston, 1986, p. 62. See also Edie et al.,1965, I, p. 179. Kireevsky was an adamant anti-Cartesian.
4. Arseniev in Khomiakov, *Izbraniye sochininiya*, p. 13.
5. L. N. Shestov, *Sochineniya*, Moscow, 1993, II, p. 262 ('Job's Balances', part iii, On the Philosophy of History).
6. Nikolai Efremovich Andreev, *To Chto Vospominayetsya*, Tallinn, 1996, I, p. 271.
7. Semyon Frank, *Reality and Man*, tr. Natalie Duddington, London, 1965, pp. 85–9; B. P. Vysheslavtsev, *The Eternal in Russian Philosophy*, tr. Penelope V. Burt, Grand Rapids Michigan, 2002, esp. pp. 157–76.
8. Berdyaev, 1955, p. 11.
9. See below, p. 170.
10. Berlin, 1978, p. 68.

11. Berdyaev, *Sub specie aeternitatis*, 2002, p. 218.

12. Cf. Khomiakov to Samarin, 15 August 1943, in *Izbraniye sochineniya*, p. 325; PSS, VIII, p. 228ff.

13. Solovyov uses the term *syzygy*. See Vladimir Solovyov *The Meaning of Love* [1892], tr. Janet Marshall, New York, 1947; Walicki, 1980, p. 385; Edie et al., 1965, III; V. V. Zenkovsky, *A History of Russian Philosophy*, London, 1953, II, 'The Concept of Sophia'. *Syzygy* is the desire for the other, the cosmic Eros, which seeks the mystery of the other person. Sophia is reality willing itself to be known. Her attributes include knowability and a yearning for man's response.

14. Michael Ignatieff, *Isaiah Berlin. A Life*, London, 2000, p. 71.

15. Isaiah Berlin, *Three Critics of the Enlightenment*, London, 2000. For Maistre, see Berlin, *Russian Thinkers*, pp. 57–81 and 'Joseph de Maistre and The Origins of Fascism' in Berlin, *The Crooked Timber of Humanity*, London, 1990.

16. Berlin, 1999, p. ix (Editor's Preface).

17. See Andrew Bowie, *Schelling and Modern European Philosophy*, London, 1993, pp. 17–25.

18. Berlin, 1999, p. 307.

19. Goethe ('*teilnehmende Betrachtung*' and '*geistige Teilnahme*'), *Goethes Werke*, Hamburg, 1952, X, p. 529 and XIII, p. 25.

20. Goethe bemoans '... impatience, overhastiness, complacency, stiffness, the form of one's thoughts, preconceived opinion, taking the easy option, triviality, changeability...' *Goethes Werke*, 1952, XIII, pp. 14–15.

21. The poem 'Epirrema' – variously and repeatedly quoted in Russian discourse by Herzen, Solovyov, Frank and others.

22. *Goethes Briefe*, Hamburg, 1962–7, II, p. 20.

23. *Goethes Werke*, 1952, XII, p. 406, 'Maximen and Reflexionen', No. 299.

24. Hegel to Goethe, 24 April 1825, *Briefe von und an Hegel*, ed. Johannes Hofmeister, Hamburg, 1952–61, III, p. 83.

25. Gertsen, PSS, 1955, II, p. 355 and XII, p. 128.

26. Schelling, 1958, IV, p. 54, 'Aphorisms by way of an Introduction to Nature Philosophy' (xxxx).

27. Schelling, 1958, I, p. 242, 'Philosophical Letters on Dogmatism and Criticism' (1795).

28. Schelling, 1958, I, p. 705–6, 'Ideas on a Philosophy of Nature' (1797).

29. *Poems of Hölderlin*, tr. Michael Hamburger, London, 1943.

30. 'The Oldest Systematic Programme of German Idealism' in *Schelling: Briefe und Dokumente*, ed. Horst Fuhrmans, Bonn, 1962–75, I, pp. 69–71. The passage

was found in Hegel's handwriting but appears to have been Schelling's work.

31. Schelling, 1958, IV, pp. 383–4.
32. Schelling, 1958, I, p. 265. Schelling uses *der Gerechte* and *Gerechtigkeit*.
33. Hegel, *Sämtliche Werke*, Stuttgart, 1927–40, I, p. 44.
34. See chapter 2 note 29.
35. Ibid.
36. Edie et al., 1965, I, p. 258.
37. Edie et al., 1965, I, p. 252.
38. Berdyaev, 1950, pp. 99, 199; Berdyaev, 1955, pp. 301–6.
39. Cornwell, 1986, p. 81; Copleston, 1986, p. 40; Walicki, 1980, p. 78. Russian mystical interests are so clearly delineated in the alternative tradition that one generation after another carries the torch. Frank, for instance, worked on the fifteenth-century mystic Nicholas of Cusa. Similar work was also pursued by Alexandre Koyré in Paris, as it was by Aleksei Losev: a translation of Nicholas of Cusa was the only work Losev could publish in the Stalin years. See James P. Scanlan (ed.), *Russian Thought after Communism. The Recovery of a Philosophical Heritage*, New York/London, 1994, p. 191. Koyré was lecturing on Cusanus (1401–64) in the last term before he handed over in Paris in 1933 to another Russian with a fundamental underlying interest in mysticism, Alexandre Kojève. See Dominique Auffret, *Alexandre Kojève. La philosophie, l'état, la fin de l'histoire*, Paris, 1990.
40. Ware, 1963, p. 32; Fedotov, 1946, I, pp. 46ff., pp. 123–29.
41. See chapter 2 note 33.
42. Ware, 1963, pp. 30–32.
43. Leszek Kolakowski, *Positivist Philosophy*, Harmondsworth, 1972, pp. 252–4.
44. 'The first step towards a positive aesthetic consists in rejecting the fantastic separation of beauty and art from the general movement of universal life and in acknowledging that artistic activity in itself has no particular, allegedly higher object, but that it serves the general life goal of humanity in its way and by its means.' Solovyov, *The First Step Towards a Positive Aesthetic* (1894).
45. Berdyaev, 'Philosophical Truth and the Pravda of the Intelligentsia' in *Vekhi* (1909), p. 7. See also *Landmarks*, 1977.
46. S. L. Frank, 'Etika nigilisma' in *Vekhi Sbornik statei o russkoi intelligentsii*, 2nd ed., Moscow, 1909, reprinted Moscow, 1990, p. 179. In English, 'The Ethic of Nihilism: A Characterization of the Russian Intelligentsia's Moral Outlook' in *Landmarks*, 1977. By 'nihilism' Frank meant 'the negation of, or failure to recognize absolute values' and the habit of allowing 'moralism' to rule consciousness.

47. Ibid, p. 182.
48. Théophile Funck-Brentano, *Les sophistes allemands et les nihilistes russes*, Paris, 1887.
49. Jean-Paul Sartre, 'La liberté cartesienne' in *Introduction à des textes choisis de Descartes*, 1946, reprinted in *Situations philosophiques*, Paris 1990. In English, in Jean-Paul Sartre, *Literary and Philosophical Essays*, London, 1955. See also *Existentialism and Humanism*, tr. Philip Mairet, London, 1973, pp. 44–5.
50. Berdyaev in *Vekhi*, 1909, p. 18 (See above note 45.)

Chapter 9   *The Contest of Good and Evil*

1. A. S. Akhiezer, 'On the Particularities of Contemporary Philosophizing – A View from Russia', *Voprosy filosofii*, 1995, (12), p. 7.
2. Copleston, 1986, pp. 377–84, considers the meaning of 'groundlessness' in a positive anarchistic sense which sets human freedom above the power of any state. Piama P. Gaidenko 'The Philosophy of Freedom of Nikolai Berdiaev' in Scanlan (ed.), *Russian Thought after Communism*, cites N. O. Lossky and Dmitry Merezhkovsky as critics of Berdyaev's 'obscurantism of freedom' and fails to clarify Berdyaev's position positively. This might be done in connection with understanding a similar idea in Shestov whose *Apofeoz bezpochvennosti* (1905), 'The Apotheosis of Groundlessness', was translated into English as *All Things are Possible*, London, 1920.
3. Berdyaev, 1950, pp. 49, 56, 84.
4. Ibid., p. 123.
5. Frank, 1965, p. 17.
6. See above, p. 164.
7. Frank, 1965, pp. 33–4.
8. Berdyaev, 1950, p. 50.
9. Joseph Frank, *Dostoevsky. The Years of Ordeal 1850–1859*, Princeton, NJ, 1990, pp. 50ff., 105–6.
10. L. N. Shestov, *Sochineniya*, 2 vols, ed. A. V. Akhutin and E. Patkosh, Moscow, 1993. The editors' notes to volume I, printed in volume II, survey assessments of Shestov by other Russian thinkers (vol. II, pp. 407–9). Shestov is 'the philosophizing anti-philosopher' whose approach is 'radical adogmatism' and whose subject is 'belief stripped of metaphysical postulates, belief without guarantee'. The religious historian Georgy Fedotov is quoted there as saying that Shestov spent his whole life battling Idealism and that his counter-advocacy was a way to live with terror. He was not interested in saving people.

11. R. N. Carew Hunt, *The Theory and Practice of Communism*, Harmondsworth, 1963, p. 142.

12. Both Prince Myshkin in *The Idiot* and Kirilov in *The Devils* were epileptics. See e.g. *The Devils*, Harmondsworth, 1953, p. 586.

13. See Boobbyer, 1995, pp. 64–5.

14. Compare Michel Foucault, *The Order of Things*, London, 1970, reprinted 2002, p. 373: 'To all those who still wish to talk about man, about his reign or his liberation, to all those who still ask themselves questions about what man is in his essence, to all those who wish to take him as their starting point in their attempts to reach the truth, to all those who on the other hand refer all knowledge back to the truths of man himself, to all those who refuse to formalize without anthropologizing, who refuse to mythologize without demystifying, who refuse to think without immediately thinking that it is man who is thinking, to all these warped and twisted forms of reflection we can answer only with a philosophical laugh – which means, to a certain extent, a silent one.'

15. Momme Brodersen, *Walter Benjamin. A Biography*, tr. Malcolm R. Green and Ingrida Ligers, London, 1996, p. 219.

16. The term *knizhnost'* specifically Dostoevsky uses most often in his journalism about education and national authenticity. See e.g. 'Knizhnost i gramotnost' (1861) in *Polnoe sobranie sochinenii Dostoevskogo*, St Petersburg, 1906, X. *Knizhnost'* stands in close relation to the *knizhnoe delo* of the Populists, for whom it meant the supply of key political texts to the peasants and workers. Dostoevsky develops the idea more ironically in his fiction. In *The Underground Man*, having announced in Chapter I (Underground), Section ii, that 'Petersburg [is] the most abstract and concocted city in the whole wide world', he carries forward the theme of book-fed unreality with the terms 'literary', 'literature', 'out of a book', coupled with his ongoing satire of the popularity of German Idealism in Russia as 'everything beautiful and elevated'. The word *knizhy* means 'artificial' and 'self-deceiving' in Chapter II, especially the final sections viii and ix.

17. Modern philosophy has mostly ignored the topic of evil. See as a recent exception Susan Neiman, *Evil in Modern Thought*, Oxford, 2002, p. 10: 'Descartes' evil demon is not a thought experiment but a threat. Unlike its pale heir, the brain in the vat, the devil was a real concern.'

Chapter 10 *Lenin and the View from No One*

1. *Vekhi*, 1909, p. 95. See also *Landmarks*, 1977. In the Preface to the first edition

NOTES

Gershenzon would insist on 'the theoretical and practical pre-eminence of spiritual life over the external forms of community' and 'the sense that the individual's inner life is the sole creative force of human existence and that it, and not any self-sufficient principle of a political order, is the only firm basis for any social construction'.

2. Chapter 4 note 7.

3. Lenin didn't read Hegel until 1914, five years after writing *Materialism and Empiriocriticism*. He felt the need to acquaint himself with the philosopher who had a greater influence in Russia than any other, not least over Plekhanov. Lenin's mindset was never directly affected by Hegel. But the type of philosophy Hegel brought into being was concerned with a desire for social and political effectiveness, which was especially what Lenin wanted for Russia.

4. Friedrich Engels, 'Ludwig Feuerbach and the Outcome of Classical German Philosophy' (1886). The translations are mine. For the standard version in English, see *Marx Engels Collected Works*, Moscow, 1990, XXVI, p. 398.

5. Ibid., p. 380.

6. Ibid., p. 381.

7. Richard T. De George, *Patterns of Soviet Thought*, Ann Arbor, MI, 1963, p. 146.

8. Berlin, 1978, p. 125. Maurice Baring quoted in G. S. Smith, *D. S. Mirsky*, Oxford, 2000, p. 5.

9. Lenin, 1962, XIV, p. 120.

10. Lenin, 1962, XIV, p. 340.

11. Ibid.

12. Lenin, 1962, XIV, pp. 342–3.

13. Lenin, 1962, XIV, pp. 43, 47, 49, 56, 59.

14. Copleston, 1986, p. 285.

15. Lenin, 1962, XIV, p. 343.

16. Lenin, 1962, XIV, p. 20. He credited the phrase to an anonymous Marxist.

17. The blockheads were Russian Marxists V. Chernov, V. Bazarov, P. Yushkevich and S. Suvorov.

18. Leonid Plyushch, *History's Carnival*, London, 1979, p. 391. Bergson was one of the great enthusiasms of the Silver Age intelligentsia with works published in 1909 and 1911. See, as always, Berdyaev, 1950 and 1955, and Alexander Haart, 'Appearance and Sense and Phenomenology in Russia' in Gustav Shpet, *Appearance and Sense*, Dordrecht, 1991, p. xxvii.

19. Bogdanov took sides against Abram Deborin. See De George, 1963, p. 180; and below.

20. Lenin, 1962, XIV, p. 67.

302

21. Lenin, 1962, XIV, p. 69.
22. Ibid.
23. Lenin, 1962, XIV, pp. 69–70.
24. Quoted in Louis Althusser, *Lenin and Philosophy and Other Essays*, tr. Ben Brewster, London, 1977, p. 37.
25. Kolakowski, 1981, II, p. 449.
26. Vladimir Bukovsky, *To Build a Castle: My Life as a Dissenter*, tr. Michael Scammell, London, 1978. For Plyushch, see above note 18.

Chapter 11   *How the Long Tradition Survived*

1. Ervin Laszlo (ed.), *Philosophy in the Soviet Union. A Survey of the Mid-Sixties*, Dordrecht, Holland, 1967, p. 196: *Realism* – the world exists independently of its perception and is objectively knowable. *Materialism* – reality reduces ultimately to an ontic stratum or substratum which can be denoted 'matter'. *Historical Subjectivism* – true knowledge is dependent on historically determined cognitive processes.
2. For a recent comment on party-mindedness see Simon Sebag Montefiore, *Stalin. The Court of the Red Tsar*, London, 2003, p. 77.
3. Section 2 of chapter 4 of the *Short Course*. See De George, 1963, p. 186.
4. De George, 1963, p. 193.
5. Ibid.
6. Ibid.
7. De George, 1963, p. 97: *Dialectical materialism* studied the general laws of dialectics and their application to nature and thought. *Historical materialism* studied the specific development of dialectics in history or in the development of human society.
8. Laszlo, 1967, p. 196.
9. De George, 1963, p. 193.
10. De George, 1963, p. 3.
11. Leonid Plyushch, *History's Carnival*, London, 1979.
12. See J. W. Boag, P. E. Rubinin, D. Shoenberg (editors and compilers), *Kapitsa in Cambridge and Moscow. Life and Letters of a Russian Physicist*, Amsterdam/Oxford, 1990, p. 67; Richard Lurie, *Sakharov. A Biography*, London, 2002, p. 104.
13. Lurie, 2002, pp. 62, 181.
14. Alasdair MacIntyre, *Marxism and Christianity*, Harmondsworth, 1968, p. 88.
15. Alexandre Koyré, *L'Occidentalisme d'Ivan Tourgeneff*, Paris, 1922, p. 47fn. 'Philosophy has never been very well regarded in Russia; a foreign product, recently imported, introduced into a country where the primary conditions and

the most essential bases for its development were missing, it has always lived a very precarious life, profiting in certain moments from a craze as thinly spread as it was shallow, subject to the vicissitudes of fashion, considered sometimes suspect, often dangerous, and always perfectly useless.'

16. Laszlo, 1967, p. 101.

17. Quoted in Lurie, 2002, p. 62.

18. Aleksandr Solzhenitsyn, *The Russian Question*, London, 1995.

19. See e.g. Alasdair MacIntyre, 'Hume on Is and Ought' in *Hume*, ed. A. C. Chappell, London, 1966. Philippa Foot, 'Moral Beliefs' in P. R. Foot (ed.), *Theories of Ethics*, Oxford, 1967. In a more recent interview with Jonathan Rée, BBC Radio 3, 19 September 2000, Foot considered Hume must be wrong in view for instance of the Nazi death camps. Did the camps exist, or didn't they? If they did they were evil. At the Royal Institute of Philosophy, October 2002, she argued that morality is not a discrimination of reason. Her example was of a young German refusing to join a Nazi death squad, knowing this would mean his own death. Foot's examples tend to come from moral emergencies – the Holocaust and the Second World War. Significantly Russia has been – in the moral and social sense – a chronic emergency ever since its modern birth.

20. MacIntyre, 1968, p. 94–5.

21. Arthur Koestler, *Darkness at Noon*, tr. Daphne Hardy, Harmondsworth, 1964, pp. 53, 71, 27, 70, 40, 153.

22. Ibid., p. 52.

23. Andrei Sinyavsky, *Soviet Civilization*, New York, 2000, p. 140.

24. Laszlo, 1967, p. 196.

25. De George, 1963, p. 10; Baron, 1963, p. 289, shows how Plekhanov admired Hegel.

26. The term was easy to transpose into Russian as *otmenyat'* or *predostanavlivat'*. French successfully used the verb *relever*, but the English 'sublation' never worked well. The meaningfulness of the translation surely has much to do with how well Hegel was understood in those countries. Thomas Carlyle's *Sartor Resartus* (1833–4) was actually an expression of English enthusiasm for German Romanticism, make of that aspect of the English psyche what you will.

27. Laszlo, 1967, pp. 76–8. The idea of *praxis* supported the fluid concept: '*Practice* is the line between theoretical and empirical concepts and propositions. It is in the [sic] human activity that the [sic] insight into essences and necessary structures of reality is made possible for man. A Cartesian static subject–object relation together with a general mechanist view makes the fact

of knowledge and science unintelligible. Practice is the dynamic transcendental relation between consciousness and material world which makes knowledge possible. This is certainly an interesting idea (and a long way from the Marxian concept of Praxis in the direction of something like Whitehead's "causal efficacy").' Ibid., p. 101.

28. Laszlo, 1967, p. 58.

29. For Derrida and *différance*, see Christopher Norris, *Derrida*, London, 1987, p. 108.

30. That the serious heart of post-structuralism is rooted in the need for philosophy to come to grips with twentieth-century political evil is why it should not be dismissed lightly, even if Derrida's solution seemed only to be a return to Hegel, giving new status and nomenclature to never-finished concepts. The Russian equivalent to postmodernism was mystical/religious anarchism in philosophy.

31. See George Kline, *Spinoza in Soviet Philosophy*, London, 1952.

32. 'The Teaching of Spinoza on Attributes' in *Voprosy filosofii i psikhologii*, 1912, kn 114, pp. 523–67. For an analysis of all the philosophical ingredients that went into *The Object of Knowledge* (1915), see Boobbyer, chapter 8. Frank, *Reality and Man*, pp. 48–51 rejects Spinoza as 'iron' like Parmenides and 'monistic' and 'abstract' – compare Berdyaev's judgement of the different strains in Western mysticism.

33. Walicki, 1980, p. 421.

34. Kline, 1952, p. 15.

35. Kline, 1952, p. 25; De George, 1963, p. 180.

36. Kline, 1952, p. 26: the Deborinites exaggerated the dialectical element and the mechanicists neglected it.

37. Derrida insisted it wasn't a concept. See Norris, 1987, p. 15, and on its vulgarization, p. 119.

38. The Marxist Sebastiano Timpanaro, *The Freudian Slip*, 1976, argues, against unconscious reasons for making mistakes in transmission, that the mind naturally simplifies. The study of copied medieval manuscripts shows repeated reversion to simpler, more familiar forms of words. The same seems to be true in the non-professional memory of music. The tune one sings is a simplified version of, say, the subtle original of Schubert.

39. Victor Terras, *A History of Russian Literature*, New Haven and London, 1991, p. 509.

40. I. I. Blauberg, Introduction to V. F. Asmus, *Vladimir Solovyov*, Moscow, 1994, p. 5.

41. Boris Pasternak, *An Essay in Autobiography*, tr. Manya Harari, London, 1959. See also *Marburg Borisa Pasternaka*, ed. E. L. Kudryavtseva, Moscow, 2001.

42. Boris Pasternak, *Doctor Zhivago*, London, 1961. For Vedenyapin, see part 2, p. 79.

43. Blauberg, 1994, p. 6.

44. Ibid. The description of Soviet philosophy is Blauberg's own, followed by a quotation from Asmus's memoirs.

45. V. V. Zenkovsky, *A History of Russian Philosophy*, tr. George L. Kline, 2 vols, London, 1953.

46. Yury Mann, *Russakya filosofskaya estetika*, Moscow, 1969, p. 51.

47. Laszlo, 1967, pp. 2, 142.

48. Mann, 1969, p. 178ff. Not that Marx and Engels were always wrong. Engels was a brilliant writer. But they were most often inappropriate.

49. Mann, 1969, p. 171.

50. Mann, 1969, p. 122.

51. *Marx Engels Collected Works*, London, 1975, III. For their publishing history, part in 1927 and the rest in 1932, see De George, 1963, p. 32.

52. Plyushch, 1979, pp. 63–4.

53. Plyushch, 1979, p. 86.

54. Plyushch, 1979, p. 64.

55. James P. Scanlan, *Marxism in the USSR. A Critical Study of Current Soviet Thought*, London, 1985, p. 269.

56. Plyushch, 1979, p. 215.

57. Hegel, *Phenomenology of Spirit*, 1977, p. 242 [para 404].

58. Edie et al., 1965, II, p. 97.

59. Dostoevsky, *The Devils*, tr. David Magarshack, Harmondsworth, 1953, p. 262. Part II, i, 'Night'.

60. Edie, et al., 1965, III, p. 31.

61. De George, 1963, p. 5.

62. De George, 1963, p. 223 from *Fundamentals of Marxist Philosophy*.

63. De George, 1963, p. 237.

64. Compare the Russian protagonist in the story 'What's the Matter?' in Lesley Chamberlain, *In a Place Like That*, London, 1998.

65. Laszlo, 1967, p. 5.

66. N. A. Berdyaev, *The Origins of Russian Communism*, London, 1937, p. 48.

67. S. V. Utechin, *Russian Political Thought*, London, 1964.

68. Bernice Glatzer Rosenthal (ed.), *Nietzsche in Russia*, Princeton, 1986, pp. 32ff.

69. Shklar, 1976, p. 72.

70. Odoevsky, 1980, p. 66.

71. Tim McDaniel, *The Agony of the Russian Idea*, Princeton, 1996, p. 33.

72. Andrei Sinyavsky, *Soviet Civilization*, New York, 1990, p. 113.

73. McDaniel, 1996, p. 160. McDaniel, p. 24, characterizes the Russian 'idea' from a sociologist's point of view as resting on six concepts: the rejection of egoistic utilitarianism; the desire for community; the suspicion of private property; the hatred of formalism in social relations, especially as concerns law; the desire for a state which will protect its subjects against social elites; and the idea of a distinctive national essence.

74. On voluntarism required to complement historical materialism, see De George, 1963, p. 139.

75. Jean-Paul Sartre, *Existentialism and Humanism*, tr. Philip Mairet, London, 1973, p. 67.

76. *Witness to My Life. The Letters of Jean-Paul Sartre to Simone de Beauvoir 1926–1939*, ed. Simone de Beauvoir, tr. Lee Fahnestock and Norman MacAfee, London, 1992, I, p. 316.

77. Sartre, *Existentialism*, 1973, p. 48.

78. For Feuerbach, see Eugene Kamenka, *The Philosophy of Ludwig Feuerbach*, London, 1970, p. 110.

79. *Goethes Werke*, 1952, XII, p. 43.

80. Berdyaev, 1950, p. 93, regarded his own 'true' existentialism as of the kind of Pascal, Kierkegaard and Nietzsche, not Jaspers, Sartre and Heidegger.

81. Ken Hirschkop, *Mikhail Bakhtin. An Aesthetic for Democracy*, Oxford, 1999, pp. 140–44 notes that Bakhtin may not have studied at university at all.

82. Ibid. pp. 168–9.

83. *Tvorchestvo Fransua Rable i narodnaya kultura srednevekoviya i renessansa*, Moscow, 1965, reprinted with new pagination in 1990. Quoted in Hirschkop, 1999, pp. 283–4. It was first written in 1940–46 under the title 'Rabelais in the History of Realism'.

84. Quoted in 'Forms of time of the Chronotope in the Novel' (1937–8) in *Four Essays on the Dialogical Imagination*, ed. Michael Holquist, Austin, Texas, 1981, p. 20. Russian original in M. M. Bakhtin, *Literaturno-kriticheskie stat'i*, compiled by S. G. Bocharov and V. V. Kozhinov, Moscow, 1986. On 'carnival' forms see also Hirschkop, 1999, pp. 180–83.

85. Holquist, 1981, p. 60.

86. Holquist, 1981, p. 60.

87. Holquist, 1981, pp. 47, 49.

88. Hirschkop, 1999, p. 4.

89. Caryl Emerson, 'The Making of M. M. Bakhtin as Philosopher' in Scanlan (ed.), *Russian Thought after Communism*, New York/London, 1994: Bakhtin's interest in linguistics was partly a tactical decision to benefit from Stalin's published interest ('Marxism and the Question of Linguistics', 1950). See also Hirshkop, 1999, p. 187.

90. Holquist, 1981, p. 161.

91. 'The existence of a man who is in life but not of it' may be a conscious echo of Schiller, *On The Aesthetic Education of Man*, ed. E. Wilkinson and L. Willoughby, Oxford, 1967, pp. 57–9: 'But how is the artist to protect himself against the corruption of the age which besets him on all sides? . . . Live with your century; but do not be its creature.'

92. 'Epic and Novel' in Holquist, 1981, pp. xxxii, 22, 24.

93. Martha Nussbaum, *Love's Knowledge*, Oxford, 1990.

94. Sinyavsky, 2000, p. 159.

95. Elena Bonner, 'The Remains of Totalitarianism', *New York Review of Books*, 8 March, 2001.

96. Plyushch, 1979, p. 92.

97. Plyushch, 1979, p. 43.

98. Venedikt Yerofeev, *Moscow Stations. A Poem*, tr. Stephen Mulrine, London, 1997, pp. 116–17.

99. Translated by Andrew Bromfield, London, 1994 and 1999 respectively. Andrew Meier, *Black Earth*, London, 2004, p. 47.

100. Masha Gessen, *Dead Again. The Russian Intelligentsia after Communism*, London, 1997, p. 19.

101. Solzhenitsyn, London, 1995, p. 108: 'We must build a moral Russia or none at all' and p. 115 'Among the Russian people . . . the phrase to live by the truth [zhit' po pravde] – has never been extinguished.'

Chapter 12 *On the Edge of Reason*

1. Nicholas Dent in *The Oxford Companion to Philosophy*, ed. Ted Honderich, Oxford, 1995, p. 516. Alasdair MacIntyre, *After Virtue*, 2nd (corrected) ed., London, 1985, p. 58: 'Moral arguments within the classical, Aristotelian tradition – whether in its Greek or its medieval versions – involve at least one central functional concept, the concept of *man* understood as having an essential nature and an essential purpose or function . . . but once the notion of essential human purposes or functions disappears from morality, it begins to appear implausible to treat moral judgements as factual statements.'

2. *Voprosy filosofii*, 1996, No. 1, contained an interview with MacIntyre.

3. See chapter 11, note 19.
4. MacIntyre, 1968, p. 88.
5. *Russian Thought after Communism. The Recovery of a Philosophical Heritage*, ed. James P. Scanlan, London, 1994, cites the enthusiasm for Leontiev of Evegeny Troitsky in *Vozrozhdenie russkoi idei: Sotsial'nie-filosofskie ocherki* [The Resurrection of the Russian Idea: Socio-Political Studies], Moscow, 1991.
6. See Scanlan, 1994, especially Scanlan, 'Interpretations and Uses of Slavophilism in Recent Russian Thought', pp. 31–61. In 1991 a leading member of the Academy of Sciences, Dmitry Likhachev, expressed a common fear that the West might be far more destructive of Russian national characteristics than ever Communism was. The contrary Westernizing position was defended in 1992 by, for example, E. V. Barabanov, who had catalogued the European influences on Russian philosophy from Plato to Husserl and argued that the pursuit of truth in Russia rested on acknowledging and joining this great tradition.
7. Scanlan notes (p. 8) the new attraction of religious thought and, at p. 9, alas, 'a new abuse of Russian religious philosophy to support illiberal political programmes'. Generally it is clear the debate between Slavophiles and Westerners is far from over.
8. François Dosse, *History of Structuralism*, Paris, 1997, I, p. 354.
9. For post-Soviet Russian interest in Bakhtin, see Emerson (see chapter 11 note 89) and *M. M. Bakhtin kak filosof* [M. M. Bakhtin as a Philosopher], Moscow, 1992.
10. Dominique Auffret, *Alexandre Kojève. La philosophie, l'état, la fin de l'histoire*, Paris, 1990; Shadia B. Drury, *Alexandre Kojève. The Roots of Postmodern Politics*, London, 1994. For the dystopic vision see Alexandre Kojève, *Introduction to the Reading of Hegel*, assembled by Raymond Quéneau, tr. James H. Nichols, Jr, with an introduction by Allan Bloom, New York, 1969, p. 40 and Mark Lilla, pp. 134–6 (see full reference in note 11 below). Another mischievous twentieth-century Russian cultural figure, though not a philosopher, was Prince Dmitry Svyatopol-Mirsky, who while he was teaching at the School of Slavonic Studies in London in the 1920s, told the art critic Roger Fry: 'I don't believe in science and I don't think it can contribute anything of value for thought. To tell the truth I get far more from theology.' 'Russia will not want science. It will have theology.' See G. S. Smith, *D. S. Mirsky*, Oxford, 2001, pp. 102, 207. Smith comments (p. 210) on Mirsky's 'love of intellectual mischief'. Mirsky, an émigré, returned willingly and blindly to Stalin's Russia where he was arrested and died in a labour camp.

11. Mark Lilla, 'The End of Philosophy', *Times Literary Supplement*, 5 April 1991, reprinted in *The Reckless Mind: Intellectuals in Politics*, New York, 2001.

12. Habermas quoted in Andrew Bowie, *Schelling and Modern European Philosophy*, London, 1993, p. 3.

13. Plato, *The Republic*, tr. H. D. P. Lee, Harmondsworth, 1955, pp. 92–3 (Part One, Book Two, paras 361–2).

14. See John Keane, *Václav Havel. A Political Tragedy in Six Acts*, London, 1999, pp. 253–66. It is used in Russia by Solzhenitsyn. See above, chapter 11 note 101.

15. Berdyaev, *The Creative Act*, 1955, pp. 254–5; also Berdyaev, *The Bourgeois Mind*, London, 1934, p. 13 and compare also Marc Raeff, *The Origins of the Russian Intelligentsia: the Eighteenth-Century Nobility*, New York, 1966, p. 115.

16. Quoted in Hirschkop, 1999, p. 121.

17. For instance when pop singers and models are asked to judge literary prizes.

18. Jonathan Kvanvig, *Intellectual Virtues and the Life of the Mind*, Savage, Md, 1992, p. 169. Kvanvig's argument *for* epistemic virtue as social virtue seems to me to be an argument in favour of primitivism and social manipulation. It is expressly non-Cartesian.

19. Chapter 9, note 12.

20. Chapter 7, note 37.

21. Odoevsky, 1981, I, pp. 64–5, 134–9.

22. Bowie, 1993, pp. 60–61, has shown this was also Schelling's approach to knowledge: that it could not proceed from a division between the thinking subject and the thought-about world; and that it should not, because the split made thought aggressive and unattuned to its material.

23. Walicki, 1980, p. 218. The term was coined by Apollon Grigoriev.

24. Konstantin Asadowski, *Rilke und Russland*, Berlin and Weimar, 1986; George K. Epp, *Rilke und Russland*, Frankfurt am Main, 1988.

25. Rilke, *Gesammelte Briefe in sechs Bänden*, ed. Ruth Sieber-Rilke und Carl Sieber, Leipzig, 1936–9, IV, 1938, p. 292.

26. Rilke, *Die Aufzeichnungen des Malte Laurids Brigge*, Frankfurt am Main, 1963, p. 217.

27. Rilke, *Das Stundenbuch* (The Book of Hours), 1899–1903, I.

28. 'Schmargendorff Diary' in *Diaries of a Young Poet*, tr. Edward Snow and Michael Winkler, New York, 1998, p. 163.

29. *Das Stundenbuch*, I.

30. Rilke, *Duino Elegien* (Duino Elegies), I.

31. *Diaries of a Young Poet*, 1998, p. 88.

32. Letter to Ellen Key, 15 August 1903, quoted in S. L. Frank, 'R. M. Rilke und die russische Geistesart', *Germano-Slavica*, Brünn, 1932–3, II, Heft 4, pp. 481–97. See also Epp, 1988, pp. 48–52 and a similar letter to Aleksei S. Suvorin, 5 March 1902, *Gesammelte Briefe*, Leipzig, 1939, I, p. 438 (also in Asadowski, 1986, p. 337). The 1903 letter to Ellen Key cited by Frank does not appear in *Gesammelte Briefe*.

33. *Das Stundenbuch*, II.

34. Paima P. Gaidenko, 'The Philosophy of Freedom of Nikolai Berdiaev', in Scanlan, 1994, p. 116.

35. See Frank, 1965, chapter 2 *passim*.

36. *Goethes Werke*, 1952, X, p. 529; XIII, p. 25; XIII p. 30. The relevant essays are 'Erfahrung und Wissenschaft' (Experience and Knowledge) and 'Aschauende Urteilskraft' (Intuitive Judgement). Also *Goethes Briefe*, II, p. 297.

37. Copleston, 1986, pp. 356–7; *Sbornik pamyati Semena Lyudvigovicha Franka*, Munich, 1954, p. 2.

38. Belinsky, PSS, 1953–9, XI, pp. 307ff.

39. See below, note 46.

40. See, in particular, the early story 'Tonio Kröger'.

41. Berdyaev, 1955, p. 30.

42. *Martin Heidegger Basic Writings*, revised and expanded edition ed. David Farrell Krell, London, 1993, p. 110.

43. George Steiner, *Martin Heidegger*, with a New Introduction, Chicago, 1991, p. 70.

44. My translation is from Heidegger, 'Was ist Metaphysik?', 1929, in *Gesamtausgabe*, Frankfurt-am-Main, 1975, Band 9 (1976), p. 122. See also Farrell Krell, p. 109. Steiner, 1991, p. 71 explores the interpretative possibilities.

45. N. O. Lossky, *History of Russian Philosophy*, 1952, p. 179.

46. *Goethes Briefe*, Hamburg, 1962–7, II, p. 297: 'I have exactly observed [such] objects which bring forth such an effect and to my astonishment I have noticed that they are actually symbolic. That is, as I hardly need say, they are eminent cases which, in a certain characteristic multiplicity, stand there as the representatives of many others; they contain a certain totality within themselves and invite a certain order. They awaken in my mind similarities and differences and so from both without and within they lay claim to a certain unity and universality. They are therefore, what a good choice of subject is for a writer, fortunate objects for humanity.'

47. See M. J. Inwood, 'Hermeneutics 3. Heidegger' in *The Oxford Companion to*

Philosophy, Oxford 1995, for Heidegger's preference for 'pre-predicative simple seeing'. The phrase exactly captures the simple 'pre-logical' knowledge of which Khomiakov and Kireevsky were in favour.

48. Berdyaev, 1955, p. 274.
49. Berdyaev quoted in Edie et al., 1965, III, p. 190.
50. Kamenka, 1970, pp. viii, 121ff.
51. See p. 253.
52. Emmanuel Levinas, 'Ethics as First Philosophy' (1984) ed. Sean Hand, *The Levinas Reader*, Oxford, 1989, p. 78.
53. J. S. Mill, 'Coleridge' in *Utilitarianism and Other Essays*, ed. Alan Ryan, London, 1987, p. 185.
54. Berlin, 2000, p. 15.
55. Ibid., pp. 210, 227–8.
56. *Marx Engels Collected Works*, 1975, III, p. 232.
57. Berlin, 1978, p. 170.
58. 'Two Concepts of Liberty' in Isaiah Berlin, *Four Essays on Liberty*, Oxford, 1969, p. 122.
59. Berlin, 1969, p. 172.
60. Berdyaev, 1950, p. 87.
61. Copleston, 1986, pp. 394–5: 'For Shestov, positivist philosophy, turning itself into the handmaiden of science, eliminated human freedom, considered as an exception to the operation of natural law and determining causality. What is precious to the human being is rejected in the name of science. But natural science is a mental construction. Hume showed that necessity is not to be found in the world but that it is a subjective contribution. The theory of evolution has [further] undermined the old thesis that like produces like, and effects must always resemble their causes. As far as possibility goes, anything might follow from anything … Hume was concerned with epistemological problems, however, whereas Shestov was motivated by religious considerations. Once science is seen as a mental construction, the God of the Bible, bound by no laws of nature, can return to the centre of the picture and human freedom can be reasserted.'

Suggested Reading

General

There are a few indispensable sources in English:

Copleston, Frederick, *Philosophy in Russia*, Notre Dame, 1986.

Edie, James M., James P. Scanlan and Mary-Barbara Zeldin, with the collaboration of George L. Kline, *Russian Philosophy*, 3 vols, Chicago, 1965.

Walicki, Andrzej, *A History of Russian Thought from the Enlightenment to Marxism*, Oxford, 1980.

Isaiah Berlin's writing on Russian thought is idiosyncratic, tailored to a British audience. See *Russian Thinkers*, London, 1978, and also *Vico and Herder*, 1976 and *The Magus of the North*, 1993, published together as *Three Critics of the Enlightenment*, London, 2000. 'Artistic Commitment: A Russian Legacy' and 'Marxism and the International in the Nineteenth Century' are two interesting essays reprinted in *The Sense of Reality*, London, 1996.

Lossky, Nicholas, *A History of Russian Philosophy*, London, 1952.
Zenkovsky, V. V., *A History of Russian Philosophy*, London 1953.
Both are histories written by early twentieth-century émigrés, idiosyncratic in their refusal to distinguish religious thought from philosophy but usefully detailed on minor figures.

Primary texts in English:

Berdyaev, N. A., *The Meaning of the Creative Act*, tr. Donald Lowrie, London, 1955.

—*Dream and Reality*, London, 1950.

—*Christian Existentialism. A Berdyaev Anthology*, selected and translated by Donald A. Lowrie, London, 1965.

Bulgakov, S. N., *Philosophy of Economy. The World as a Household*, translated, edited and with an introduction by Catherine Evtuhov, London, 2000.

Herzen, Alexander, *My Past and Thoughts*, tr. Constance Garnett, London, 1968.

—*From the Other Shore*, tr. Moura Budberg. London, 1956.

McNally, Raymond T., *The Major Works of Peter Chaadaev*, London, 1969.

Scanlan, James P., translated and with an introduction and notes, *Peter Lavrov Historical Letters*, Berkeley, 1967.

Shestov, Lev, *In Job's Balances. On the sources of the eternal truths*, tr. C. Coventry and C. A. Macartney, London, 1932.

Shragin, Boris, and Albert Todd, *Landmarks*, tr. Marian Schwarz, New York, 1977.

The religious background

Fedotov, G. P., *The Russian Religious Mind*, 2 vols, Cambridge, Mass., 1946, 1966, is still the standard work in English on Russian Orthodoxy. Also in English, Timothy Ware, *The Orthodox Church*, Harmondsworth, 1963, is a pleasure to consult. In Russian, see Georgy Florovsky, *Puti russkogo bogosloviya*, Paris, 1937; Vilnius, 1991.

The German background

The influence of Goethe and Schiller, and the German Idealists in Russia has been too vast and diverse to contain in any one study. On Schiller, see Elizabeth M. Wilkinson and Leonard A. Willoughby (eds.), *Friedrich Schiller On the Aesthetic Education of Man*, Oxford, 1967. Judith N. Shklar, *Freedom and Independence. A Study of the Political Ideas of Hegel's Phenomenology of Mind*, Cambridge, 1976, is a fine introduction to Hegel. Edward Craig, *The Mind of God and the Works of Man*, Oxford, 1987, encapsulates the Idealist world and its relation to poetry, with special reference to Goethe and Hegel. Andrew Bowie, *Schelling and Modern*

European Philosophy, London, 1993, is a recent technical study accounting for postmodern interest in Schelling. In German, *Hegels Theologische Jugendschriften*, edited by H. Nohl, Tübingen, 1907, explores the roots of Idealism. Classic studies are Emil Steiger, *Der Geist der Liebe und das Schicksal*, Leipzig, 1935; Paul Kluckhohn, *Das Ideengut der deutschen Romantik*, Halle, 1942; and H. O. Burger, *Die Gedankenwelt der grossen Schwaben*, Tübingen, 1951. Another useful work is Wolfgang Schadewaldt, 'Goethes Begriff der Realität', in *Goethestudien Natur und Altertum*, Zurich, 1963.

The Marxist background

Kolakowski, Leszek, *Main Currents of Marxism*, translated from Polish by P. S. Falla, 3 vols, Oxford, 1981, is lucid and indispensable, and also covers the earlier German period.

The Soviet period

De George, Richard T., *Patterns of Soviet Thought*, Ann Arbor, MI, 1966.

Laszlo, Ervin (ed.), *Philosophy in the Soviet Union. A Survey of the Mid-Sixties*, Dordrecht, Holland, 1967.

Scanlan, James P., *Marxism in the USSR. A Critical Survey of Current Soviet Thought*, London, 1985.

Post-Soviet thought

Scanlan (ed.), James P., *Russian Thought after Communism. The Recovery of a Philosophical Heritage*, New York/London, 1994.

Individual thinkers

Auffret, Dominique, *Alexandre Kojève. La philosophie, l'état et la fin de l'histoire*, Paris, 1990.

Baron, Samuel H., *Plekhanov. The Father of Russian Marxism*, London, 1963.

Boobbyer, Philip, *S. L. Frank. The Life and Work of a Russian Philosopher*, Ohio, 1995.

Cornwell, Neil, *The Life, Times and Milieu of V. F. Odóevsky*, 1804–1869, London, 1986.

Evtuhov, Catherine, *The Cross and the Sickle: Sergei Bulgakov and the Fate of Russian Religious Philosophy 1890–1920*, London, 1997.

Hirschkop, Ken, *Mikhail Bakhtin. An Aesthetic for Democracy*, Oxford, 1999.

Kelly, Aileen, *Mikhail Bakunin. A Study in the Psychology and Politics of Utopianism*, Oxford, 1982.

Kostalevsky, Marina, *Dostoevsky and Soloviev. The Art of Integral Vision*, London, 1997.

Malia, Martin, *Alexander Herzen and the Birth of Russian Socialism*, Cambridge, Mass./ Oxford, 1961.

Pomper, Phillip, *Peter Lavrov and the Russian Revolutionary Movement*, London, 1972.

References to many more specialist works will be found in the notes to the text.

Index

INDEX